W9-CVA-731

POSITIVISM AND CHRISTIANITY

A STUDY OF THEISM AND VERIFIABILITY

POSITIVISM AND CHRISTIANITY

A STUDY OF THEISM AND VERIFIABILITY

by

KENNETH H. KLEIN

MARTINUS NIJHOFF / THE HAGUE / 1974

To my father

ISBN 90 247 1581 4

PRINTED IN BELGIUM

CONTENTS

INTRODUCTION

This essay is conceived as a critical exposition of the central issues that figure in the ongoing conversation between Logical Positivists and neo-Positivists on the one hand and Christian apologists on the other. My expository aim is to isolate and to describe the main issues that have emerged in the extended discussion between men of Positivistic turn of mind and men sympathetic to the claims of Christianity. My critical aim is to select typical, influential stands that have been taken on each of these issues, to assess their viability, and to isolate certain dilemmas which discussion of these issues has generated. I am convinced that the now commonly rejected verifiability theory of meaning is very commonly misunderstood and has been rejected by and large for the wrong reasons. Before it is cast off—*if* it is to be cast off—what is needed is a reconsideration of that theory and of the objections that its several formulations have elicited. Furthermore, at least partially because of a misconstruing of the verifiability doctrine, there have been some interesting—though in my opinion unsuccessful—claims advanced about the testability-status of sentences expressive of Christian belief. Moreover, in their haste to vindicate Christianity, some apologists have been fairly cavalier, in my opinion, about what "Christianity" involves. This volume offers what I hope will be a clear statement and analysis of the principle points at issue between Positivism and Christianity, together with my own assessment of where the argument stands now. My attempt throughout has been to provide for teachers, students, and interested laymen an orderly, concise discussion of several of the most crucial, interrelated issues that figure prominently in this manifestly vivid, still-unclosed chapter of contemporary analytic philosophy of religion. My claim will be that the problems posed by Positivism for Christianity, and for any theism of this type, have not yet been resolved either by the alleged discrediting of Positivism or by the apologetic efforts formulated thus far.

The issues examined here are historically associated with the formulation, dissemination, and eventual widespread influence of the doctrines of Logical Positivism, a philosophical movement which enjoyed prominence in Austria, England, and America during the second and third decades of this century. Although Logical Positivism, considered as a philosophical movement, is passé, its influence upon recent philosophy of religion is massive, its philosophical afterbirth—linguistic analysis—has been sanguine, and some of its own tenets are still defended, albeit in usually sharply modified form. The doctrines of Logical Positivism have a complicated genealogical history, stemming not only from the writings of Kant and the tradition of British empiricism, but also from writers of more recent vintage—physicists, logicians, sociologists, and philosophers of science. The immediate progenitors of Positivism were a small group of philosophers, scientists, and mathematicians more or less loosely gathered together by Moritz Schlick in the early 1920's at the University of Vienna who gave themselves the name of "the Vienna Circle." The officially recognized precursors of Positivist ideas are remembered in a sort of Positivist manifesto—*Wissenschaftliche Weltauffassung, Der Wiener Kreis*—written in 1929 by Rudolf Carnap, Otto Neurath, and Hans Hahn.

No attempt will be made in this volume at historical completeness, completeness either with respect to the full evolution and variety of Positivist doctrines or with respect to the burgeoning variety of responses offered in service to Christian apologetics. Readers interested in the broader conceptual picture would do well to look at A. J. Ayer's *Logical Positivism* and at Frederick Ferre's *Language, Logic, and God* and to follow up some of the generous bibliographical leads provided there. My focus in this essay is with—so to speak—hard-core Positivism as it bears on Christianity and with more or less direct, first-generation responses to Positivism in defense of Christian orthodoxy. Developments in Christian apologetics within the last decade or so have been very interesting indeed. These developments, however, open an entirely new chapter and I have thought it best, in the interest of preserving singleness of theme, to neglect them in this study.

My book takes a dual look at one of the central doctrines of Logical Positivism—dual, in that I will be looking both at the doctrine itself (the verifiability-doctrine) and also at the impact which this doctrine has made in one field of inquiry (Christian apologetics). That portion of the book which will be devoted to examining the doctrine itself will try to ascertain whether or not the doctrine is tenable and, if so, in what form. If the doctrine is tenable, it constitutes, or appears to constitute, a challenge to—indeed an attack upon—the intelligibility of that type of religious belief exemplified by Christianity. Of course the Positivists' attack upon Christianity was but one instance of their hostility to "metaphysics" in general. By focusing upon this one instance of their attack, I do not mean to suggest that Christianity was singled out for special disfavor. But since the Positivistic bite was forcefully felt by philosophers of religion and particularly by Christian apologists, it is appropriate to field the argument at the point of one of its foci of conflict, even though there were others as well.

Whether or not the doctrine which the Positivists employed to undermine Christianity is tenable, there are many writers of contemporary philosophy of religion who certainly *think* that it is. Certain writers are sufficiently worried about the potential destructive fecundity of the doctrine in question that they have tried to answer the Positivists in some way or another. What these answers characteristically have in common is the attempt to vindicate Christianity, or some more general religious orientation of which Christianity is a special case, from Positivist objections. Given this common concern, however, two quite different types of response occur. Some hold that Christianity is not really susceptible to the Positivist's attack in the first place, since Christians are not really disposed to hold what the Positivists think they hold, although they sometimes appear to do so. Others hold that although Christianity is susceptible, in principle, to the Positivists' objection, sentences expressive of a Christian's basic beliefs are not unintelligible in the way the Positivists alleged since these sentences, in their typical use, meet the requirements of intelligibility. These replies to the Positivists' argument, whether the argument is initially sound or not, are interesting in their own right since they highlight topics of concern both to Christian theologians and to philosophers of religion, notably the distinction between the first and the second persons of the Trinity and, more generally, the topic of the *transcendence* of God.

There is another sort of reply to the Positivists which is relevant to their attack upon Christianity. One might raise objections to the doctrine from which the Positivists argued. Professional philosophers have in fact raised such objections, although not necessarily for the purpose of vindicating Christianity or metaphysics. The raising of objections to Positivist doctrine will be considered here as a type of response relevant to their sort of attack upon Christianity, first, because it was indeed a response to Positivism, albeit not one offered in behalf of Christianity, and second, because this type of response is obviously adaptable to the intent of the Christian apologist: if there is no satisfactory formulation of a Positivist type criterion of factual significance, then the Positivist attack upon Christianity fails. Assaying the force of the Positivist attack, therefore, requires assaying the force of the principal objections that have been raised against the several formulations of the Positivists' criterion of factual significance.

The organization of the five chapters of this book is as follows: The purpose of chapter one is to set forth the Positivists' attack upon that type of religious belief exemplified by Christianity and in particular to describe the Positivists' stand on each of the three issues upon which their argument turns. Chapters two, three, and four will discuss each of these three issues in turn by examining three different types of reply, each keyed to one of the constituent issues. The reply considered in chapter two is illustrated by reference to several kinds of meta-theological approach which were influential during the early years of the last decade. Writers who took approaches such as these either explicitly deny, or tend to deny by suggestion, that sentences expressive of a Christian's fundamental belief are of the sort that would make Christianity even *open to* objections of the Positivist type. The reply considered in chapter three consists in urging that the various formulations of the criterion of factual significance, upon which the Positivists' program rests, are open to very strong objections. The reply considered in chapter four is exemplified by certain attempts neither to circumvent the attack, nor to nullify it, but rather to meet it directly, that is, by trying to show how statements expressive of Christian belief might be tested. Chapter five looks back over my argument and attempts to concede the force of certain recent non-trivial objections to some of its crucial steps without conceding their individual or collective force to overthrow it altogether. I have also tried there to isolate certain dilemmas which the issues discussed generate.

A few words of explanation about my notational devices might be in order. I have tried to restrict the employment of *single* quotation marks, over and above the usual occasions of marking quotations-within-quotations and direct quotations from authors who use them normally, to occasions when the expression so quoted—a word or sentence—is *mentioned*, as they say, rather than *used*; that is, when the *expression itself* is talked about. *Double* quotation marks acknowledge direct quotation or, where undocumented, indicate the *use* of the expression so designated in some typical, atypical, or merely specially featured sense. An example might help to make this clear. 'There is a God' (note single quotation marks) is a use-neutral utterance-inscription, or a verbal token when spoken, which could be and normally would be used by someone to make the statement that there is a God. "There is a God" (note double quotation marks) is an inscription of the statement made by someone who uses the utterence 'There is a God' (single quotes) to assert that there is a God. Since I shall usually be discussing not the use-neutral utterance-inscriptions but the statements which typical Positivists and theists could use and normally would use such inscriptions to make, these inscriptions will ordinarily be enclosed within double quotation-marks. I have also found it convenient to employ some shorthand conventions for locating sources; these are explained in the footnotes where they are introduced. In all cases the pagination of each citation will always be to the volume originally mentioned in locating the citation; for example, all references to an article cited from its reprinting in a larger volume will be to the pagination of that larger volume, even though that volume is mentioned only on the occasion of its first reference.

I would like to express my thanks to the many colleagues and students who furthered my labors and to exculpate them one and all for faults and shortsightednesses which remain. Special thanks are due in three quarters. First and foremost, I wish to remember Rogers Albritton, who was my mentor at Harvard University where this book took its original shape as my doctoral dissertation. I should also like to thank the Committee on Creative Work and Research—notably John Strietelmeier— at Valparaiso University, which released me from my teaching duties for half a year to revise the manuscript. I also give thanks to my wife, Mary, whose encouragement and patience were crucial in bringing this phase of the work to completion.

Valparaiso University
July, 1973

CHAPTER ONE

STATEMENT OF THE ISSUES

The Logical Positivists' attack upon that type of religious belief exemplified by Christianity—or, to put it more simply, their attack upon *theism* —turns upon the Positivists taking a particular stand on each of three issues. It will be helpful to set out these issues clearly at the beginning, since certain writers, whose views will be examined in chapters two, three, and four, have proposed that the argument should be countered, or might be averted altogether, by taking a different stand on each issue in turn. To see how the Positivists stood on each, consider first a brief overview of their attack, concluding with a statement of the issues. The Positivist stand on each issue will then be developed in greater detail. For expository purposes it will be convenient to speak of *the Positivist* and *the theist*. This idiom is not intended to slide over important differences among Logical Positivists and differences among theists on the doctrines discussed. Yet I do not think excessive violence will be done to the mainline positions characteristically endorsed by Positivists and theists by setting forth the substantive issues by reference to some imagined paradigmatic Positivist and paradigmatic theist. Where the argument requires greater precision of reference the idiom will shift accordingly.

A. OVERVIEW OF THE POSITIVIST ATTACK UPON THEISM

The principal vehicle of the Positivist attack upon theism, which was one instance of its attack upon metaphysics in general, was a certain canon or standard of meaning, which will be called here the *criterion of factual significance*. It was suggested that this canon could be used as a criterion for deciding whether a putative statement of fact is a genuine statement of fact. A genuine statement of fact, according to the Positivist classification of sentences, is a sentence which succeeds in asserting something about the world, about what is the case. More commonly, a genuine statement of fact declares that a particular state of affairs obtains, and not that a different state of affairs obtains. The statement that it is raining outside typically declares that it is raining outside, not that it is snowing, hailing, sleeting, etc. A statement of fact says something which might be true or false, but not, as was variously phrased, "analytically" or "necessarily" or "formally" true or false.[1]

The hallmark of genuineness in putatively factual statements, or for their *meaningfulness*, as the Positivist was wont to put it, was that they must be *testable*. The Positivist advanced a criterion of factual significance according to which, in A. J. Ayer's very general formulation, "... if a sentence succeeded neither in expressing something that was formally true or false nor in expressing something that could be *empirically* tested ... it did not express any proposition at all ... Their point was that ... it did not state anything that was either true or false...."[2] That a genuine factual statement must be empirically testable was essential; according to the various formulations of the criterion, a necessary condition of a putative factual statement's being a genuine statement of fact is that it must be, at least in principle, verifiable,[3] or it must be, at least in principle, falsifiable.[4] A genuine non-

[1] A. J. Ayer offers a brief introduction to the Positivist view of "tautologies" in "The Vienna Circle," *The Revolution in Philosophy*, ed. A. J. Ayer (London: Macmillan & Co., Ltd., 1957), pp. 76-77, as does Richard von Mises, *Positivism. A Study in Human Understanding* (New York: George Braziller, Inc., 1956), pp. 114-116. The analytic-synthetic distinction has been widely discussed in recent years. Interested readers will find a bibliography of some of the more popular sources in Paul Edwards and Arthur Pap, eds., *A Modern Introduction to Philosophy* (New York: The Free Press, third edition, 1973), pp. 740-747.

[2] Editor's introduction to *Logical Positivism*, ed. by A. J. Ayer (Glencoe, Illinois: The Free Press, 1959), p. 10.

[3] Possible documentation for this point is rich. For one classical instance see Moritz Schlick: "Every proposition has meaning only in so far as it can be verified, and it *says* only what is verified, and simply nothing more." "Positivismus und Realismus," *Erkenntnis*, vol. III (1932-1933); trans. by David Rynin as "Positivism and Realism" in *Logical Positivism* [pp. 82-107], p. 90.

[4] The suggestion that falsifiability, rather than verifiability, might be viewed as a criterion of factual significance is generally credited to Karl R. Popper, *Logik der Forschung*, 1934; trans. by the author as *The Logic of Scientific Discovery* (London: Hutchinson & Co., Ltd., 1958). Popper suggested a falsifiability-criterion as a criterion of demarcation between scientific and non-scientific theories. He did not also claim that falsifiability might be employed as a general test for factual significance. See Israel Scheffler's discussion of this point in his *The Anatomy of Inquiry* (New York: Alfred A. Knopf, 1967), pp. 127-150. There is also some dispute as to whether Popper should even be called a Positivist at all. Ayer, for example, makes the following historical note: "Popper was not in fact a member of the Circle [the Vienna Circle] and would at no

analytic *statement*, that is, must be at least in principle capable of being *shown* true or false by reference to specifiable empirical data under specifiable conditions. Moritz Schlick declares that "The criterion of the truth or falsity of the proposition ... lies in the fact that under definite conditions ... certain data are present, or not present."[5]

Empirical testability is generally regarded as a *sufficient* condition for a sentence's possessing factual significance; what the Positivist maintained is that it is also a *necessary* condition. Necessary and sufficient conditions are standardly defined schematically as follows: If condition A is a necessary condition for condition B, then if A does not obtain, B cannot obtain; if condition A is a sufficient condition for condition B, then if A obtains, B will also obtain.

Now the Positivist presumed that at least some of the sentences expressive of that type of religious belief exemplified by Christianity make a factual claim or, more precisely, are characteristically used by those who hold that type of belief to make putative statements of fact. *Look* at the documents constituting the corpus of traditional Christian theology, the Positivist said. *Listen* to theists expressing their beliefs about God. "God," in that tradition, obviously purports to name, or to refer. "There is a God" typically purports to state a fact.

If sentences expressive of that type of religious belief exemplified by Christianity are used to make putative statements of fact, how might they be verified or falsified? God is assuredly not a material being located in the world, so statements about Him or His actions in the world cannot be verified or falsified in the way that statements about some historical person might be verified or falsified. The Positivist claimed that 'God,' in theistic usage, purports to name a transcedent being. But if God is a transcendent being, then statements about God are untestable. Arthur Pap writes, "No conceivable observations can be described that have a clear bearing on the truth or falsehood of the theistic hypothesis, ... It follows that the theologian is not saying anything about the world when [for example] he utters the sentence 'the world was created by an infinite spirit.' "[6]

The Positivist claim is that no empirical observations are available, or could ever become available, which would settle the question of the existence

---

time have wished to be classed as a positivist, but the affinities between him and the positivists whom he criticized appear more striking than the divergencies." Editor's introduction to *Logical Positivism*, p. 6.

[5] Schlick, "Positivism and Realism," p. 87.

[6] Editor's introduction to sec. viii of *A Modern Introduction to Philosophy*, p. 753.

or the non-existence of a transcendent being. But nothing other than empirical observations can be accepted as constituting the requisite verification or falsification. "The theist," Ayer declares, "... may believe that his experiences [of God] are cognitive experiences, but, unless he can formulate his 'knowledge' in propositions that are empirically verifiable, we may be sure that he is deceiving himself.... For no act of intuition can be said to reveal a truth about any matter of fact unless it issues in verifiable propositions. And all such propositions are to be incorporated in the system of empirical propositions which constitutes science."[7]

By and large, then, the Positivist answer to the questions "Are sentences expressive of theistic belief empirically testable?" and "Could sentences expressive of theistic belief conceivably be empirically tested?" was "*no*". Consequently, sentences expressive of theistic belief fail to meet the requirement for saying something which could be true or false. They could not be genuine statements of fact, regardless of their purport. Ayer summarized the view curtly: "To say that 'God exists' is to make a metaphysical utterance which cannot be either true or false."[8]

Consider now, by way of summary, the following three contentions :

A. The statement that God exists—or any statement of the fundamental claim or claims of Christianity—is a genuine factual statement.

B. A necessary condition of a genuine factual statement is that it must be Verifiable—i.e., either verifiable or falsifiable or both.[9]

C. The statement that God exists is not Verifiable.

The Positivist turned these three incompatible contentions into a case against theism. The Positivist himself held B and C; and because he presumed that Christians, or most of them anyway, hold A, the Positivist charged the theist, in effect, with falling into inconsistency. The Positivist did not say, to be sure, that the theist *consciously* holds an inconsistency, since it was unclear what position the theist himself takes on B and C. The argument was, instead, that a theist is *committed* to holding an inconsistency

[7] A. J. Ayer, *Language, Truth, and Logic* (New York: Dover Publications, Inc. n.d. [first published, 1936; second edition, 1946]), p. 120.

[8] *Ibid.*, p. 115.

[9] This version of the criterion of factual significance was proposed by David Rynin in "Vindication of L*G*C*L*P*S*T*V*SM", *Proceedings and Addresses of the American Philosophical Association*, vol. 30, 1957). Rynin's formulation expresses what is common to two formulations built, respectively, upon verifiability or upon falsifiability. Rynin's criterion will be discussed in detail in chapter three.

since, first, a theist presumably holds A, or at least, would want to hold A; second, a theist *should* hold B, whether he wants to or not, since everybody should; third, a theist should concede the truth of C when he stops to consider what is implied in God's transcendence. The Positivists do not appear to have maintained that the average theist either consciously holds or does not hold C. The claim is, rather, that if God is the kind of being theists describe, namely, a transcendent being, then C is true.

What the Positivist did, then, was to use contentions B and C as premises in an argument against A. (1) A necessary condition of a genuine factual statement is that it must be Verifiable; (2) The statement that God exists is not Verifiable. Therefore, (3) the statement that God exists is not a genuine factual statement. The statement that God exists, in theism, purports to be genuinely factual, he conceded, but given B and C it *cannot* be genuinely factual. Judged as a statement of fact, he concluded, the statement that God exists is meaningless. Meaningless, too, is any statement that logically presupposes the truth of the statement that God exists; for example, any of a theists's beliefs, and statements expressive of them, about God's actions or dispositions. Theological statements may function in some other manner serviceable to those who traffic in them. But considered as genuine *statements*—that is, as utterances of which it makes sense to claim that they are true or false—theological sentences are unintelligible.

Is it plausible to hold that the statement that God exists—or any statement of the fundamental claim or claims of Christianity[10]—is, at least putatively, a statement of fact? Is it plausible to hold that a necessary condition of a genuine statement of fact is that it be Verifiable? Is it plausible to hold that the statement that God exists is not Verifiable? These are the crucial issues involved in the attack. The Positivist stand on each issue may now profitably be examined in greater detail.

B. EXPOSITION OF THE POSITIVIST STAND ON THE ISSUES

1. "The statement that God exists is, at least putatively, a statement of fact"

The Positivist assumed that sentences expressive of theistic belief are characteristically used by exponents of that type of belief to make putative statements of fact. Why would he have made this assumption about a theist's employment of religious language? What was he thereby assuming?

[10] For example, "God was in Christ reconciling the world unto Himself," "For God so loved the world that He gave His only begotten Son ...," "In Christ God became manifest," etc.

The Positivist appears to have assumed, first, that the principal religions of the western world—Judaism, Christianity, and Islam—are characterized by certain common themes; second, that by virtue of these common themes one might employ expressions pertaining to these religions such as 'religious belief,' 'religious experience,' 'theological statement,' 'religious knowledge,' etc. without falling into crippling vagueness; third, and most important, that there is one feature common to all western religions and presupposed by every tenet within their various doctrinal schemas, namely, that all explicitly or implicitly assert the existence of God. It seemed quite safe to assume that the *behavior* of an exponent of one of these religions as well as most of the things he *says* about this religion are backed up by a number of assertions about God. It seemed quite correct to assume that "There is a God," when spoken by an exponent, say, of the Christian religion, purports to state a fact. The Positivists themselves do not seem to have been much interested in defending this assumption. What might be said in defense of it? Whether or not they would have argued in the way suggested here, of course, is conjectural, but it is at least plausible given some of the things they did say.

It is plausible to hold that a Christian acts in the way he does because he holds certain beliefs, and that fundamental to many of these beliefs is his believing in the existence, reality, or being of God. That a Christian believes that there is a God—indeed, that he presupposes it in the many things he says and does while expressing his religion—might plausibly be surmised from the sort of justification Christians characteristically give for their acting as they do, or which they might naturally give under questioning. When a Christian prays, for example, it seems evident that he typically believes himself to be addressing a Person of some sort. For if asked why he is praying, a Christian normally would sooner or later advance his belief that there is a God who hears and answers prayer. He would offer that belief as his ultimate justification for his praying. When a Christian confesses one of the classical creeds, in the context of worship, for example, it seems evident that he typically believes himself to be making *statements*, asserting that certain things are the case and that the condition expressed by the denials of those statements is not the case. It would not be surprising to find him characteristically advancing his belief that these statements are *true* as his justification for making them. When a Christian reports that God has spoken to him during a moment of mystical experience or worship, it is evident that he is claiming to have encountered something or someone in that experience. If he is asked to explain why he interprets a particular devotional experience as an encounter with God, it would not be surprising to find that the man falls back, as a kind of ultimate justification for his interpreting the experience in just the way he did, upon his belief that there is a God who sometimes reveals himself, or his will or disposition, to men in experiences of this sort. On the whole, then, it seems reasonable and fair to assume that someone who subscribes to Christian doctrine and practices or advocates Christian piety holds certain beliefs, and that among these beliefs there is one which all the rest presuppose, namely, that there is a God. Only in unusual circumstances, to be sure, would a Christian *say* that God exists, or that God is real, or that there is a God in so many words. But when asked why he speaks and behaves in the manner he does speak and behave, a Christian would characteristically back up his behavior and speech by advancing his fundamental belief that there is a God. And he might aver that if there were no God, then some of his behavior would be inappropriate. It is plausible to assume, then, that "There is a God," when thus advanced by a Christian as an ultimate justification for his verbal and non-verbal behavior, does the job of asserting something. Such an utterance, to adopt another idiom, purports to state a fact.

The Positivist assumed that "There is a God" purports to be a fact-stating sentence, that when a Christian normally utters a sentence like this he is presumably making an assertion of some sort. But of what sort? Everything turns upon what, exactly, that sentence is used to putatively assert. The remarks of two spokesmen for Positivism, one early and one more recent, illustrate the characteristic Positivist way of construing the putative assertion in question.

A) *A. J. Ayer.* Consider, first, the following selected passages from *Language, Truth, and Logic*[11]:

[1.0] It is sometimes claimed ... that the existence of a certain sort of regularity in
nature constitutes sufficient evidence for the existence of a god. But if the
[1.1] sentence "God exists" entails no more than that certain types of phenomena
occur in certain sequences, then to assert the existence of a god will be
[2.0] simply equivalent to asserting that there is the requisite regularity in nature;
and no religious man would admit that this was all he intended to assert in

[11] In order to facilitate convenient reference to thoughts in these passages, I have imposed upon them a decimal notation, in brackets, similar to that employed by Wittgenstein in his *Tractatus Logico-Philosophicus*. The argument of the *Tractatus* is extremely obscure, and the exact relation between the thoughts of that work, which are alleged to have been seminal for Positivists, and the early teachings of the members of the Vienna Circle, is difficult to ascertain. Wittgenstein was never a member of the Circle. It will be better to avoid discussing the Positivist-sounding passages of the *Tractatus* and concentrate instead upon the somewhat more lucid, certainly more characteristically Positivistic, writings of Ayer, Carnap, Schlick, Kraft, Feigl, etc.

[2.1] asserting the existence of a god. He would say that in talking about God, he was talking about a transcendent being who might be known through certain empirical manifestations, but certainly could not be defined in terms of those manifestations.[12]
[3.0] It is to be remarked that in cases where deities are identified with natural objects, assertions concerning them are allowed to be significant. If, for ex-
[3.1] ample, a man tells me that the occurrence of thunder is alone both necessary and sufficient to establish the truth of the proposition that Jehovah is angry, I may conclude that, in his usage of words, the sentence "Jehovah is angry"
[4.0] is equivalent to "It is thundering." But in sophisticated religions, though they may be to some extent based on man's awe of natural processes which they cannot sufficiently understand, the "person" who is supposed to control
[4.1] the empirical world is not himself located in it; he is held to be superior to the empirical world, and so outside it; and he is endowed with super-empirical attributes.[13]
[5.0] ... If the man who asserts that he is seeing God is merely asserting that he is experiencing a peculiar kind of sense content, then we do not for a moment
[5.1] deny that his assertion may be true. But, ordinarily, the man who says that he is seeing God is saying not merely that he is experiencing a religious emotion, but also that there exists a transcendent being who is the object of
[6.0] this emotion; just as the man who says that he sees a yellow patch is ordinarily saying not merely that his visual sense-field contains a yellow sense-content, but that there exists a yellow object to which the sense-content belongs.[14]

In these three parallel passages Ayer explains what he takes a "religious man" [2.0] to be characteristically talking about when he talks about God. When an exponent of a "sophisticated religion" [4.0] says "God exists," or some roughly equivalent expression, he is not primarily asserting that there are regularities in nature, although he might be asserting that as well [1.0], or that certain more or less awe-inspringing events occur [3.0, 3.1], or that people have perceptual or introspective experiences of such and such a description [5.0]. If a man's assertion that God exists "entails" no more than that such events occur, then "God exists," so used, functions as a sentence which states facts of a familiar sort, although it states them in an unfamiliar manner.

Ordinarily, however [5.1] a religious man—and this is Ayer's main point—does *not* use 'God exists' to assert that there are specifiable regularities in nature; nor to assert that there occur certain events which dazzle and confound many a beholder; nor to assert that men have, upon occasion, anomalous perceptual or psychological experiences. A religious man ordinarily

[12] *Language, Truth, and Logic*, p. 115.
[13] *Ibid.*, p. 116.
[14] *Ibid.*, p. 119.

uses that expression to assert something quite different. He uses the expression, or kindred ones, putatively to assert that there is a transcendent being who stands in a certain relationship to these occurrences—a relationship, Ayer's illustrations suggest, analogous to the relationship of a maker to what he makes [2.1], or to the relationship of a material object to someone's perception of it [6.0]. God is a " 'person' who is supposed to control the empirical world" (4.0], but is Himself distinct in some manner from the world He allegedly controls. This is an important point deserving of further development.

At one point, Ayer employs a spatial metaphor to describe the respect in which he takes a religious man to hold that God is to be distinguished from the world: "not Himself located in it ... and so outside it." [4.1.] Ayer here invokes one of the prominent classical metaphors of Christian thought. Christian theologians would by and large hasten to add, however, that God *is in* the world in some sense as well as outside it, that He is acting in the world, or something of that sort. Most theists, at least, would flatly deny that the spatial metaphor, taken by itself, exactly expresses the kind of distinction which they want to make between God and the world. It is not clear whether Ayer anticipates this likely rejoinder or not. He does, however, couch the distinction between God and the world in still another way, a way which travels some distance toward taking into consideration the theological rejoinder just mentioned.

On Ayer's view of "sophisticated religion," of which he would surely count Christianity as one, the exact sense in which God is held to be distinguished from the world comes out at [2.1]. When a religious man talks about God, "he would say that ... he was talking about a transcendent being who might be known through certain empirical manifestations but certainly could not be defined in terms of these manifestations." The exact import of that remark, which Ayer does not develop at any length, might be clarified by looking at some remarks of T. R. Miles, a more recent, Positivistically-inclined writer. Miles develops two analogies which illustrate the distinction adumbrated in the citation from Ayer. Consideration of Miles' remarks will help to explain the sort of putative assertion the Positivist took a sentence like "There is a God" to be commonly used by theists to make.

B) *T. R. Miles.* Professor Miles' own position about the function of sentences containing the word 'God' will be discussed in chapter two. Prior to formulating his own view, Miles offers an interpretation of sentences containing the word 'God' according to which 'God' might be said, following Ayer's idiom, to be *defined* in terms of certain empirical manifestations.

On this view, God is a "theoretical construct" analogous to "the unconscious."[15] "The unconscious," according to this view, serves to link together different phases of a person's behavior—his dreams, slips of tongue, hypnotic and post-hypnotic behavior, neurotic compulsions, physical symptoms, and the like. Miles offers the following example:

> A person, let us say, makes the sort of slip of tongue that Freud was interested in; when he was trying to say 'The honourable member for Central Hull' he inadvertently says 'The honourable member for Central Hell'. To explain this behaviour we invent a theoretical construct—the unconscious. There are forces, we say, emanating from his unconscious, which make him act in this inappropriate way. Freud admittedly speaks sometimes as though the unconscious was an extra entity in addition to familiar ones; but for purposes of argument let us assume that he is wrong, and that the words 'the unconscious' stand for ... a 'theoretical construct'. This construct serves to link together this particular slip of the tongue with other parts of the person's behaviour, e.g., his irrational failure to cooperate with the honourable member in question.... The words 'the unconscious' function, that is, as an explanatory concept as a result of which these two separate events can be brought under the same general law.[16]

The way in which invoking of "the unconscious" explains a piece of behavior is different, however, from the way in which the hypothesis that one's house has been burglarized explains the mangled lilies, the jimmied window latch, and the missing silver. The cash-value of "the unconscious," on this view, *is* observable occurrences of a certain sort, segments of a person's behavior. But "the unconscious" is not anything of which one could conceivably have independent experience. The cash-value of "the burglar," by contrast, *is not* lillies, latch, and loot. The burglar is a man, distinct from the damage attributed to him :

> In the case of the unconscious, however, there is nothing comparable to actually catching the burglar.... The activity of the unconscious does not explain ... events in the same sense of 'explain' as that in which the activity of the burglar explains the missing spoons. The unconscious is not an independently discoverable entity at all, and while 'There are hostile feelings in his unconscious' can be given 'cash-value' in terms of slips of the tongue, his failure to co-operate with the honourable member, etc., 'There has been a burglar' cannot be given 'cash-value' in terms of 'The spoons are missing,' 'There are footprints on the flower-beds,' or any conjunction of similar assertions.[17]

[15] Miles' illustration turns upon a particular use of 'theoretical construct' and 'the unconscious.' He acknowledges that there are other ways of construing these expressions.

[16] T. R. Miles, *Religion and the Scientific Outlook* (London: George Allen & Unwin, Ltd., 1959), pp. 150-151.

[17] *Ibid.*

We may speak about the unconscious *as if* it were some sort of entity operating to produce certain kinds of behavior. But there is, we suppose, no such entity.[18] There is only a general law connecting X-behavior, Y-behavior, and Z-behavior.

The application is as follows. If "God" were construed as a theoretical construct along the lines indicated by the analogy, the sentence 'There is a God' typically would be used to say something about events in this world. It would have its cash-value in "answered" prayers, opportune occurrences, numinous experiences, and the like.[19] God would be analogous to the unconscious in the following way: On the view that "the unconscious" is a theoretical construct, to talk about John's unconscious hatred for his father is to talk *as though* there were an entity of some sort behind the behavioral scene to produce X-, Y-, and Z-behavior of John relative to his father, but not to say that there is such an entity. John's "unconscious hatred" just *is* behavior-events of X-, Y-, and Z-description. On the view that "God" is a theoretical construct, to talk about God's acting in history is to talk *as though* there were a being of some sort behind the historical scene operating to produce or helping to produce events of X-, Y-, and Z-descriptions, but not to say that there is such a being. "God's acting in history," on this view, just *is* events of X-, Y-, and Z-description. For example, the references to the deity in "The Lord is my shepherd, I shall not want," "God is our refuge and strength," and "He restoreth my soul," etc. are not claims, on this view, about a being behind the scene *doing* these things in the world. They are references—oblique ones at that—to experiences of wants which people have fulfilled, strength which people sometimes find in times of duress, morale-boosting experiences people often enjoy. To talk about "God" on this view *is* to talk about certain features of this world.[20]

[18] It is hard to see how "the unconscious" can operate, on this view, as an explanatory concept at all. Can Miles say *both* that the activity of the unconscious *explains* slips of tongue, etc., *and* that the cash-value of sentences referring to the unconscious is *given in terms of* slips of tongue, etc.? Miles clearly wants to get away from viewing the unconscious as an "entity" *causing* behavior of such-and-such a sort. But he also seems unwilling to relinquish the claim that "the unconscious" is an explanatory notion referring to something other than what it is adduced to explain. To accomplish the former, he speaks as if sentences about the unconscious *mean* behavior of a certain sort. To preserve the latter, he speaks as if sentences about the unconscious are not "cashable" into behavior-events at all, but refer to a "general law" which "links" certain behavior-events together. Can he have both? Compare Alasdair MacIntyre's discussion of the notion of the unconscious in his *The Unconscious* (London: Routledge & Kegan Paul, 1958), pp. 71-79.

[19] *Religion and the Scientific Outlook*, p. 151.

[20] The theological view expressed in Henry Nelson Wieman's *The Source of Human*

Concerning this view, Miles makes the following observation, which is surely correct:

> ... I am quite sure that this is not the way in which people ordinarily think of God.... The ordinary person regards God as the explanation of answered prayers not in the sense in which the unconscious is the explanation of slips of the tongue, but in the sense in which the burglar is the explanation of the missing spoons. Answered prayers are *evidence*, it would be said, for the existence of God, much as footprints in the flower-beds are evidence for the existence of a burglar.[21]

The straw-man view which Miles has sketched comes to this: sentences containing the word 'God' might be given cash-value in terms of certain independently describable empirical and psychological occurrences. Miles' assessment of this view, which is developed in an imaginary dialogue between a philosopher and a theologian, concurs with Ayer's judgment of the view according to which God might be *defined* in terms of "certain empirical manifestations." Miles' philosopher remarks to his theologian: "I find it hard to take this view seriously. I suppose one *could* use the word 'God' in some such way, but I am sure it would not be a sense acceptable to you as a theologian."[22]

SUMMARY. The Positivist maintained that when the theist makes statements about God, these statements are advanced, at least putatively, as *truths*, as statements of fact. The question was what fact or facts did such sentences purport to assert. The Positivist interpreted the theist's use of sentences about God as purporting to assert the existence, disposition, or activities of something or someone, a *being* of some sort, although the being concerned was perhaps not, to be sure, an *ordinary* being in the sense in which an historical person or a material object or even a reflection or dream might be called ordinary beings. Accordingly, the Positivist did not take the word 'God' to refer, on the theist's usage, either directly or obliquely to any being in the material world or to any occurrences in the world either of a public or of a private sort. The Positivist assumed that "There is a God" typically functions as an assertion, that it typically asserts the existence of

---

Good (Chicago: The University of Chicago Press, 1946) is strikingly similar to the view just described.

[21] *Religion and the Scientific Outlook*, p. 152.

[22] *Ibid.*, p. 150.

a being of some sort, albeit perhaps an extraordinary being.[23] "There is a God" functions as a putative statement of fact.[24]

But if "There is a God" functions as a putative statement of fact, the Positivist argument continued, the statement must be *testable*. What does the requirement of statement-testability involve?

2. *"A necessary condition of a genuine statement of fact is that it must be Verifiable"*

In denying factual significance to a large number of sentences which plausibly were thought by their speakers to claim that status, the Positivist was employing a criterion of significance expressive of his view of the conditions under which any sentence at all may be said to make an intelligible assertion. "A criterion of significance," Paul Marhenke writes, "is a statement to the effect that a sentence is significant if it satisfies such and such conditions, and that it is meaningless if it does not satisfy the specified conditions."[25] Behind the various formulations of the criterion, the variety of which almost prompts one to speak of criter*ia* instead, there lies a common theory of factual meaningfulness which animates them all. On matters of detail, to be sure, there were differences among the views of the Positivists. But beneath the differences, a consensus prevailed on the question as to how the "meaningfulness" of an assertion is ultimately to be assayed. This consensus is summed up in the very early slogan that the meaning of a proposition is the method of its verification.[26] The slogan has in common with others that it can be easily misunderstood. It has been claimed, for example, that the slogan must surely be false since we commonly distinguish between what a statement means and how we ascertain whether that statement is

[23] The question as to what the Positivists took sentences about God to putatively assert is developed further, and from a slightly different point of view, in section three of this chapter and in section F of the Appendix.

[24] Ayer has been the chief spokesman for Positivism in this section. It is noteworthy that Ayer has characterized his *Language, Truth, and Logic*, from which the argument here has largely been drawn, as an attempt to present "the classical position of the Vienna Circle." Editor's introduction to *Logical Positivism*, p. 8.

[25] Paul Marhenke, "The Criterion of Significance," *Proceedings and Addresses of the American Philosophical Association*, 23 (1950); reprinted in *Semantics and the Philosophy of Language*, ed. by Leonard Linsky (Urbana, Illinois: The University of Illinois Press, 1952 [pp. 139-159]), p. 139.

[26] *Logical Positivism*, p. 13. Also see M. Schlick, "Meaning and Verification," *The Philosophical Review*, 45 (1936), reprinted in Herbert Feigl and Wilfrid Sellars, eds., *Readings in Philosophical Analysis* (New York: Appleton-Century-Crofts, Inc., 1949 [pp. 146-170]), p. 148.

true or false. We commonly tell how old a tree is, for instance, by counting its annual growth-rings. But it is clear that "Duncan's oak is 75 years old" is not cashable without loss of meaning into "Duncan's oak has 75 growth-rings" or any of the sub-activities involved in someone's ascertaining that Duncan's oak has that many growth-rings. This sort of reply betrays a fundamental misunderstanding of the Positivist slogan. To grasp its purport, one must look very carefully at the intimate connection which the Positivist held to obtain between the question as to a proposition's *meaningfulness* and the question as to its *testability*. The more or less official view may be seen in some early remarks of Rudolf Carnap and Moritz Schlick.

The central features of the official view appear in two parallel passages written by Carnap, the first in 1932 and the second in 1936:

> ... The meaning of a statement lies in the method of its verification. A statement asserts only so much as is verifiable with respect to it. Therefore a sentence can be used only to assert an empirical proposition if indeed it is used to assert anything at all. If something were to lie, in principle, beyond possible experience, it could be neither said nor thought nor asked.[27]
>
> Two chief problems of the theory of knowledge are the question of meaning and the question of verification. The first question asks under what conditions a sentence has meaning, in the sense of cognitive, factual meaning. The second one asks how we get to know something, how we can find out whether a given sentence is true or false. The second question presupposes the first one. Obviously we must understand a sentence, i.e., we must know its meaning, before we can try to find out whether it is true or not. But, from the point of view of empiricism, there is a still closer connection between the two problems. In a certain sense, there is only one answer to the two questions. If we knew what it would be for a given sentence to be found true then we would know what its meaning is.... Thus the meaning of a sentence is in a certain sense identical with the way we determine its truth or falsehood; and a sentence has meaning only if such a determination is possible.[28]

[27] Rudolf Carnap, "The Elimination of Metaphysics," trans. by Arthur Pap from "Ueberwindung der Metaphysik durch Logische Analyse der Sprache," *Erkenntnis*, II, (1932), reprinted in *Logical Positivism* [pp. 60-81], p. 76.

[28] Rudolf Carnap, "Testability and Meaning," *Philosophy of Science*, 3 (1936) and 4 (1937); reprinted, with omissions, in Herbert Feigl and May Brodbeck, eds., *Readings in the Philosophy of Science* (New York: Appleton-Century-Crofts, Inc., 1953 [pp. 47-92]), p. 47. Readers interested in the official view of these matters should consult the articles cited in this note and the note above, as well as three others, to which reference will occasionally be made: R. Carnap, "Truth and Confirmation," adapted by the author and trans. by H. Feigl from "Wahrheit und Bewährung," *Actes du Congrès International de Philosophie Scientifique* (1936), reprinted in *Readings in Philosophical Analysis* [pp. 119-127]; M. Schlick, "Meaning and Verification," and M. Schlick, "Positivism and Realism."

What is the exact sense of "verify" and its variants that makes it plausible for Carnap, and the Positivists generally, to equate the meaning of a proposition with the method of its verification? In Positivist writings, the force of "verify" is *show to be true*. It is important to get clear on the purport of "show" in that definition. It is crucial, the Positivist would insist, to distinguish what *shows* a proposition to be true and that which, more weakly, merely *attests to* or *certifies* its truth. That "certain sense" in which the meaning of a proposition is held to be "identical with the way in which we determine its truth or falsehood" emerges only by observing this distinction. What does the distinction involve?

There is a more or less conventional sense of "verify" according to which one might plausibly say that the claim that Caesar crossed the Rubicon can be verified by looking into a history book. It is perfectly proper to say that the statement made by uttering the sentence 'Caesar crossed the Rubicon' is verifiable, and that the way one might verify it—assay its truth or falsehood—is by checking what the sentence asserts against the relevant claims recorded in a book about Caesar's life. Similarly, it is proper to say that the statement made by uttering the sentence 'Sam Snead bogeyed the 18th hole today' might be verified by listening to the evening sportscast, and that the statement made by uttering the sentence 'Dr. Lambert told John that he (John) has pleurisy' might be verified by telephoning Dr. Lambert and asking him what he said about John's illness. The sense of "verify" at work in this conventional manner of speaking is that of consulting a creditable record or checking with someone who is in a position to know the facts and is veracious in his reporting of them.

Let that sense of "verify" be re-christened "certify" in order to distinguish it from another, more restricted usage of the word. In the more restricted usage, "Sam Snead bogeyed the 18th hole today" could be verified only by being at the golf course and by watching Sam Snead bogey the 18th hole. It could not be verified by listening to the evening sportscast, for *that* procedure only certifies the fact in question, attests to it. Similarly, "Dr. Lambert told John that he has pleurisy" could be verified, on this usage, only by having heard Dr. Lambert say that John has pleurisy, not by calling him later and asking what he said about John's illness. "Caesar crossed the Rubicon," similarly, could be verified only by watching Caesar cross the Rubicon, not by looking into a book or hearing some authority on Caesar's life allege this of him.

For expository purposes, let us adopt the somewhat awkward expression 'the fact asserted' and let its usage be illustrated as follows. The fact asserted by "Dr. Lambert told John that he has pleurisy" is a certain man's (Dr.

Lambert's) saying that another man (John) has pleurisy. The fact asserted by "Caesar crossed the Rubicon" is a certain man's (Caesar's) crossing a certain river (the Rubicon). The fact asserted by "Sam Snead bogeyed the 18th hole today" is a certain man's (Sam Snead's) going one over par on a certain hole (the 18th) at a specified time (today). Let us say, furthermore, that anyone hearing Dr. Lambert tell John that he has pleurisy *confronts* the fact asserted by "Dr. Lambert told John that he has pleurisy." Anyone seeing Sam Snead go one over par on the last hole today confronts the fact asserted by "Sam Snead bogeyed the 18th hole today." Anyone seeing the man Caesar cross the river Rubicon confronts the fact asserted by "Caesar crossed the Rubicon." Let us say, finally, that confronting the fact asserted by a proposition, as illustrated by the examples given, constitutes a test-procedure for determing the truth of that proposition.

The use of 'confront' employed here is not entirely without Positivistic precedent. In "Truth and Confirmation," for example, Carnap describes the process of statement-confirmation as one of "confrontation of a statement with observation. Observations are performed and a statement is formulated such that it may be recognized as confirmed on the basis of these observations."[29] Carnap later notes that "confirmation is understood to consist in finding out as to whether one object (the statement in this case) properly fits the other (the fact); i.e., as to whether the fact is such as it is described in the statement or, to express it differently, as to whether the statement is true to fact."[30] For variety, let the expression "confronts the fact" be equivalent to the expression "confronts the state of affairs."

When the Positivist equated what he called "the meaning of a proposition" to what he called "the method of verifying that proposition," it was *verification*, not certification, that he had in mind: *to verify proposition-p just is to confront the fact asserted by p*. What made it plausible for the Positivist to hold that "the meaning" of *p* exactly matches "the method of verifying" *p* was presumably the view that, first, "the meaning of p" *is* the fact asserted by *p*, and second, "the method of verifying *p*" is the confrontation of the fact asserted by *p*. The test-procedure for determing the truth of *p*, in short, is nothing less than confronting the fact asserted by *p*, which implies that nothing of what is included in "the meaning of *p*" is left unverified because nothing of what is included in "the meaning of *p*" is unconfront*able* or unconfront*ed*.

Two passing points might be noted at this juncture. First, the doctrine

[29] Carnap, "Truth and Confirmation," p. 124.
[30] *Ibid.*, p. 125.

that to verify a proposition is to confront the fact asserted by it posed serious difficulties for the Positivists, difficulties which the expression 'verifiable in principle' was calculated to overcome. These difficulties will be discussed in detail in chapter three; to discuss them here would necessitate discussing several things at once. Second, it is difficult to formulate an introductory parallel statement of a proposition's falsification-condition. Following the pattern set by "to verify *p* is to confront the fact asserted by *p*," it is tempting to say that "to falsify *p* is to confront the absence of the fact asserted by *p*." Schlick may have had something like this in mind when he wrote "... it is simply impossible to give the meaning of any statement except by describing the fact which must exist if the statement is to be true. If it does not exist then the statement is false."[31] But this formulation might be misleading. If it were false that Sam Snead bogeyed the 18th hole today —say he birdied it instead—one would not normally describe its falsification-condition as confronting the absence of Sam Snead's going one over par on the 18th hole today. One cannot confront the absence of a fact. It is closer to the truth to say that one confronts *other* facts which are incompatible with its being true that Sam Snead bogeyed the 18th hole today. A more acceptable formulation, then, of the falsification-condition for proposition-*p* might be this: to falsify *p* is to confront a state of affairs *O* such that if *O* obtains then *p* is false. To confront the state of affairs correctly described by "Sam Snead birdied the 18th hole today" would be one of the possible states of affairs which would show that "Sam Snead bogeyed the 18th hole today" is false.

It might be illuminating to dwell at greater length upon some of the Positivists' thinking behind their contention that the test-procedure for determining the truth of proposition-*p* is the confronting of the fact asserted by *p*, which implies that nothing of what is included in the scope of "the meaning of p" is left unverified. This view might be elucidated further by considering some remarks of Moritz Schlick in his article "Positivism and Realism."

> The criterion of the truth or falsity of a proposition then lies in the fact that under definite conditions (given in the definition) certain data are present, or not present.... The statement of the conditions under which a proposition is true is *the same* as the statement of its meaning, and not something different.[32]
>
> A proposition has a statable meaning only if it makes a verifiable difference whether it is true or false. A proposition which is such that the world remains the same whether it be true or false simply says nothing about the world; it is empty

[31] Schlick, "Positivism and Realism", pp. 86-87.
[32] *Ibid.*, p. 87.

and communicates nothing; I can give it no meaning. We have a *verifiable* difference, however, only when it is a difference in the given, for verifiable certainly means nothing but "capable of being exhibited in the given."[33]

Within Positivist writings it is difficult to find a more succinct exegesis of the doctrine that the meaning of a proposition is the method of its verification. Some of the theses here expressed by Schlick have already been explored: for example, that a proposition stakes out a definite state of affairs; that the "meaning" of a proposition is the fact or state of affairs it stakes out; that the verification of a proposition consists in the confronting of the fact or state of affairs which the proposition asserts to obtain. The doctrine that the state of affairs which a proposition asserts to obtain must, in the end, be capable of being indicated *ostensively* should now be elucidated at greater length.

An important question for someone who maintains, with the Positivist, that the factual "meaningfulness" of a proposition is a function of its being verifiable in the sense explained, is whether an assertion can *say more* than what is verified, or what is verifiable, with respect to it. Schlick's attack upon "realism" is a paradigm of Positivist analysis. It is summed up in this sentence: "Every proposition has meaning only in so far as it can be verified, and says only what is verified, and simply nothing more."[34] Against what view is this objection directed, and what does Schlick propose in its place?

Schlick attacks a particular version of the belief in the reality of the external world, a version, as he says, which "assume[s] something further to exist behind the empirical world." Schlick does not himself deny the meaningfulness of the assertion that there is a real external world, nor does he think that such a denial is entailed by anything properly called Positivism. The external world which he holds to exist is the empirical world, "the realm of the observations of everyday life and science." The existence of the world of nature and human artifacts is not denied. "There are, quite evidently, houses, clouds and animals existing independently of us and ... any thinker who denied the existence of the external world in this sense would have no claim to our respect." Schlick's attack is directed against the meaningfulness of the assertion that there is a real external world "in the transempirical sense of that word." He contends that metaphysicians have long maintained that behind the veil of empirical reality "lies some-

[33] *Ibid.*, p. 88.

[34] *Ibid.*, p. 90. The several brief quotations cited in the following three paragraphs of the text are drawn from "Positivism and Realism," pp. 91-107.

thing more, the transcendent reality." Schlick calls this view "metaphysical realism" and its adumbration of classical theological claims should be at once evident. "Realism," on this view, designates "something altogether independent of experience," a "transcendent world," something which "lies beyond a boundary line which separates the accessible from the inaccessible." Schlick mentions two variant forms which this view has taken. It has been formulated as a doctrine to the effect that behind the empirical world "there is something which is to be designated, say, 'independent existence' or 'transcendent being.' " It has also been formulated as a doctrine about existential propositions, that is, that existential propositions may be interpreted as referring, ultimately, to something non-empirical. The latter formulation has the consequence that what is legitimately included within the "meaning" of an existential proposition "is not exhausted by what can be verified in the given, but extends far beyond it." Schlick's argument is directed principally against the latter formulation, since that formulation, more explictly than the former, involves a denial of the Positivist thesis that "the meaning of every proposition is finally to be determined by the given, and by nothing else." To have that thesis fail would be to give up the core position since, as Schlick remarks, "the justified unassailable nucleus of the 'positivistic' tendency seems to me to be the principle that the meaning of every proposition is completely contained within its verification in the given."

Schlick counters the thesis of metaphysical realism with an argument in support of the conclusion that a proposition can intelligibly say no more than what can be given in experience with respect to it. Carnap's earlier remark that a sentence can be used only to assert an empirical proposition, if indeed it is used to assert anything at all, finds its mate in a parallel, more polemical passage by Schlick : "Even to speak of any other world [than the empirical world] is logically impossible. There can be no discussion concerning it, for a non-verifiable existence cannot enter meaningfully into any possible proposition."

The argument here appears to be as follows. The claim that a proposition can refer to more than what might be contained in the empirically "given" invites the query "what more?" "For one cannot assert the existence of something without saying *what* one asserts to exist." The answer to the query "what more?" will always make reference to what might be given in some possible experience. Schlick concedes, to be sure, that there is an obvious sense in which assertions can and normally do *say more* than what is "given." Statements about physical objects provide a case in point. "Strictly speaking, the meaning of a proposition about physical objects would be exhausted only by an indefinitely large number of possible verifications." For example, "Michelangelo's *David* is in the Florentine Academy" obviously says more than—its meaning is not exhausted by—what is given in any finite collection of empirical data in any *one visit*, say, to the Academy to look at the piece. "The meaning of every physical statement is lodged in an endless concatenation of data." But what more can an assertion intelligibly assert, Schlick implies, than "an infinitely large number of possible verifications" *of the sort* exemplified by the finite collection? To say that something more is meant, where the 'more' is used to convey the suggestion of something of a *different* (*super-empirical*) *sort altogether*, is again to invite the question "what more?" or "what sort?" and each response to these queries, however far the series is extended, would appear to involve making reference to the familiar categories of the empirically given, upon pain of falling into unintelligibility:

> If anyone is of the opinion that the meaning of a proposition is nevertheless not exhausted by what can be verified in the given, but extends far beyond it, he must at least admit that this additional meaning cannot be in any way described, stated, or expressed in language. For let him try to communicate this additional meaning: To the extent to which he succeeds in *communicating* something about this additional meaning he will find that he has indicated certain conditions which can serve for verification in the given, and thus he finds our position confirmed. Or else he believes himself to express only that *something* more is there, concerning whose nature simply nothing is said. And then in fact he has communicated nothing, and his assertion is meaningless. For one cannot assert the existence of something without saying *what* one asserts to exist.[35]

SUMMARY. This section has examined several aspects of the doctrine that the meaning of a proposition is the method of its verification. That was the early Positivist formulation of the doctrine which, in later Positivist writings, became a doctrine to the effect that a necessary condition of a genuine—that is, a meaningful—statement of fact is that it must be Verifiable. The empiricism embraced by the Positivists is more radical and thoroughgoing than that involved in some philosophical views plausibly labeled empiricistic. According to the Positivists' variety of empiricism, the meaningful employment of words within the language rests on the specification of their criterion of application, or, as was sometimes said, upon *definitions*. Definitions, in turn, must be, as Kraft maintains, "ultimately reducible to ostentation of what is designated."[36] What a proposition con-

[35] *Ibid.*, p. 92.

[36] Victor Kraft, *The Vienna Circle*, trans. by Arthur Pap (New York: The Philosophical Library, 1953), p 32.

veys, in turn—the fact or state of affairs it designates or asserts to obtain —is ultimately specifiable in terms of what might be observed. The "meaning" of proposition-*p consists in* the empirical conditions which, if confronted in the matrix of a broader empirical setting, would show *p* to be true, and if *not* confronted in that matrix, would show *p* to be false. Having determined by observation, for example, that the specimen brought back from the moon is an animal with a segmented body and jointed legs and an exoskeleton, I correctly assert that the specimen brought back from the moon is an *arthropod.* Having been a member of the gallery and having watched Sam Snead shoot one under par on the 18th hole today, I correctly deny that Sam Snead bogied the 18th hole today. One must be able to *point out* the state of affairs a proposition designates. "... The state of affairs designated by it [the proposition] ... is equivalent to the conditions under which it is accepted as true or false. The meaning of a proposition is determined by the method of its verification."[37] This requirement restricts the intelligible reference made by a particular proposition to the domain of the empirical. As Kraft declares, "... what assertions can possibly mean is tied to experience, there can be no super-empirical meaning. No meaning can be given to that which is not reducible to experience."[38] The requirement also restricts the *range* of meaningful propositions, *a fortiori,* to those for which it is possible to specify a method of verification or falsification. "Only assertions about empirical facts admit of verification. Hence sentences about what is in principle beyond experience have no meaning."[39] A necessary condition of a genuine factual statement is that it be possible to specify the empirical conditions which would constitute its verification or its falsification.

3. "*The statement that God exists is not Verifiable*"

The Positivist maintained that the statement that God exists is, at least putatively, a statement of fact. He contended, in effect, that the entire class of theological sentences depended either for their truth or for their appropriateness upon its being a fact that there is a God. By "theological sentences" in that sort of formulation he would have meant that class of sentences which make direct or indirect reference to God, such as "God is love," "The Kingdom of God is among you," "Forgive us our trespasses ...," "God was incarnate in Jesus Christ," "The Lord moves in a

[37] *Ibid.,* p. 31.
[38] *Ibid.,* p. 33.
[39] *Ibid.,* p. 34.

mysterious way ...," etc. Theological sentences "depend for their truth" upon its being a fact that there is a God in the sense, say, that statements about the fabled Loch Ness monster ("... appeared near the beach on December 19, 1899," "... was seen by two fishermen, and photographed by them, on May Day, 1936," etc.) depend for their truth upon the truth of the statement that there is, or was, a monster in Loch Ness. Theological sentences "depend for their appropriateness" in the sense, say, that hte appropriateness of advertising "Fly Braniff to Bangkok" depends upon its being true that Braniff schedules flights to Bangkok: the appropriateness of sincerely saying "Let us pray ..." depends, similarly, upon its being true that there is a God who hears (answers) prayer, or at least upon the speaker's believing so. The Positivist construed sentences like "There is a God," naturally enough, as typically asserting the existence of something or someone. He maintained, furthermore, that a necessary condition of a genuine statement of fact is that it must be empirically testable. Any *prima facie* statement which fails to meet that condition becomes, factually speaking, meaningless. What remains to be explained in his reasoning in support of the conclusion that the statement that God exists is, factually speaking, meaningless.

a) The classical position

(1) *The first argument: The transcendence of God.* The prevailing Positivist line of argument was that the untestability of the statement that God exists follows directly from one indefeasible feature of the theistic concept of God, a feature commonly designated by the term 'transcendence'. Nothing intelligible could be said, the Positivist maintained, about a non-empirical or super-empirical reality. If "transcendent" is construed to mean "lying beyond the scope of possible human experience," then *any* talk about transcendent objects, be they substrata of material objects or entities of any sort, falls to the charge of unintelligibility. "... No statement which refers to a 'reality' transcending the limits of all possible sense experience can possibly have any literal significance," Ayer declares, "from which it must follow that the labours of those who have striven to describe such a reality have all been devoted to the production of nonsense."[40] The very word "metaphysical" suggested to the Positivists the attempt to say something about the existence or nature of something allegedly transcending the reach of possible empirical observation. In "Demonstration of the Impossibility of Metaphysics", Ayer wrote, "... I *define* a metaphysical enquiry as an en-

[40] *Language, Truth, and Logic*, p. 34.

quiry into the nature of a reality underlying or transcending the phenomena which the special sciences are content to study."[41] John Passmore observed that "The logical positivists, when they spoke of 'metaphysics,' had in mind the unabashed transcendentalism, the sort of metaphysics which glories in its superiority to the merely experiential...."[42] Why did it strike the Positivist that the writings of many theologians seemed a susceptible target for the kind of attack against metaphysics which they were eager to press? More briefly, why was theology thought to be metaphysical?

It seemed clear to the Positivist that God is often construed by many *metaphysicians* as a transcendent being. Carnap, for example, writes that "In its *metaphysical* use ... the word 'God' refers to something beyond experience. The word is deliberately divested of its reference to a physical being or to a spiritual being immanent in the physical."[43] Similarly, that God is usually understood as a transcendent being in the mainstream of Christian theology was also quite clear to the Positivists, or to most of them. At any rate, it is the assertion of the existence of a transcendent God, wherever it occurs, which the Positivist was zealous in pronouncing to be meaningless. Admittedly, the extent to which God, as conceived in the Judeo-Christian tradition, is held to have entered into relations with the world often fostered the suspicion that the God of that tradition is not *wholly* transcendent. A God who is alleged to have made himself visible to persons in the Old Testament times and/or to have become incarnate in Jesus Christ is surely different in important respects from an utterly transcendent God. What Passmore calls the "many transactions between the natural and the supernatural order" alleged by classical Christian theologians, made some Positivists—Rudolf Carnap, for example—wary of generalizing about the distinctive meaning of 'God' in its theistic usage. He writes:

> The theological usage of the word "God" falls between its mythological and its metaphysical usage ... Several theologians have a clearly empirical (in our terminology, "mythological") concept of God.... The linguistic usage of other theologians is clearly metaphysical. Others again do not speak in any definite way, whether this is because they follow now this, now that linguistic usage, or because they express themselves in terms whose usage is not clearly classifiable since it tends towards both sides."[44]

[41] A. J. Ayer, "Demonstration of the Impossibility of Metaphysics," *Mind* (1934); reprinted in *A Modern Introduction to Philosophy* [pp. 760-769], p. 761.

[42] John Passmore, *Philosophical Reasoning* (London: Gerald Duckworth & Co., Ltd., 1961), p. 87. Passmore does not here observe the distinction sometimes made between "transcendent" and "transcendental" as, for example, in the philosophy of Kant.

[43] Carnap, "The Elimination of Metaphysics," p. 66.

[44] *Ibid.*, pp. 66-67.

On the whole, however, the Positivists regarded "God" as typically purporting to designate a unique, transcendent being whom Christians hold, it was presumed, to be distinguished from the world and from anything in the world, regardless of God's relations with the world. As was already noted, the Positivists were not themselves much concerned with providing documentation for that contention. But finding such documentation would surely not be difficult; one strong theme within the history of Christian thought is the theme of the sharp distinction—sometimes a muted distinction—between the divine and the human domains, although there are, to be sure, tendencies running in the other direction, too. These tendencies are important and will be discussed in some detail in chapter four.

The conception of God, then, which the Positivists seem generally to have attributed to Christians is a conception according to which God is a transcendent being. Passmore expressed what could be taken as the prevailing Positivist view of the matter when he writes, "According to traditional theology, the supernatural is of a completely different order from the natural,"[45] which might be re-tooled slightly to fit the Christian context and read, rather: According to traditional Christian theology, God belongs to a completely different order from the natural. But problems arise precisely in virtue of that thesis. The supposition that God exists, as Passmore observed, "... creates philosophical problems only when he is said to have a mode of existence quite different from that of other beings."[46] The problem the Positivist pointed out is one that follows, he alleged, directly from God's being characterized as transcendent. If God is conceived as a transcendent being, then it follows immediately that nothing that might be indicated ostensively could be God. Anything which might be ostensively indicated falls, by that fact, within the reach of human experience, and therefore could not be a transcendent being. The same thing that Passmore observed about "substance," the Positivist would have said, *mutatis mutandis*, about God: "If ... 'substance' is defined as 'that which underlies all the objects of experience,' it at once follows that the metaphysician cannot point to a sample of substance. Anything to which he draws our attention would automatically be a particular object of experience, not something which underlies such objects.... Anybody who says 'I can produce a sample of substance' is automatically denying that substance is the sort of thing he has taken it to be."[47]

45 Passmore, *Philosophical Reasoning*, p. 47.

46 *Ibid.*, p. 50.

47 *Ibid.*, pp. 86-87.

But why should the alleged transcendence of God constitute a problem? An answer formulated with an eye to the more or less official Positivist position reflected in the passages quoted earlier from Carnap and Schlick might proceed as follows. "... It is simply impossible to give the meaning of any statement," Schlick said, "except by describing the fact which must exist if the statement is to be true." A factually significant statement, Schlick holds, conveys, so to speak, a *description* of some "definite state of affairs," where Schlick means by that expression something which might conceivably be "pointed at,"[48] given by ostension. A statement conveys or contains a description by virtue of the meaning of its constituent words. Accordingly, following this line of approach, if one wants to know what a statement says, one might ask what description it conveys. What description is conveyed by "There is a God?" Something is obviously being *said* in that words are spoken, but how might one "describe the fact which must exist if the statement is true?" In the nature of the case we are denied that ultimate, terminal ostensive step by which what a factually significant statement says is tied, by an act of indication, to what might be given in experience, tied to what it is ultimately all about. Passmore observed that "... there is an incompatibility between the nature of the description and the possibility of its applying to a particular instance, e.g., there can be no true proposition of the form 'this is a transcendental being' because a transcendental being is so defined that it can never appear as a 'this', something to which attention can be drawn, a sample, a particular case."[49] If "There is a (transcendent) God" were factually significant, then it would convey a description of some state of affairs; indeed, it would refer to some definite state of affairs, and not another, if what it says is true. But the supposed state of affairs in question is such that neither it nor anything of the sort could conceivably be pointed at. Surely, the Positivist concluded, we have here no intelligible assertion. The sentence conveys nothing, describes nothing, refers to nothing.

(2) *The theist's response*. The theist might fairly respond to such a charge, however, in the following manner: All you have shown, he might say, is that we do not take "God" to name an empirical being. On my usage "God" obviously purports to name a transcendent being. God is a transcendent person who created the world, who loves men, who sent His Son, etc. You have *yet* to persuade me that, in Ayer's strong words, "the notion of a person whose essential attributes are non-empirical is not an intelligible

[48] Schlick, "Positivism and Realism", pp. 86-87.

[49] Passmore, *Philosophical Reasoning*, p. 91.

notion at all."[50] You have perhaps shown that the statement that God exists is untestable; some theists might concede that this follows from God's transcendence. But you have not yet shown that statements about God are, for that or for any other reason, meaningless, unintelligible, or anything of that sort. The meaningfulness of statements about God is clearly a different matter from their testability.

(3) *The second argument: The erosion of key-expressions down to a vanishing point.* It is clear that the Positivist needed a somewhat sharper argument to convey his disquietude about theological sentences. He had to show why and in what sense theological sentences are really unintelligible in consequence of their being about a transcendent being. He had to show why and in what sense theological sentences, insofar as they lack reference to empirical facts, fail to communicate. A sharper line of argument is available in some of the early Positivist writings, although it is neither elucidated fully nor applied so specifically to theological sentences as it has been more recently by neopositivist thinkers. In a nutshell, the argument reduces to the following claim: certain key expressions that figure in theological sentences are void of content. Theological sentences indeed *look* as though they conveyed informative descriptions, but on closer inspection they turn out to be uninformative. The *prima facie* statement that God exists, or that God loves us, etc., is uninformative because, in Passmore's words, "The meanings of its constituent words are so refined away by successive metaphysical re-definition that there is no longer any possible way of discovering whether anything answers to the description: it no longer directs us anywhere in particular."[51] When elucidated in the manner of Antony Flew, whose argument will be examined in detail shortly, the contention becomes even stronger than Passmore's formulation suggests. Flew will deploy the argument in such a way that the verdict about any given theological sentence should be not so much that it conveys a description, albeit a description about which there is no way of discovering whether anything answers to the description; rather, the verdict should read: "If we cannot test it, this is only because we cannot see what it is being used to assert; ... The set of words does not suggest anything to us which we could

[50] *Language, Truth, and Logic*, p. 116.

[51] Passmore, *Philosophical Reasoning*, p. 91. Let it be clear that Passmore does not himself explicitly attack the intelligibility of theological statements on the grounds under consideration, at least not on the occasion of this citation. I have taken the apt wording of his general argument and applied it to the specific point at hand. However, see n. 52 below.

set about trying, and failing, to test."[52] That more apt formulation of the problem, incidentally, is the one offered by Passmore in elucidation of Carnap's notion that an expression may be meaningless when it commits a breach of logical syntax. Before turning to Flew, let us look briefly at Carnap's contention.

In 1932 Carnap pressed the line of argument suggested by Passmore's formulation when he argued against the intelligibility of the metaphysician's use of the word 'principle.' The metaphysician refined the meaning of this word beyond the possibility of intelligible application. He deprives the word of one use and then of another and does not himself specify the criterion of application which governs *his* use of the word. Accordingly, the word remains "as an empty shell."[53] Metaphysical writings are rife with expressions that are thus "devoid of meaning" for the reason that their empirical truth conditions cannot be specified."[54] Consequently, "the alleged statements of metaphysics which contain such words have no sense, assert nothing, are mere pseudo-statements."[55]

What needs further elucidation is the connection between an expression's having no empirical truth-conditions and the allegation that *prima facie* statements employing it have no sense, assert nothing. Ronald Hepburn, for example, claims that "... it has been argued that a proposition like 'God loves me' appears at first sight to be rich in meaning but it is in fact qualified out of existence as soon as we attempt to describe in detail what precisely it claims."[56] What is the argument in support of that contention? What is involved in his charge that "the proposition 'God exists' is eroded away to emptiness by successive qualification: 'he exists—*but* is invisible, inaudible, intangible, not *in* the world nor a name for the world as a whole ...' "[57]? Antony Flew, too, has recently made the same allegation. His vigorous attack upon theism seems to trade, moreover, upon what was implicit in the original Positivist attack. Flew's two celebrated essays, reprinted in *New*

[52] *Ibid.*, p. 89. Passmore does indeed show some sympathy with the Positivist's verdict about metaphysical descriptions, namely, that a metaphysical description might conceivably be "refined beyond the possibility of application" and that if this happens "we might well conclude 'it has no sense' or 'it is not really a description at all.' " *Ibid.*, p. 94.

[53] Carnap, "The Elimination of Metaphysics," pp. 65-66.

[54] *Ibid.*, p. 67.

[55] *Ibid.*

[56] Ronald Hepburn, "Demythologizing and the Problem of Validity," *New Essays in Philosophical Theology*, ed. by Antony Flew and Alasdair MacIntyre (London: SCM Press, 1955), p. 238.

[57] *Ibid.*

Essays in Philosophical Theology,[58] exemplify the erosion-argument mentioned above. His remarks will be examined in some detail.

b) Antony Flew's restatement of the attack

A prefatory word or two about the mood of the Positivists would be in order at this point. First, Positivists are remembered, in part, for their militancy, perhaps in large part because of the youthful vigor of one of their early popularizers, A. J. Ayer, notably in his *Language, Truth, and Logic*. Some of the Positivists, but certainly not all, were intentionally abusive in their attack upon metaphysics. Some, however, were assuredly not militant. Richard Von Mises' *Positivism, A Study in Human Understanding* is an example of the less pugnacious wing of the Positivist movement. Second, there is good reason to believe that one of the guiding considerations in the Positivists' search for a criterion of factual significance was that an adequate criterion should rule out metaphysics *en bloc*. Whether or not Positivists were guided *simply* by a desire to rule out metaphysics will be discussed in Chapter three, section A.

Antony Flew's Positivistic reflexes are moderate. In the first place, Flew appears genuinely concerned to understand what theological sentences are characteristically used to assert, rather than to poke fun at them or dismiss them by a canon consciously contrived to do just that job. Also, Flew shows no inclination to limit the range of "potential falsifiers" to sense-experience, as many of the Positivists were wont to do. A number of the Positivists, particularly neo-Positivists of recent vintage, have adopted a fairly generous standard as to what should be included in "observation" and "experience."[59] In his search for potential falsifiers, Flew is obviously drawing upon Karl Popper, although he goes beyond Popper in one respect. Popper would apparently not claim that falsifiability is a general criterion of cognitive meaningfulness. If one attributes to Popper, as one should, solely the intention of using falsifiability as a criterion for demarcating scientific from

[58] Antony Flew, "Theology and Falsification," reprinted in *New Essays in Philosophical Theology* [pp. 96-108]. "Theology and Falsification" is a symposium provoked by Flew's article, and consists of that article, responses to it by R. M. Hare, Basil Mitchell, and I. M. Crombie, plus a rejoinder by Flew to Hare's and Mitchell's contributions. In what follows references to the items of that symposium are indicated by the rubric "Theology and Falsification," and pinpointed by the author and page designations.

[59] Herbert Feigl, "Empiricism versus Theology," printed in *A Modern Introduction to Philosophy*, first edition (1957), p. 536. References to *A Modern Introduction to Philosophy* are normally to the third edition (1973), from which Feigl's essay, elsewhere unpublished, was eliminated.

non-scientific theories, one must attribute to Flew the more ambitious hope that a falsifiability-criterion would serve to distinguish genuine statements from pseudo-statements. Flew's argument, in brief, is this: the intelligibility of an assertion is a function of its falsifiability. A statement informs to the extent that it delimits a state of affairs. A statement whose truth nothing could conceivably count against, delimits no state of affairs and cannot be informative; hence, it cannot be true. Theological sentences turn out upon inspection to be uninformative, vacuous.

Flew is perplexed by sentences like "God has a plan," "God created the world," and "God loves us as a father loves his children." He formulates his perplexity in two ways: 1) "... we are in doubt as to what someone who gives vent to [such] an utterance is asserting"; 2) "... we are skeptical as to whether he is really asserting anything at all...."[60] Between those two formulations falls the whole block of Positivist argument against metaphysics. The early Positivists sometimes added the denigrating claim that such sentences are nonsensical. Flew avoids the third step. Nevertheless, he begins with the fairly innocuous "doubt" mentioned in 1), but then shifts his final declaration to the less innocuous "skepticism" mentioned in 2). Why does he make that shift?

The Positivist attack upon theological sentences, as was indicated, is predicated upon the supposition that such sentences are typically used to make assertions, that they are typically used by the theist putatively to declare one state of affairs to obtain and not another, that they are typically used by the theist putatively to say something true or false. Flew's rejoinder, in effect, is that he does not understand what they assert. Moritz Schlick had said much earlier, "The empiricist does not say to the metaphysician 'what you say is false,' but 'what you say asserts nothing at all!' He does not contradict him, but says, 'I don't understand you.' "[61] Flew delivers the same charge to the feet of the theologian. He offers two illustrative examples:

(1) "*Some gardener must tend this plot.*" Flew's first example is drawn from John Wisdom's now famous parable about two explorers,[62] of which Flew gives his own briefer version:

> Once upon a time two explorers came upon a clearing in the jungle. In the clearing were growing many flowers and many weeds. One explorer says, 'Some

[60] Flew, "Theology and Falsification," p. 98.

[61] Schlick, "Positivism and Realism," p. 107.

[62] John Wisdom, "Gods," *Proceedings of the Aristotelian Society* (1944-45); reprinted in *Logic and Language*, first series [Two volumes: first series, 1951; second series, 1953], ed. by Antony Flew (Oxford: Basil Blackwell, 1955).

gardener must tend this plot'. The other disagrees. 'There is no gardener'. So they pitch their tents and set a watch. No gardener is ever seen. 'But perhaps he is an invisible gardener.' So they set up a barbed-wire fence. They electrify it. They patrol it with bloodhounds. (For they remember how H. G. Wells's *The Invisible Man* could be both smelt and touched though he could not be seen.) But no shrieks ever suggest that some intruder has received a shock. No movements of the wire ever betray an invisible climber. The bloodhounds never give cry. Yet still the Believer is not convinced. 'But there is a gardener, invisible, intangible, insensible to electric shocks, a gardener who has no scent and makes no sound, a gardener who comes secretly to look after the garden which he loves'. At last the Sceptic despairs, 'But what remains of your original assertion? Just how does what you call an invisible, intangible, eternally elusive gardener differ from an imaginary gardener or even from no gardener at all?' [63]

It is clear from the parable that explorer A, say Jones, who asserts that X—"Some gardener must tend this plot"—does not expect any *happening* in the forest clearing other than what might equally be expected by explorer B, Smith, who asserts that Y—"There is no gardener." A difference in expectations would give Smith an important clue as to what Jones's remark asserts: the difference in expectations would be part of the cash-value of X. Denied a difference in expectations, Smith is unable to ascertain what Jones *means* by X.[64] His only clues are misleading ones: he is in the position

[63] Flew, "Theology and Falsification," p. 97.

[64] This point comes out most lucidly in Wisdom's original parable. It might be helpful to quote that fecund story, once again, in its entirety: "Two people return to their long neglected garden and find among the weeds a few of the old plants surprisingly vigorous. One says to the other 'It must be that a gardener has been coming and doing something about these plants'. Upon inquiry they find that no neighbour has ever seen anyone at work in their garden. The first man says to the other 'He must have worked while people slept'. The other says 'No, someone would have heard him and besides, anybody who cared about the plants would have kept down these weeds'. The first man says 'Look at the way these are arranged. There is purpose and a feeling for beauty here. I believe that someone comes, someone invisible to mortal eyes. I believe that the more carefully we look the more we shall find confirmation of this'. They examine the garden ever so carefully and sometimes they come on new things suggesting that a gardener comes and sometimes they come on new things suggesting the contrary and even that a malicious person has been at work. Besides examining the garden carefully they also study what happens to gardens left without attention. Each learns all the other learns about this and about the garden. Consequently, when after all this, one says 'I still believe a gardener comes' while the other says 'I don't' their different words now reflect no difference as to what they have found in the garden, no difference as to what they would find in the garden if they looked further and no difference about how fast untended gardens fall into disorder. At this stage, in this context, the gardener hypothesis has ceased to be experimental, the difference between one who accepts and one who rejects it is now not a matter of one expecting something the other does not expect. What is the difference between them?

of someone misled by a false French cognate; *demander*, for example. X does not imply that a man will come carrying a hoe, or that a hoe will simply float out of the woods and commence to weed the garden, or any such thing. What, then, does X assert? If one strips away, one by one, all the signs by which one might tell whether there is or is not a gardener who tends the plot, one liquidates, *ipso facto*, the cash-value of "Some gardener must tend this plot."

Explorer Smith reflects as follows. I wonder what explorer Jones means by "gardener" in this instance. When Jones says "Some gardener must tend this plot" he is saying more than that there are flowers here, or that it's almost as if a gardener did all this. He is saying that indeed a gardener *did* it. He believes that there is something or someone responsible for these flowers other than spores in the wind, sprouts in the ground, and the busy bees. Who or what is responsible? I understand the connection that sometimes obtains between flowers and gardeners. But I do not see it here. I can't find the gardener. All I find is flowers. I account for their being here by explaining about spores, sprouts, and bees. Jones knows *that* explanation all right. But the account of germination and reproduction in flowers does not satisfy him in this instance. He wants to put in some other explanatory factor. He calls it a "gardener." Now I can conceive of a gardener. I sometimes even get a sort of picture in my mind when I hear the word. But I cannot conceive of an invisible, intangible gardener. He denies me the appropriateness of anything which would be included in a mental picture, or a physical perception, of a gardener, but what does he leave me? Gardeners are made of sterner stuff. If he had said that her Majesty's gardener tends this patch, I would know how to test that statement: I know what it would be like for *that* gardener to arrive on the scene and perform his tasks. But I do not know what it would be like for Jones' "gardener" to arrive, to sleep late and miss a day's work, or to do anything else. None of the "gardener's" *actions* make any sense until I have some prior idea of what sense "gardener" makes, what the gardener in question is like. What is the difference between there being such a gardener and there being none? I haven't the foggiest idea. What would I be asserting if I asserted it, or, for that matter, what would I be denying if I denied it? Each is as obscure as the

---

The one says 'A gardener comes unseen and unheard. He is manifested only in his works with which we are all familiar', the other says 'There is no gardener' and with this difference in what they say about the gardener goes a difference in how they feel towards the garden, in spite of the that fact neither expects anything of it which the other does not expect." John Wisdom, "Gods," *Logic and Language* I, pp. 192-193.

other. If I have no difference in mind, as I surely do not, between what would be the case if it were true that a "gardener" comes and what would be the case if it were false, then I do not appear to be asserting anything. Therefore, I will ask Jones, "Just how does what you call an invisible, intangible, eternally elusive gardener differ from an imaginary gardener or even from no gardener at all?"

(2) "*God loves us.*" Flew has the same problem with the statement made by theists uttering sentences such as "God loves us as a father loves his children," hereafter "God loves us." So long as Jones is unable to indicate what could conceivably happen to extract the concession "There is no gardener," just so long does Smith remain confused about what Jones' assertion asserts. Similarly, so long as a theist is unable to indicate what could conceivably happen to compel him to concede that it is false that God loves us, just so long will Flew remain confused as to what "God loves us" asserts.

Nothing could conceivably happen, Flew avers, to induce the theist to concede that God does not love us. If indeed this is the case, this *shows* something about theological sentences, Flew maintains. So long as the theist is not able to *conceive* at least of a state of affairs incompatible with the truth of his assertion(s), his assertion fails to assert. Sentences like "God loves us" and its negation, on theistic usage, are typically putatively fact-stating sentences. But since they fail to conform to the logic of other sentences of the form 'X loves Y' and 'X does not love Y', it follows—so the allegation runs—that theological sentences are defective.

There are two ways of couching this defectiveness, first, in terms of *testability*, and second, in terms of *meaning*. One might say, first, that there is no test, no conceivable test, for determining their truth or their falsity. Or one might say, second, that what they assert is unclear, unintelligible, meaningless, vague, or something of that sort. The Positivist wants to insist, as was explained in section 2, that there is but one problem here. Flew's way of speaking steers, as it were, between the two idioms. He wants to say that one's inability to test the truth or falsity of putative statements like "God loves us" is a function of one's not knowing what such sentences assert. His argument, of course, is not that the opacity of theological sentences is due to some difficulty which *he*, Flew, has with them; it is attributed, on the contrary, to the sentences themselves, or rather, to those who speak them and the use to which they would put them. Certain examples will help to elucidate Flew's point.

(a) "*John loves Mary*" *versus* "*God loves us.*" There are certain things one looks for in order to ascertain whether some specific John does or does not love some specific Mary. The case of ascertaining whether someone loves someone else is a complicated case; it is far more difficult than ascertaining, say, whether there is a scorpion in my desk drawer. But the difficulties must be shouldered to display as much symmetry or asymmetry as possible with the case of God's loving men. Although, first, the circumstances in which one correctly asserts *p*—"John does not love Mary"—are more difficult to specify than the circumstances in which one correctly asserts "No gardener tends this plot"; and although, second, it seems difficult to find a case for correctly asserting *p* whose "correctness" could not be shaken fairly by an argument of the form "John does indeed love Mary, and if you knew the whole story of their relationship you would understand that in this case John's loving Mary is not incompatible with John's behaving in such-and-such a fashion towards Mary under these circumstances"; nevertheless, there is a series of tests which asymptotically help us to determine the truth or falsity of *p*. No one test, taken by itself, establishes *p* as true. But several tests, taken together, yield increasing assurance that *p* is true or that it is false. If John does this and that to Mary, and fails to do this and that, then we can be increasingly confident that "John loves Mary" is true, or false.

But the case is different, Flew alleges, with "God loves us." *Nothing* compels its withdrawal; *nothing* constitutes a sufficient reason for denying that God loves us. "God loves us" is compatible with every peril flesh is heir to. Ronald Hepburn writes:

> Although there are certain sorts of human behavior which give good grounds for denying that one human being loves another, the Christian is expected to go on saying that 'God loves me' even when his child is born blind and he himself succumbs to an incurable disease.[65]

Flew's formulation is stronger:

> ... sophisticated religious people ... tend to refuse to allow, not merely that anything actually does occur, but that anything could conceivably occur, which would count against their theological assertions and explanations. But in so far as they do this their supposed explanations are actually bogus, and their assertions are really vacuous.[66]

If no *conceivable* contingency compels the withdrawal of "God loves us," then the *prima facie* statement becomes vacuous. That is Flew's allegation. John Wilson agrees, presumably, when he writes that "... statements are

[65] Hepburn, "Demythologizing and the Problem of Validity," p. 238.

[66] Flew, "Theology and Falsification," p. 106; cf. p. 98.

informative to the same degree as they are falsifiable or vulnerable.... If, then, a statement's truth is consistent with any evidence that might be forthcoming, it cannot be at all informative."[67] But why are unfalsifiable statements uninformative, vacuous?

First, empirical statements exclude some contingencies. A successful, informative statement satisfies two conditions: first, that I, the speaker, claim that things stand thus and so, and not otherwise; second, that you, the hearer, know what it would be like to find that what I assert is *not* the case, that things stand otherwise. Under normal circumstances, my asserting that John loves Mary of a John and a Mary known to both of us satisfies the conditions. Difficult as it might be to tell whether John loves Mary, the claim that it is so, spoken under normal circumstances, raises no *special* testability problems in that the statement has what might be called a limited-contingency-range. That is, it excludes John's doing certain things with respect to Mary. By knowing what to look for on the supposition that a proposition of the form 'X loves Y' is true or false, by knowing John and Mary, and by knowing what is here being asserted about them, you are able, given sufficient access to the relevant information, to test "John loves Mary." It is likely, of course, that sentences of the form 'X loves Y' have a plurality of accredited uses in everyday discourse. If one wishes to test a proposition of that form, one must first know, or be able to find out, which of the several possibly closely related sorts of things sentences of this form *might* be saying is being said in the case at hand; hence, one needs the qualifying phrase "by knowing what is here asserted about them."

But "God loves us" appears to exclude no contingencies. When Flew asks whether any conceivable contingency would falsify "God loves us," he is asking whether there is any limit to the state of affairs which that statement could correctly describe. In short, what is the breaking-point of the statement with respect to the evidence; could any evidence ever compel its withdrawal? Does "God loves us" have a limited-contingency-range or not? If it does, it is informative; if it does not, it is uninformative, vacuous. Flew does not know what "God loves us" *excludes*. He understands that it does not exclude being in pain, enduring misfortune, or dying. As he wondered earlier what "Some gardener must tend this plot" excludes, he now wonders what contingencies, if any, are ruled out by "God loves us." If *nothing* is ruled out, then the delimited state of affairs which a statement stakes out becomes in this case undelimited—unlimited—which is to say

[67] John Wilson, *Language and Christian Belief* (London: Macmillan & Co., 1958), pp. 7-8.

that no single state of affairs satisfies the assertion as distinguished from any other state of affairs. The assertion is "vacuous" in the sense that it is evacuated of any *specific* claim.

Of course, to say that "God loves us" excludes "It is not the case that God loves us" misses the edge of Flew's perplexity. As a response to Flew's problem, such an answer is as much beside the point as answering a boy's query, "What is a *cupreous* rock?" by saying "It's a rock that's not a non-cupreous rock." To ask for what the locution "God loves us" excludes or denies, is to ask for the cash-value of the claim which that putative statement makes, which would be analogous to asking for the cash-value of "Father loves me"—that is, father will do such-and-such, and not do such-and-such, and will think and feel such-and-such while he acts—and analogous to asking for the cash-value of "This is a cupreous rock"—that is, this rock is either reddish-brown, or contains copper, or both.

(b) "*My wife loves me.*" The perplexity that drives Flew to ask what would show that "God loves us" is false may perhaps be illustrated by one final example. If I say, "My wife loves me," and you say, "She was unfaithful to you last week," and I say with a broad smile, "Yes, I know," you are likely to be confused. My blithe countenancing of infidelity as compatible with my wife's loving me may lead you to wonder about something you may not have sufficiently considered initially, namely, what I am asserting when I say the familiar words 'My wife loves me.' If I reply, "Yes, I know," but say it with a frown, a frenetic pause, and a glazed, tortured look and then I add, "But you don't know the whole story; she still loves me very much," you would not be quite so perplexed as before. You would surmise from my behavior that for me, as for the ordinary man, a wife's infidelity "counts against" one's wife's loving one. You would not have good reason to suspect that you do not understand my assertion, since my behavior indicates that I regard my wife's infidelity as counting against her loving me. But something that counts against "My wife loves me" need not *falsify* it. Fidelity is but one element in the montage of marital compromises; there are others. You know that different people might weigh the matter of fidelity quite differently.

Now the following takes place. Suppose that it emerges during our conversation that my wife has been unfaithful to me every week for a year, has refused to cook breakfast any longer, takes long trips alone and unannounced, has grown sullen and petulant, and grievously overtaxes the checking account. I continue to say, "My wife loves me." I still furrow my brow, sputter helplessly, and look more agonized with each succeeding disclosure of domestic squalor. Increasingly you might wonder what I count as a necessary and sufficient condition for saying "My wife loves me." Let us call it the *criterion* for making the statement. Actually, you are wondering not so much what I count as a necessary and sufficient condition for *affirming* that my wife loves me as what I count as a sufficient condition for *denying* it. The point is that you have become progressively confused about what I am asserting, for I have erased several more good candidates for the criterion of saying "My wife loves me." But there are some still remaining. Now, if I were to confess as we talk further, that I hold my wife's loving me to be compatible not only with the conjugal indiscretions mentioned so far, but also with my wife's ceasing to *think* or to *feel* or to be favorably disposed in any particular fashion about me, then you would be in a muddle. For I have denied you your last clues about what I might be asserting when I say that my wife loves me. Your understanding my assertion depends upon your understanding what I would hold as incompatible with that assertion. You did not see that at the outset, for you presumed that I meant, when I said that my wife loves me, pretty much what you would mean if you said this of your wife. But if I deny you a criterion for making, or for denying, the assertion, and then deny you another, and still another, you will land in confusion, not knowing any more *what* I am saying. My statement has been drained of the factual significance it appeared to have at first; it has been evacuated to the point of inscrutibility. Flew calls this condition, aptly, "death by a thousand qualifications."[68]

The Positivist asked, in effect, for the criterion for saying "God loves us," "God exists," "God sent forth his Son," etc. Flew trades on the underside of that request; he asks, specifically, for the sufficient condition for denying it. Flew's request dovetails with that of the Positivists generally, since the absence of a state of affairs satisfying some necessary condition for affirming a statement becomes a sufficient condition for denying it. If one recognizes nothing as falsifying "God loves us," then one admits no criterion for affirming it. "God loves us" thus fails to declare that things stand thus and so, and not otherwise. It declares that *however* things stand, God loves us.

But if that is the case, then Flew and the Positivists land in exactly the same position with respect to theological sentences as the baffled man in the example about "My wife loves me." Failing a description of the state of affairs with which theological sentences are incompatible there is a collapse in communication: without some apprehension of what facts a statement holds *not* to obtain—without some sense of what a statement *denies*—one is by that fact unable to tell what a statement asserts. What Flew asks of the

[68] Flew, "Theology and Falsification," p. 97.

theist, what the Positivists in general ask, is for a description of that evidential crisis which *would* compel the acceptance or the rejection of "God loves us" ("There is no God," etc.). Where is the crux, the experiential watershed such that *if* the evidence were to fall one way, we would be entitled to say that God loves us, and if the evidence were to fall the other way it would "not merely (morally and wrongly) ... tempt but also (logically and rightly) ... entitle us to say 'God does not love us' or even 'God does not exist' "?[69] Since the Positivist thought that *there is no such crux*, he concluded that theological sentences are without factual significance.

RETROSPECT. The argument in this section, elaborated principally by reference to Antony Flew, may be summarized as follows. The ability of men to use some sentences of ordinary discourse to do something we commonly call "stating facts" is a function of there being, first, ascertainable uses to which words and combinations of words are put; second, conventions governing the circumstances under which a word, or a combination of words, may be intelligibly employed; and third, conventions governing the combination of words into sentences designed for this or for that job. The *prima facie* intelligibility of theological sentences arises from the fact that, first, many of their constituent words are common to ordinary discourse; second, many of their constituent words are put to the same use as words in ordinary discourse; and third, theological sentences are constructed according to the conventions governing the combination of words into sentences. Sometimes, however, theological sentences appear to be formulated with disregard to the conventions governing the circumstances under which a word, or combination of words, may be intelligibly employed for a certain use. The putative statement that God loves us, for example, appears to employ the word 'loves' in a way which deviates from at least one important convention governing the intelligible assertive-employment of 'loves' in typical sentences of the form 'X loves Y.' That convention might be stated as follows: use an assertion-sentence of the form 'X loves Y' to describe state-of-affairs-S if and only if you know what it would be like to find some state-of-affairs-*not-S* which is incompatible with its being true that X loves Y. A speaker who makes an assertion of the form 'X loves Y' and disregards that convention fails to meet the minimum requirement for asserting, namely, to declare that things stand thus and so, *and not otherwise*. His assertion, under that condition, fails to assert. A passage written by Arthur Pap might serve as a fitting concluding statement of the Positivists' case against theism:

[69] *Ibid.*, p. 99.

> If a sentence by which a speaker purports to state a fact, to make an assertion, is not empirically verifiable ... then nothing is asserted by it at all; it is neither true nor false.... If, for example, the statement that 'there is an infinite spirit which is omniscient, omnipotent, and good, and this spirit is the creator of the universe' is not empirically verifiable in the sense that observations can be described that would, if they were made, confirm or disconfirm it, then nothing that is either true or false is asserted by it. There is only a cognitively meaningless sentence which seems to many people to be meaningful because it is grammatically similar to unquestionablty meaningful sentences, and because *emotions* of a religious kind, as well as mental pictures, are associated with it. The sentence is cognitively meaningless, according to the positivist, in the sense that no conceivable state of affairs is described by it....[70]

The Positivist claimed, in brief, that (1) theological sentences are characteristically used to make putative assertions; (2) these putative assertions are neither verifiable nor falsifiable; (3) consequently, theological sentences are uninformative. As statements of fact, they are meaningless, unintelligible. [71]

C. APPENDIX:
UNINTELLIGIBLE WORDS AND UNINTELLIGIBLE SENTENCES

The doctrine that the intelligibility of a statement is a function of its testability was now and again developed within Positivist writings by reference to sentences especially selected for their extreme obscurity. As surely as the Positivist criterion of factual significance was developed with an eye to ordinary, everyday empirical sentences, so too was the criterion formulated with another eye to patently nonsense utterances and near-nonsense utterances. Additional clarity may come to the claim that testability and factual meaningfulness are two sides of the same coin by looking closely at certain sentences which, by Positivist standards, are unintelligible, factually meaningless sentences. There is no new argument in this section; the examples are offered and discussed for illustrative purposes only. The Positivist indictment of theological sentences is clearly evidenced in the last example; within a little imagination, it may be discerned in some of the other examples as well. Some lengthy quotations are submitted.

a) "*Some things are teavy.*" The first example is drawn from Carnap's essay, "The Elimination of Metaphysics":

[70] Introduction to Section VIII of *A Modern Introduction to Philosophy*, pp. 750-751.

[71] Philosophers of a Positivistic turn of mind sometimes advanced this thesis by likening theological sentences to other, non-theological sentences especially selected or constructed for their "metaphysical" obscurity. See the Appendix immediately following for a brief discussion of some sample sentences of this type.

Let us suppose ... that someone invented the new word "teavy" and maintained that there are things which are teavy and things which are not teavy. In order to learn the meaning of this word, we ask him about its criterion of application: how is one to ascertain in a concrete case whether a given thing is teavy or not? Let us suppose to begin with that we get no answer from him: there are no empirical signs of teaviness, he says. In that case we would deny the legitimacy of using this word. If the person who uses the word says that all the same there are things which are teavy and there are things which are not teavy, only it remains for the weak, finite intellect of man an eternal secret which things are teavy and which are not, we shall regard this as empty verbiage.... If no criterion of application for the word is stipulated, then nothing is asserted by the sentences in which it occurs, they are but pseudo-statements.[72]

What is wrong with "some things are teavy"? From the information given, the claim which the sentence makes is patently unclear. There is the strong suspicion that some predication is being made, perhaps something like "heavy," "soapy," or "sleepy." But since there are no empirical signs of teaviness, it cannot be such as these. What is teavy *appears* no different, in any respect, from what is not teavy. The things which are allegedly teavy will remain unrecognizable, eternally. All we know, or rather, all we *say*, is that some things are teavy and some are not, and that we cannot decide which, for any given thing. But with no further information given about teaviness, one is strongly inclined to echo Carnap's perplexity as to what "Some things are teavy" asserts. If there are no empirical signs of something's being teavy, as distinguished from its being not teavy, we have no clues to work on. We simply cannot understand the assertion. Moreover, the "assertion" is also obscure to the speaker; he neither understands it nor claims to do so.

b) "*There is a disopholus in the cupboard.*" Consider a similar passage from T. R. Miles' book, *Religion and the Scientific Outlook*:

... If I were to say to you 'There is a disopholus in the cupboard', you may suspect from the context that I mean some strange animal—like a Jabberwock, perhaps; but unless criteria are given for recognizing a disopholus you will be at a loss. In this case no such criteria exist, for 'disopholus' is a word which I have invented. 'The Absolute is incapable of evolution and progress' is similar to 'There is a disopholus in the cupboard' in that in neither case are we told what operations to perform. The verification principle, when applied in these cases, can be thought of as a kind of protest. It is as though someone said 'You are using words as if you knew how to give them "cash-value" when it appears suspiciously as though you do not'. If someone asks, 'How would you verify whether the Absolute is incapable of evolution and progress?', he is making a request, not for advice on

[72] Carnap, "The Elimination of Metaphysics," p. 53-64.

procedure, but for information on the meaning of words. Sometimes 'How would you verify?' is asked rhetorically, with the suggestion that the words in question mean nothing at all.

If 'The Absolute is incapable of evolution and progress' referred to a state of affairs, that state of affairs—so long as we are not told how to recognize it—would be forever unknown and unknowable. If we choose, we may think of the verification principle as an attack on 'permanently unknowables.'[73]

As in the first case, the difficulty is that "There is a disopholus in the cupboard" is unclear as to the claim the sentence makes. There are certain slight hints available in the context as to what is being asserted, or the sort of thing that might be hereby asserted. There is the strong suspicion that a disopholus is spatially discrete, an entity that mingles with empirical things; it is small enough to be in the cupboard, for example. That's a clue. Only one disopholus is said to be in the cupboard, but perhaps there might be more, either there or somewhere else—else the sentence would have required the definite article, not the indefinite one. Beyond these clues there are no more. The complication is that Miles has made up the word. If we do not know that 'disopholus' is simply an invented term, we should be in roughly the same situation as in the first case, except that we would know *where* to go to *look*. There might be a disopholus in the cupboard all right, but since we do not know what we ought to look for ("... no criteria for recognizing ..."), we might just pass by one when we look. It's like a treasure hunt with no description of the treasure. One knows where to go to pursue the quarry, but one does not know when one has arrived or, for that matter, what the pursuit consists in. Would one *look*, visually? Would one smell? Listen? Feel? Where is a clue, even a remote clue? Does a disopholus bite, warble, shimmer, reek, bleed? Something's there, perhaps, but what? More information is needed. So far, we know not what to look for, nor what counts as finding it. It might at first look as though "There is a disopholus in the cupboard" is only extremely though tolerably vague. After all, whatever a disopholus is, there's one of them in the cupboard. But the criteria for recognizing a disopholus must be supplied, as Miles says, else the sentence's claim is not merely opaque; it is inscrutable. We must not confuse knowing-where-to-look with knowing-what-to-look-for. The point is sometimes exploited in children's literature, as for example, by A. A. Milne:

"Have you seen Small anywhere about?" "I don't think so," said Pooh. And then, after thinking a little more, he said : "Who is Small?" "One of my friends-and-relations," said Rabbit carelessly. This didn't help Pooh much, because Rabbit

[73] T. R. Miles, *Religion and the Scientific Outlook*, p. 21.

has so many friends-and-relations, and of such different sorts and sizes, that he didn't know whether he ought to be looking for Small at the top of an oak-tree or in the petal of a buttercup. "So I want you, Pooh, to search by the Six Pine Trees first, and then work your way towards Owl's house, and look out for me there. Do you see?" "No", said Pooh.[74]

c) "*This table is cotilaginous.*" W. T. Stace offers this sentence as illustrative of what the Positivist would call a meaningless sentence. He makes the following remarks:

Now suppose I were to say "this table is cotilaginous," and you were to ask me what I mean by this new word. If I were able to describe some possible experience which in some possible circumstances might be received from the table, and were to say that the character of yielding that experience in those circumstances was what I meant by "being cotilaginous," you would then understand me and I should have succeeded in communicating to you a meaning for my word. But if I were unable to specify any experienceable character of the table which I meant to convey by the word "cotilaginous," if I were unable to tell you what would be the difference in experience between a table which is cotilaginous and one which is not, would you not conclude that the word was in fact nothing but a meaningless noise? [75]

As in the first two examples, some hints come to mind which, upon reflection, one is forced to discount. We ask ourselves: Is being 'cotilaginous' like being oleaginous or cartilaginous, or like being gelatinous or diaphanous? These hints—they are hints rather than clues—suggest themselves to us because of certain rhyming words that come to mind, or words that have common orthographic features. This is sometimes helpful as a device for learning a foreign word and we try it out here, perhaps, for want of anything else to go on. Upon reflection, we discount these hints. Rhyme and orthographic similarity, like homonymy, offer no clue to meaning: why should 'oleaginous' provide a hint to the meaning of 'cotilaginous' when it provides no hint to the meaning of 'cartilaginous'? Sounding similar does not help. We have nothing else to go on, except the vague hint that the quality of being cotilaginous is obviously something that applies to tables. But if some tables are cotilaginous and some are not, and if the difference between a cotilaginous and a non-cotilaginous table is an unexperienceable difference, then we stand uninformed as to wherein the difference consists. For a table's being cotilaginous, like something's being teavy, there are no

[74] A. A. Milne, *The House at Pooh Corner* (New York: E. P. Dutton & Co., Inc.), pp. 37-38.

[75] W. T. Stace, "Metaphysics and Meaning," *Mind* (1935); reprinted, with omissions, in *A Modern Introduction to Philosophy*, second edition [pp. 695-704], p. 697.

empirical signs, Had we said of a table that it is fusty, ichthyoid, made of lemon verbena, or inflammable, we could have *shown* the meaning of our claim to someone who challenged our assertion. As Schlick says, "... there is no way of understanding any meaning without ultimate reference to ostensive definitions, and this means, in an obvious sense, reference to 'experience' or 'possibility of verification.' "[76] Had we judged the table ugly and found ourselves at a loss to say exactly why, we could have struck an informative contrast, perhaps, by displaying tables we judge not-ugly. But unless we are able to show *some* difference between a table's being cotilaginous and a table's being not-cotilaginous, then the difference we presumably intend to mark off by bothering to make, or to deny, the predication cannot be ascertained by someone who hears our "assertion." As it stands, "This table is cotilaginous" is unintelligible.

d) "*An electron is a sort of ultramicroscopic bullet*". C. I. Lewis discusses the vexed case of electrons, on which more is said below in chapter three. His discussion is informative and merits quoting in full:

> The existence of electrons is inferred from the behavior of oil-droplets between charged plates, tracks registered on photographs of the discharge from cathodes, and other such actually observed phenomena. But what is it that is inferred; or is anything really inferred? Some physicists, for example, Bridgman, would say that our concept of the electron comprehends nothing more than these observable phenomena, systematically connected by mathematical equations in verifiable ways. The layman, however, and probably most physicists, would not be satisfied to think of "electron" as merely a name for such observable phenomena. But what more may they suppose themselves to be believing in? An electron is too small to be seen through any microscope which ever can be made, and it would not stay put if a beam of light were directed upon it. It is equally beyond the reach of the other senses. But is the phrase "too small to be directly perceived" meaningful or is it not? And how direct must a "direct verification" be? ... A hypothetical conception of an empirical reality cannot be definitely ruled out unless we can say categorically that the conditions of its verification could never be realized.... If those who believe in the electron as a sort of ultra-microscope bullet cannot envisage this object of their belief in such wise that they would be able to recognize certain empirical eventualities as the verification of it, in case the conditions of verification *could* be met, then they deceive themselves and are talking nonsense. But if they can thus envisage what they themselves believe in, then the fact that such verifying experience is highly improbable, and even that the detail of it must be left somewhat indefinite, is no bar to its meaningfulness. Any other decision would be a doctrinaire attempt to erect our ignorance as a limitation of reality.[77]

[76] Schlick, "Meaning and Verification," p. 148,.

[77] C. I. Lewis, "Experience and Meaning," *The Philosophical Review*, 43 (1934); reprinted in *Readings in Philosophical Analysis* [pp. 128-145], pp. 139-140.

The issue here posed by Professor Lewis is not the question of what can be gained or lost by conceiving of electrons as entities. The issue is whether a certain conception of an electron is intelligible. The conception in question is that of an electron as an ultramicroscopic bullet. Let us call an electron, so conceived, an Electron.

Lewis has two almost contradictory beliefs about electron microscopy. On the one hand he appears quite certain that, while we have been able to see molecules directly, we shall never produce a microscope powerful enough to see Electrons directly. Even if the lens problem were solved, we would never develop a method of illumination without disturbing the view, since the "illumination" in an electron-microscope is itself of a stream of electrons. On the other hand, Lewis cannot abandon the hope that both problems might conceivably be solved. The experimental conditions for verifying or falsifying sentences asserting the existence of Electrons, therefore, cannot be categorically ruled out.

Given this starting-point, Lewis argues as follows: It is meaningful to assert the existence of Electrons even though the existence of Electrons has not yet been directly confirmed and very probably will not be so. But it is only meaningful *provided* that someone who believes in the existence of Electrons *would* be able to decide whether he was right or wrong about their existence *if* observations could be made of the kind that micro-microscopic breakthroughs would provide. Electrons are supposedly ultramicroscopic bullets which are related to the phenomena we observe, just as the burglar is related to the burglary we discover when we return from the theater, but are not themselves observed—as the burglar might conceivably not be observed. The difference between the Electron and the burglar is that the burglar *might* be observed if we set up watch, but the Electron is beyond the reach of observation by any instrument currently in use. Even so, Lewis argues, it is *still* meaningful to assert the existence of Electrons: ultramicroscopic or not, a bullet is still a bullet. Were we to be satisfied that microscope X^n made accessible that region where the bullets fly and we *still* saw no bullets, then we must be willing to concede "We were wrong about Electrons; there are none." Talking intelligibly about an Electron, however small, requires our knowing what we *would* expect of observations discriminating enough to locate these supposedly discrete, and hence isolable-in-principle entities. Supposing *that* contigency to obtain, that is, the contingency of sufficient magnification, then we must be willing to concede that we would *then* be able to see Electrons or else satisfy ourselves once and for all that there are none. To say that there is a particle smaller than we can now detect is one thing; to say that there is a particle so small that it can *never* be detected, even in principle, is quite another. If it *is* a very small particle, then surely a very-small-particle-finder might *conceivably* find one. Otherwise, what does it mean to say that an Electron is a particle? If you do not mean by "particle" something about which you might envision yourself saying, on the receipt of some conceivable experience, "There it is!" then what do you mean? Lewis reiterated substantially the same view later on when he wrote as follows: "With empiricists in general and pragmatists in particular, such references to verifiability as essential to meaning is only a roundabout way of pointing out that unless you are somehow prepared to recognize the factuality you assert, in case that factuality should be, or could be, presented to you, your verbal expression is not a matter-of-fact statement because it affirms nothing intelligible."[78]

e) "*There's a drogulus over there.*" A. J. Ayer submits the sentence in his debate with Father Copleston:

> Suppose I say "There's a 'drogulus' over there," and you say "What?" and I say "Drogulus", and you say "What's a drogulus?" Well I say "I can't describe what a drogulus is, because it's not the sort of thing you can see or touch, it has no physical effects of any kind, but it's a disembodied being." And you say, "Well how am I to tell if it's there or not?" and I say "There's no way of telling. Everything's just the same if it's there or it's not there. But the fact is it's there. There's a drogulus there standing just behind you, spiritually behind you." Does that make sense? [79]

The case is similar to the first two. A drogulus neither is nor does anything that can be observed, as distinguished, say, from Electrons. A drogulus is "a disembodied being" and it is "standing behind you." The only clues we have lie in these expressions. Let us assume that Ayer did not say "standing just behind you." Three things might be said in justification of overlooking that remark. First, as will be seen presently, his argument against the sentence does not need the phrase. Second, there is some reason to believe that "standing just behind you, spiritually behind you" is the mocking-Ayer we have seen before. Ayer has declared himself clearly and often enough on the meaninglessness of just such sentences as the one in question, that he should not seriously be construed as asserting that a disembodied being is *standing anywhere*. Third, if he were taken to be asserting that a disembodied being *is* standing somewhere, then his case against the

[78] C. I. Lewis, "Some Logical Considerations Concerning the Mental," *The Journal of Philosophy*, 38, (1941); reprinted in *Readings in Philosophical Analysis* [pp. 385-392], p. 391.

[79] Ayer and Copleston, "Logical Positivism—A Debate," p. 747.

intelligibility of the sentence would be slightly weakened. His argument is that the truth or falsity of the assertion the sentence putatively makes is one for which no empirical clues are available. But "standing behind you" is at least one empirical clue, as Ayer himself appears to realize when he adds, backpeddlingly, "*spiritually* behind you." He may have added "spiritually" to blunt the empirical hint contained in "standing behind"; but why he included the entire phrase, except perhaps to mock, is not clear.

The difficulty with "There is a disembodied being ..." may be illustrated by showing what we might conceivably do to decipher its meaning. What we might do is to break down the phrase into its component terms, as we sometimes do with a grammatically telescoped German construction (e.g., *Ab/hängig/keits/gefühl*). By combining simpler parts the problematic phrase arose; perhaps it might be deciphered by breaking it down. What follows is a description of such an analytic process. When we hear the words 'a being,' we might hastily draw up a mental list of what things "a being" is true of. The list grows ponderously long. We take a slightly different tack; we ask what property or properties are ordinarily present as pertains to anything we call "a being." Or, if we are nervous with that idiom, we try to find a sentence or a series of sentences which express the conditions under which "a being" is conventionally used. Suppose we come up with the following sentences[80]:

1. It can act or be acted upon.
2. It lasts through time.
3. It has spatial boundaries.
4. It is solid, or at least opaque to unaided vision.

We follow a similar procedure for "disembodied" and come up with nothing perhaps more discerning than the phrase "without a body," and a similar procedure again for "body," and conclude that in all the uses of "body" which we fairly countenance, what *is* a body or *has* (a) body is at least detectable by one or more of the five senses, usually the sense of vision.

Now we try to combine the lists so as to see if sense can be given to the expression "a disembodied being," What do we get? A being is solid, impenetrable to unaided vision; but a drogulus is disembodied, hence invisible. A being has spatial boundaries; but a drogulus is disembodied and has no spatial boundaries. A being can act or be acted upon; but a drogulus has no physical effects of any kind. A being lasts through time. Yes, a drogulus might last through time, but in what sense of "last through time"? Is it

[80] With minor modifications, the list is drawn from Miles, *Religion and the Scientific Outlook*.

like gold's lasting through time, or is it like a lie's lasting through time, or is it like the truth of $a^2 + b^2 = c^2$ lasting through time? If we were to say, as under certain circumstances we might, that such things last through time, we could specify the sense in which we intend to assert that they last through time. Gold lasts through time in the sense that gold is a stable metal which can be counted on to be there, pretty much unchanged in appearance, or chemical composition, to act or be acted upon for many years. But a drogulus cannot act or be acted upon. Lies last through time in the sense that they can be remembered, recalled, forgiven, taught, recorded, passed on, etc., by people; they produce certain physical effects. But a drogulus has no physical effects of any kind; nor, presumably, does a drogulus have any other kind of effects. The truth of $a^2 + b^2 = c^2$ lasts through time in the sense that it will always be a true formula for right triangles. But what is always true, or *ever* true, for that matter, of being a drogulus? If you say "being a disembodied being," I shall ask "Of what is that true?" and if you continue to say nothing except "a drogulus" then I fail to understand you, as I did when we began. If I had said "There's a lepidopteron over there" and you had failed to understand my words about butterflies, moths, and skippers, I could procure a specimen-lepidopteron for you to inspect. I could point out that state of affairs which my assertion covers. But what can you *show* me such that, failing to grasp the meaning of your words or to locate the referent by myself which they presumably denote, I can determine what state of affairs your assertion covers, as distinguished from what it does not cover?

f) "*God intervened at Dunkirk.*" The Positivist request for ostensive definition is also evidenced in the final example to be considered. T. R. Miles offers the following remarks about the sentence in question, which he heard from an English clergyman during the war:

> Now the difficulty with 'God intervened at Dunkirk' is that, if understood literally, it clearly purports to be factually significant, and yet it admits of no verification or falsification by observational means. If we agree that the word 'God' indicates something invisible and intangible, there are just no criteria for deciding whether God intervened; and in the absence of such criteria it is as pointless to assert that he did intervene as to assert that he did not. A person who was told to inspect the facts and see if God had intervened would just not know what to look for; and even if he had microscopes, telescopes, X-ray cameras, and all the resources of modern science at his disposal he would still be none the wiser. 'God intervened at Dunkirk' is thus objectionable on linguistic grounds. It purports to be factually significant, and yet no account can be given of its 'cash-value.'[81]

[81] *Ibid.*, p. 149.

What we are in effect saying is, This is an empirical assertion, and yet it is inconceivable that any empirical test should indicate its truth or falsity; it is an empirical assertion which has no empirical 'cash-value'. I appeal to you, and to all thinking people; is it not futile to pretend to subscribe to assertions of this kind? [82]

Why does "God intervened at Dunkirk" lack cash-value? The point at issue between Miles and the clergyman is not one which might be settled by *deduction*. Miles might say, for example, "Your argument is this, isn't it?: If God intervened, then the men got away; the men got away—therefore, God intervened. That's invalid." "Correct," the clergyman might reply, "but my argument is this: If God had not intervened, then the men would have died on the beach; the men did not die on the beach—therefore, God intervened. That's valid." Miles might reply, "But what's to show your major premise to be true? Might it not be false?" "Of course it might be false," the clergyman might reply, "but I believe that it is not false."

The case is similar to the one presented in John Wisdom's parable. Explorer B might say, "Your argument is this, isn't it?: If a gardener comes, flowers will grow here; flowers are growing here—therefore, a gardener comes. That's invalid." "Correct," explorer A might reply, "but my argument is this: If a gardener did not come, there would be no flowers here; there are flowers here—therefore, a gardener comes. That's valid." Explorer B might answer: "But what's to show your major premise to be true? Might it not be false?" "Of course it might be false," explorer B might explain, "but I believe that it is not false." Another impasse—but an impasse with a difference. They decide to set up a watch in the garden to decide about the truth of the major premise. By a test, one should be able to decide whether *these* flowers originate from spores in the wind and no gardener, or from bulbs in the ground and a gardener with a bag-full. The test is inconclusive for explorer A. He keeps on saying "a gardener comes," but with the result that explorer B ceases to find in "gardener" any cash-value. "I can see the flowers, and before them I could have seen the sprouts and the falling rain. And I know the story about germination and the like. But I don't see the gardener, and I do not know what *he*—the "gardener"—*adds* to the explanation of why these flowers are here. It is *not*, mind you, simply that I don't need a "gardener" to explain the presence of these flowers; there are many things I do not understand about flowers and the conditions of their growth under various circumstances. It's merely that I don't understand how adding your kind of "gardener" helps me to under-

[82] *Ibid.*, p. 148.

stand any better. I don't comprehend what you mean by "gardener" in this instance."

The case is substantially the same, Miles holds, with "God intervened at Dunkirk." To the clergyman, he might say something like the following: "When you say 'God intervened at Dunkirk,' you are presumably saying that something else was involved in the evacuation *other* than the British Navy, the rear-guard flanking the French beach, and all those little launches. But what is this 'something else'? You know the logistic plans laid in advance by the Chiefs of Staff for the contingency that developed at Dunkirk. You know how courageous the rear-guard was, how Mr. Miniver and all those brave boatmen behaved. In a perfectly good sense of 'explain,' *all of that* explains how the British got away. You know that; but you add something else to explain the evacuation: Divine Intervention. I don't understand what part Divine Intervention adds to the explanation of the events. There were other successful retreats during the war, retreats about which you haven't said 'God intervened there,' and there were some terrible routs—Bataan, for example—about which you would probably *not* say that God intervened there. Now, how am I to tell if God intervened or not? You say that if God had not intervened, the men would have died on the beach. This strongly suggests to me that what 'God intervened' comes to—its cash-value, that is—is that the men got away. Yet you assuredly would be unhappy with that reductionistic interpretation of your words since you want 'God intervened' to come to more than the fact that the British got away, the 'more' being that *God did it*. But what do these words really *say*? Give me a criterion for saying 'God intervened here' and tell me why it is satisfied at Dunkirk but not in the North Atlantic when those 1500 poor men on the *S. S. Hood* caught the third salvo from the *Bismark* and all of them, save three men, drowned in the sea. When you say 'God intervened at Dunkirk' it seems that you're saying something about what happened at Dunkirk, and something more than that 338,226 men were safely evacuated from the beach at Dunkirk under extremely perilous conditions. But *what* more are you saying? I can't see God, and I don't know what His intervention adds to the otherwise acceptable explanation of how the evacuation was implemented. It is *not*, mind you, simply that I don't need 'God' to explain the evacuation; there are many things involved in the evacuation which I don't know about. It's merely that I don't understand how adding 'God' helps me to understand any better. I don't comprehend what you means by 'God'. "

CHAPTER II

THEISM WITHOUT BELIEF IN GOD

The Positivists' attack upon that sort of religious belief which they interpreted Christianity as involving has occasioned the growth of a certain kind of "analysis" on the part of a number of British and American philosophers of religion. Writings which feature such analysis are couched as investigations into the "nature" or "function" or "use" of the *language* of religion. Construed narrowly, "the language of religion", or some similar expression, designates those linguistic expressions, spoken or written, characteristically employed in the articulation of the fundamental tenets of a particular religion or, more vaguely, some unspecified religion. Construed more broadly, "the language of religion" designates all the linguistic elements, doctrinal and devotional, which become incorporated into the practice of a particular religion by those who conscientiously subscribe to it.

A practitioner of this sort of analysis must settle one question in his mind before he begins his investigation. He must first decide what *are* the fundamental tenets of the religion whose language he proposes to analyze. Studies animated by the question "How does the language of religion-X function?" thus either presuppose or end up in proposing, either implicitly or explicitly, an interpretation of what an exponent of a particular religion wants to stand by *as* an exponent of that religion. *Prima facie* second-order analyses, accordingly, build upon a prior answer, usually a tacit one, to a first-order question. Discussions concerning the manner in which, say, a Christian uses the language of his religion become, at least in part, discussions of what a Christian stands by *as* a Christian. In analytic philosophy of religion, then, as in other areas of analytic philosophy, adjudication of so-called linguistic questions sometimes involves making normative decisions about the subject-matter.

If analytic treatments of the language of religion, particularly the language of the Christian religion, have shown nothing else, they have made it abundantly clear that there is considerable disagreement about what are the fundamental tenets of Christianity. For example, one now fashionable way of replying to the Positivist's attack upon Christianity, indeed of evading it in the first place, is to claim that to be a Christian is not to commit oneself to holding anything even remotely like that sort of religious belief which the Positivists judged unintelligible. Writers who reply to Positivism in this manner, in behalf of some religion, do not necessarily reject Positivist teachings. On the contrary, as will become evident shortly, some of the respondents are very much attracted to Positivist doctrines. Their style of defense for Christianity, accordingly, takes the form of the double-thesis that such-and-such "simple-minded" or "unsophisticated" forms of Christianity are indeed untenable for the reasons the Positivists noted, but that some other form of Christianity, a form which is "authentic" or "essential" Christianity, is quite tenable. Either by way of giving a direct response to Positivism, then, or by way of offering an independent analysis of Christian belief, some contemporary writers have urged that one can very well be a Christian without believing those things which the Positivist thought a Christian believes, or without construing these "beliefs" in the way the Positivist thought they should be construed: that there is a God, that He sent forth His Son, etc. Their suggestion is that there is a way of being somewhat unspecifiably religious, or of being a Christian, or of accepting theological statements, or of employing sentences containing the word 'God,' etc., which does not leave one vulnerable, as "religious" or "Christian" to the sort of attack which the Positivist made. The purpose of this chapter is to sample and evaluate some early and influential forms which their suggestion has taken. Three distinguishable but related forms will be examined: first, a view fashioned by R. B. Braithwaite, second, a view suggested by certain remarks of T. R. Miles and Ronald Hepburn, and third, a view put forth by Peter Munz. The place of this chapter in the strategy of the whole essay is not so much to debate the normative question as to whether any of these views has a fair claim to being called a Christian view, as it is to highlight the peculiar force and centrality of the doctrine of God which has been an indispensable part of Christianity *traditionally*. If that doctrine is forfeited, then the Positivist's attack is indeed beside the point. But if that doctrine of God is forfeited, then traditional Christianity is also forfeited. That forfeiture, although some are prepared to make it, will be here abjured. Such a move, it seems to me, is akin to curing the disease by killing the patient.

A. RELIGIOUS BELIEF CONSTRUED AS A MORAL COMMITMENT

In 1955 R. B. Braithwaite wrote a monograph entitled *An Empiricist's View of the Nature of Religious Belief.*[1] He describes his study as an attempt to "explain, in empirical terms, how a religious statement is used by a man who asserts it in order to express his religious conviction." (11) Braithwaite's several positive doctrines are animated by one bold disclaimer, which it is well to keep in mind from the beginning: religious belief is not really belief at all. His analysis is an analysis of "the meaning of statements used to make religious assertions" or "... express religious conviction." (32) He explains why he makes such scant use of the notion featured in his title: "In disentangling the elements of this use I have found nothing which can be called 'belief' in the senses of this word applicable either to an empirical or to a logically necessary proposition." (32) This point can scarcely be overemphasized. Sentences expressive of religious belief, on Braithwaite's account, do not say something which is characteristically *believed* in the manner in which "There are tigers in Africa" or "Mont Blanc is the highest mountain in Europe" say something which is characteristically believed. The meaning of a religious statement, he says, is given in the way in which it is used [2]; but religious statements are not used for the job of asserting anything. At least "educated believers" do not "normally" use sentences expressive of their religious belief to say something true or false. Their use is quite different. The primary and normal use of religious statements is to announce the speaker's endorsement of a set of moral principles:

[1] R. B. Braithwaite, *An Empiricist's View of the Nature of Religious Belief* (Cambridge: Cambridge University Press [The Ninth Arthur Stanley Eddington Memorial Lecture], 1955). This essay is broadly reprinted, as for example in John Hick's *The Existence of God* (New York: The Macmillan Co. [pp. 228-251], 1964). References here are to the pagination of the original printing. Because of the heavy saturation of simple source citations, they are noted by page number, unadorned, in parentheses, immediately after each reference in the text. The same procedure is followed in Sections B and C for citations in Miles', Hepburn's, and Munz's books, and elsewhere where the citation-source is sufficiently clear to permit it. References are always to the same work by the respective author; identification, then, is by page number, the author and work being presumed to be clear in each case,.

[2] Braithwaite attributes his "use principle" to Wittgenstein: cf. *Philosophical Investigations* #340, 353, 559, and 560. The most succinct statement of this principle, although it pertains to "words," not "statements," is found in #43: "For a large class of cases—though not for all—in which we use the word 'meaning' it can be defined thus: the meaning of a word is its use in the language." Ludwig Wittgenstein, *Philosophical Investigations,* trans. by G. E. M. Anscombe (New York: The Macmillan Co., 1953), p. 20e.

A religious assertion, for me, is the assertion of the intention to carry out a certain behaviour policy, subsumable under a sufficiently general principle to be a moral one, together with the implicit or explicit statement, but not the assertion, of certain stories (32).

Braithwaite would concede, of course, that his "normal" usage is not necessarily the usage of Christians everywhere and at all times; "normal" usage, for him, is the use of so-called "educated believers." The selectivity here is obvious. Braithwaite is no doubt anxious to avoid the suggestions, on the one side, that he is commending a new usage and, on the other, that he is reporting and recommending the usage of a select class of people. For that reason he sometimes shifts into the anonymous passive voice, employing locutions like 'the use an expression has,' 'the job an expression does,' etc. This idiom may have certain advantages but they are purchased at the price of leaving the reader unaware of the perhaps unavoidable shading of the descriptive mode into the prescriptive mode.

Braithwaite has a strong historical case in contending that without allegiance to a set of moral principles there is no true religion. What leads him to stress the centrality of the moral element in religious belief is the correct historical judgment that religious conviction has always been intimately linked with adherence to some action-policy or, as he puts it, "declarations of commitment to a way of life." (15) But Braithwaite goes further. He is not content with the view that "the intention of a Christian to follow a Christian way of life is ... only the criterion for the sincerity of his belief in the assertions of Christianity...." (15) Rather, it is *constitutive* of that belief. "To say that it is belief in the dogmas of religion which is the cause of a believer's intending to behave as he does is to put the cart before the horse: it is the intention to behave which constitutes what is known as religious conviction." (16) The metaphor suggests that Braithwaite wishes merely to reverse cart and horse. Actually, he intends to do away with the cart altogether. Traditionally, a sentence like "God is love" has had "dogmatic" significance. Braithwaite invests it instead with only "conative" significance since he understands a religious assertion as merely "expressing the intention of the asserter to act in a particular sort of way specified in the assertion." (12) When a Christian says "God is love," for example, he is declaring his intention to "follow an agapeistic way of life." The notion of an agapeistic way of life is undeveloped, but it is not especially obscure. Presumably it designates that sort of behavior enjoined by the whole body of traditional Christian moral instruction, everything from Sunday-school brochures to Canon Law. "God is love" declares nothing about *God.* It declares something about the person saying it, namely, that he resolves to love his fellow men to the best of his ability. The point is nicely expressed by Ronald Hepburn in a comment he credits to John Wren Lewis [3]:

> St. John said, 'God is love', and so he is quite literally. He belongs to the moral world, not to the world of cosmology and impersonality. His commandments are nothing but the statement of the 'conditions in which we either do or do not encounter Love, the only Source of Life'. Religious disciplines are ways of sensitizing the believer, making that encounter more enduring, and increasing the areas of life over which love is sovereign.[4]

When Braithwaite writes "... the intention of a Christian to follow a Christian way of life is ... the criterion for the meaningfulness of his assertions" (15) he is maintaining that the principal meaning which such expressions have is that they are used to declare an agapeistic moral policy. "... The meaning of a religious assertion is given by its use in expressing the asserter's intention to follow a specified policy of behaviour." (16) The connection, then, between religious belief and religious practice, on Braithwaite's view, is the connection between wanting, intending, or resolving to do something and doing it. This is not to say that religious belief *is* religious practice; intending to do something is not the same thing as doing it. Religious belief and religious practice are related as *trying* to do X is related to *succeeding* in doing X.

As not all statements of intention are moral statements, so not all moral statements are religious statements. A religious statement is a special kind of moral statement, and derives its "religious" character from features not shared by non-religious moral statements. Braithwaite notes five contrasting features: (1) The behavior implicit in religious statements [5] includes certain "ritual practices" not included in moral statements. (2) The behavior implicit in religious statements includes not only external but also internal behavior. Whereas moral declarations imply the intention to act in a certain way, religious declarations imply, in addition, "the intention to feel in a certain way...." (21) (3) The behavior implicit in religious statements is often given in concrete examples, whereas moral teaching is often given in abstract terms. (4) The behavior implicit in a moral statement may be specified by the statement itself, but the behavior implicit in a religious

[3] The reference is to an article by Wren-Lewis in *The Philosophical Quarterly* (July, 1955).

[4] Ronald Hepburn, *Christianity and Paradox* (London: Watts, 1958), p. 194.

[5] The expression "behavior implicit in religious statements" is my abbreviation for Braithwaite's longer phrase, "principles of conduct the asserter takes the assertion to involve."

statement is characteristically not specified by the statement itself, or even by several such isolated statements. "... The body of assertions of which the particular one is a representative specimen is taken by the asserter as implicitly specifying a particular way of life." (17) An entire religious system, so to speak, must be considered in order to ascertain exactly what behavior is endorsed. "To assert the whole set of assertions of the Christian religion is both to tell the Christian doctrinal story and to confess allegiance to the Christian way of life." (24) (5) The last, and perhaps the most distinctive characteristic of a religious statement is this: "A religious assertion will ... refer to a story as well as to an intention [to behave in a certain manner]." (24) A story, in Braithwaite's sense, is presumably an account of anything that has occurred, might have occurred, or might conceivably occur. Stories need not be fictive, for Christian stories, Braithwaite concedes, "include straightforward historical statements about the life and death of Jesus of Nazareth." (26) On the other hand, stories need not be historical either: Matthew Arnold's parable of the three Lord Shaftesburys is a story. (25) Braithwaite selects the term 'story' because it is a neutral term, "implying neither that the story is believed nor that it is disbelieved." (26) Every major religion contains an enormous body of such stories as part and parcel of its heritage. Braithwaite feels it incumbent upon him, as well he might, to account for the role which such stories play in "religious belief" construed along the lines he suggests. His account is as follows.

Religious stories nurture the way of life a believer has resolved to lead. But they nurture in a different fashion than one might at first think. Consider, for example, the case of a Christian pondering the life and death of Jesus, and expressing his thoughts with the help of sentences that make reference to stories found in the gospels, by reciting, say, the Apostles' Creed. Ordinarily, Braithwaite allows, a Christian will believe that some or all of these stories are true. (26) But for the purposes of religious nurture, as Braithwaite understands the precise manner in which these stories nurture, it is not necessary that the Christian believe *any* of them. The nurture the stories provide for helping the Christian to live his chosen agapeistic way of life does not depend upon his believing the stories. "The reference to the story is not an assertion of the story taken as a matter of empirical fact: it is a telling of the story, or an alluding to the story, in the way in which one can tell, or allude to, the story of a novel with which one is acquainted." (24) The stories may in fact function more effectively if they are not believed:

> The religious man may interpret the stories in the way which assists him best in carrying out the behaviour policies of his religion.... And since he need not believe the stories he can interpret them in ways which are not consistent with

one another.... Indeed a story may provide better support for a long range policy of action if it contains inconsistencies (29-30).

A religious man will typically allude to a set of stories in his statements and employ them in his ritual. But what does the nurturing is what happens in the course of his using the stories in these and other ways, namely that he *entertains* them in his thought. He need not believe them, hold that they are true. He need only *think about* them, very much as one might think about the story of the Grand Inquisitor in *The Brothers Karamazov*. "For it is not necessary, on my view, for the asserter of a religious assertion to believe in the truth of the story involved in the assertions; what is necessary is that the story should be entertained in thought...." (15-26) How does merely entertaining a story or set of stories nurture the moral policy one has elected to pursue?

Braithwaite presumably does not hold a view suggested by his contention that the religious man will "interpret" the stories in the way which assists him best in fulfilling his behavior-policy: A religious man might conceivably use religious stories as one might conceivably use an historical record—in law, for example—to provide precedent for one's actions, thinking perhaps that to find precedent for an action is partly to justify an action of that sort. Someone's doing such-and-such under particular circumstances affords precedent for my doing that under like circumstances. Religious stories are replete with accounts of such paradigm-behavior from which one might select precedent for one's own actions. But Braithwaite rejects such a view for the reason that finding precedent for an act is not the same thing as justifying that act. That Charles Starkweather killed his father in fact, or that Smerdykov "killed his father" in fiction (in *The Brothers Karamazov*) under certain circumstances, does not justify my performing a similar act under similar circumstances. Finding precedent for an action is merely to discover that someone else has done it, which is a different matter from justifying it. Moreover, if a religious man is not obliged to believe the stories he entertains, that would remove at least one piece of "evidence" that anyone ever behaved in the way in which the story reports. Concerning the allegation that one might feel oneself to be obliged to do a particular sort of act, or live according to a certain policy, because God wills that one do so, Braithwaite holds that even if there is a God, and even if God were to will that one behave in a particular manner, *that* would not be sufficient reason for doing it:

... even when the story is literally believed ... that there is a magnified Lord Shaftesbury who commands or desires the behaviour policy, that in itself is no reason for carrying out the policy: it is necessary also to have the intention of doing what the magnified Lord Shaftesbury commands or desires. But the intention to do what a person commands or desires, irrespective of what this command or desire may be, is no part of a higher religion; it is when the religious man finds that what the magnified Lord Shaftesbury commands or desires accords with his own moral judgments that he decides to obey or to accede to it (31).[6]

Religious stories influence conduct, then, not by supplying examples of model-behavior to be emulated but merely by being entertained in thought. But how is that accomplished?

My answer is that the relation is a psychological and causal one. It is an empirical psychological fact that many people find it easier to resolve upon and to carry through a course of action which is contrary to their natural inclinations if this policy is associated in their minds with certain stories. And in many people the psychological link is not appreciably weakened by the fact that the story associated with the behaviour policy is not believed (27).

According to Braithwaite, the entertaining of stories acts directly upon the wellsprings of action, not because the stories are believed, but because there is a direct link between imagination and the disposition to act. One's behavior is affected not only by what one thinks to be true, that is, by what one believes, but also by what one merely entertains in thought, "his phantasies, imaginations, ideas of what he would wish to be and do...." (27-28) By "associating" one's moral policy, for instance, with the "pantheistic sub-set of stories in which everything is a part of God" (30), one is provided with "confidence." And one is spurred to action by entertaining the "dualistic Manichaean sub-set of stories ... [portraying] a conflict between the

[6] Braithwaite submerges the argument contained in this citation in the making of what is an apparently empirical point, a dubious one at that: while it may appear that religious men do an act because they believe that God wills that they do it, they actually have independent grounds, he seems to think, for their doing the act. Presumably Braithwaite believes that men who embrace "higher religions" conceive God's willing that one do act-*X* as strictly analogous to another man's willing that one do act-*X*. Since men generally realize that the latter, taken by itself, fails to justify one's doing act-*X*, religious men must generally realize, Braithwaite reasons, that the former fails as well. Now while it may be true that religious men have reasons for doing act-X independent of their believing that God wills that they do it, that they themselves realize this is quite probably not the case. Even unsophisticated religious persons, one would suppose, do not think of God's willing something as strictly analogous to another man's willing something. Empirically speaking, it is more accurate to say that religious men generally believe, rightly or wrongly, that because it is *God*, and not merely another man, who wills that one do act-*X*, His willing-so provides as complete a justification for one's doing that act as one might wish for.

forces of righteousness under the banner of Christ, and the forces of darkness under Lucifer's banner." (30)

What Braithwaite maintains, then, is essentially this: First, a Christian resolves to act agapeistically. Second, he also entertains Christian stories to make it easier for him to act in this manner. Entertaining the stories has a direct influence upon his behavior because and only because they "produce a state of mind in which it is easier to carry out a particular [agapeistic] course of action. ..." (30) Certain actions or sorts of actions are directly promoted by a person's contemplating Christian stories. There are two colloquialisms in the English language which capture pretty much what Braithwaite has in mind. One is "listening to mood music" and the other is "greasing the skids." Rather than believing the stories, a Christian allows himself, so to speak, to be filled with the spirit of the stories, as one might allow oneself to be filled with the spirit or mood of a certain sort of music. Merely permitting oneself to be permeated by the "mood" of the Christian stories provides nurture for a Christian's actions, fosters and promotes Christian behavior. Entertaining Christian stories greases the skids for the living out of a Christian's agapeistic moral policy.

B. RELIGIOUS BELIEF CONSTRUED AS "SLANTING"

Braithwaite's monograph expresses one view of how one might, so to speak, accept religious statements without believing them. A somewhat different view is suggested by certain remarks of T. R. Miles and Ronald Hepburn.[7] The exact import of these remarks is difficult to ascertain. Sometimes they suggest a view closer to that held by Peter Munz, which will be examined presently. But sometimes they suggest still a third view, one which is distinguishable from the views of both Braithwaite and Munz. For reasons which will become clear shortly "quasi-ritualism" might be an apt name for the view in question. Incidentally, Miles holds that his position is compatible with the Christian religion: "... there is nothing in the argument to suggest that the central truths of Christianity are invalid."[8] But Hepburn is not inclined to think that his position carries as a description of Christianity. His remarks are considered here principally for the light they shed upon the nature of religious "slanting."

The section of Miles' book which suggests the sort of view in question may be summarized as follows: A Christian is a man who "accepts ... the

[7] Miles, *Religion and the Scientific Outlook*, chapters 13 through 20; Hepburn, *Christianity and Paradox*, chapter XI.

[8] Miles, *Religion and the Scientific Outlook*, p. 138.

theistic parable—the parable of a loving father who has called us all to be like him and to become his children." (161) To accept the theistic parable, however, is not to hold that what the parable says is the case. To accept the theistic parable is to make or to accept a "parable-assertion" (179), to express an "attitude toward life" (178), an "orientation" or way of looking at the world such that "our whole way of life is affected." (169) "It is not," Miles writes, "that one person is better informed on his facts than the other; it is, rather, that they see the same facts, as it were, through different spectacles." (176)

In the concluding chapter of *Christianity and Paradox*, Ronald Hepburn offers some similar remarks about what he calls "slants". A religious slant is but one of "many possible imaginative slants on the world". (200) In one bold and perplexing passage, Hepburn writes:

> Poets and painters are endlessly singing out alternative pictures of man's relation to nature. Some are quixotic and fanicful, the plaything of a lyric or sketch: but one lingers over others, because in some way they project onto nature a vision with which one would be well content to live, which one would choose, before any other perspective, as providing the perfect backcloth to the way of life one has opted to follow.... We may, of course, realize from time to time that our slant is no more than one out of many other possible slants, and that it is sustained by the work of the imagination. But we will be fortified by recalling that the alternative to the slant we seek to maintain (the one which backs up our moral decisions) is some *other* slant, which does this task less effectively. The alternative is not 'reality' in place of 'illusion'; for *every* way of looking at nature in the round involves plumping for some slant or other (200-201).

Neither Miles nor Hepburn explains exactly what adopting, holding, or expressing a slant involves. What follows is an attempt to unravel their position.

What is striking about Hepburn's remarks on slants is the *effort*, the creative activity required for holding or adopting one: one *chooses* a slant, *plumps* for it, *projects* it into nature, seeks to *maintain* it in the face of rival, alternative slants, *sustains* it by one's imagination. Slanting is obviously *doing* something, And the sort of doing involved in adopting or maintaining a slant seems to be a somewhat different sort of activity from that involved in "entertaining stories." Slanting involves an *engineering-like* activity which is not present in Braithwaite's notion of entertaining. Slanting, presumably, is not merely an entertaining of something; it is a *constructing* of something, a "projecting" of something, a sort of thing analogous to selecting, mounting, and looking through spectacles (Miles).

What, specifically, is slanting? Looking at the world with a slant involves one in comporting oneself as one *would* comport oneself if one *believed* that such-and-such is the case, without *actually* believing that it is the case. This interpretation is supported by several of Miles' remarks about "accepting" particular Christian doctrines "parabolically." To accept particular doctrines parabolically seems to involve one in behaving—thinking and talking—*as if* one believed the doctrines to be true, without actually believing that they are true. For example, a Christian is obliged to reject the doctrine that the "Word became flesh," (199) and yet it seems that a Christian is nevertheless invited, at least permitted, to look at Jesus of Nazareth *as if* he were the Word become flesh: "... Jesus Christ is to be *treated* as an object of worship."[9] Similarly, a sophisticated Christian rejects as "meaningless" any "literal talk of 'creation by God' " (167), and yet such a Christian "accepts" the "doctrine of creation by an all-loving God," accepting it, however, as a parable-assertion. (169) And accepting the doctrine as a parable-assertion appears to have most of the same consequences for one who *accepts* it as it would have for one who believes it:

> ... the doctrine of creation, if we take it seriously, forces us to look at the world in a new way. We are forced to recognize that every event is part of God's purpose.... If we take [it] ... seriously, and if the loving father of the parable is assumed to be all-good and all-wise, it follows that we have a paramount duty to do his will. God gave himself without limit; it is our duty to do the same (168-169).

Again, Miles thinks that a Christian must reject any "literal" interpretation of what he calls "the doctrine of *grace*," any interpretation, that is, which "suggests a sort of para-physical activity by a powerful para-physical agency." (203) But, at the same time, it appears that accepting this doctrine "parabolically" issues in similar kinds of thoughts and feelings and assurances on the part of one who so accepts it as it would on the part of one who believes it:

> To speak of 'grace' is to speak the language of parable. An important member of the group of Christian parables is the parable of God as judge ... the important point, I think, in this parable is the sort of defence which we ... can hope to put up. An accused person may in many cases wish to call attention to his good character and stress that he does not deserve the rigors of the law. In this trial, however, such a defence has no place. We do not ask the judge to 'weigh our merits'. Whatever we achieve will certainly fall short of the perfection required of us, and it is a question of being dependent upon the mercy of the judge. If he takes his stand on the letter of the law there can be no acquittal. According to the parable, however, we are not under 'law' but under 'grace'. Acquittal is

[9] *Ibid.*, p. 202. Italics mine.

possible, but this acquittal stems from the mercy of the judge, not from anything that we ourselves have achieved (203).

On the surface this passage strongly suggests that someone who accepts the doctrine of grace parabolically is not only admitting to gross moral shortcomings, but is also endorsing the belief that there is, in fact, actual or proffered acquittal from some real judge. Yet this is assuredly *not* what accepting such a doctrine "parabolically" involves. The force of accepting the doctrine as a parable-assertion is the accepting of the doctrine *without* asserting or believing that there exists a para-physical judge. Thus, Miles repeatedly capitalizes upon those features of religious statements which he clearly wants to withdraw by maintaining that a Christian accepts these statements only parabolically. It is almost as if he wants to maintain that a Christian speaks, behaves, and thinks in the way he *would* speak, think, and behave *if* he believed that the parable-assertions were literal assertions, and true ones at that.

Insofar as Miles and Hepburn are, in effect, advancing a view of this sort, their remarks appear to be clearly assimilable to a view which R. C. Coburn has described recently as a "quasi-ritualistic way of construing theological statements,"[10] here abbreviated to 'quasi-ritualism.' A man who endorses quasi-ritualism acts as he *would* act if he *believed* that religious statements are true, but he does *not* believe that they are true; nor does he mean to suggest by his actions or utterances that he does. Acceptance of a religious statement, quasi-ritualistically construed, involves one in considering an X as if it were a Y, specifically *treating* an X in one's conversation, behavior, and imagination as if it were a Y. Coburn offers the example of a group of children playing "war," and taking (treating) the living-room couch as an ambulance:

> Now what does taking (treating) an *x* as a *y* in such a game come to? Fundamentally, I suggest, talking, behaving, and imagining in appropriate ways. Thus taking (treating) a couch as an ambulance for the purposes of such a game involves (i) referring to it as an ambulance, talking about various parts of the couch as if they were parts of an ambulance, etc.; (ii) behaving when one gets onto the couch as if one were getting into an ambulance by going through doors, behaving once on the couch as if one were in an ambulance by, e.g., behaving as if one were rolling down windows, etc.; and (iii) imagining when one is on the couch that one is seeing a speedometer, a gearshift, etc. This is, of course, not to say that the *x* is believed to be a *y*. Children playing "war" are quite aware that the kitchen is

[10] R. C. Coburn, "The Hiddenness of God and some Barmecidal God Surrogates," *The Journal of Philosophy*, Vol. LVII (October, 1960), pp. 705-710. Mr. Coburn describes this as a possible view; he does not endorse it.

not a battlefield—*really*; though part of the behavior which ordinarily accompanies (or is part of) such a belief is suspended during the period of the game (707).

A quasi-ritualistic acceptance of theological statements, accordingly, involves one in talking, behaving, and imagining as one would talk, behave, and imagine if one believed that religious statements were true, while all along *not* believing that they are true. Coburn's examples are again illuminating:

> That is, what the religious believer does in accepting theological statements ... is to see things in the light of the pictures these statements present, where this in turn is to take (treat) the world, e.g., as a cosmic screen behind which dwells an extra-mundane person of limitless power, complete knowledge of all happenings (past, present, and future), etc.; to take (treat) the historical figure of Jesus as somehow the same person as this extra-mundane one; to take (treat) one's own death as the beginning of a new adventure; etc. And this, it may be said, is just to talk in certain ways about such things as, e.g., the world as a whole, Jesus, death, marriage, the voice of conscience; to assume certain attitudes towards these things; to behave in certain ways—e.g., as if the wine were really the blood of a person with limitless power and unsurpassable knowledge; to imagine various things, as, e.g., that somebody knows one's inmost thoughts and feelings; etc. However, as in the case of the game of "war", the believer playing the—as it were—religious game would not necessarily have any factual beliefs which differ from those of a non-believer—though, again, he might suspend part of the behavior which ordinarily goes along with (or is part of) certain of his factual beliefs during, e.g., periods of formal or informal worship (707-708).

Coburn appears to have given here a succinct description of the root position common to both Miles and Hepburn. I have tried to interpret these writers' remarks concerning religious belief construed as a "slant," as an "orientation" chosen, plumped for, projected onto nature ("looking through spectacles"), maintained against rival slants, and sustained by one's imagination. I have suggested that these remarks adumbrate a view arguably assimilable to "quasi-ritualism." At the outset of this section it was indicated that "quasi-ritualism" is distinguishable from the views of both Braithwaite and Peter Munz. To Munz's view, contained in his stimulating book, *Problems of Religious Knowledge*,[11] we now turn.

C. RELIGIOUS BELIEF CONSTRUED AS THE CONTEMPLATING OF A "SYMBOL PICTURE"

Munz describes his book as an inquiry into the nature of religious knowledge, or, alternatively, an inquiry into the question of what religious state-

[11] London: SCM Press, 1959.

ments are about. These are alternative descriptions of the same inquiry because "religious knowledge," according to Munz, is knowledge *of* the same thing that "religious statements" are *about*, namely, "the symbol picture." 'The symbol picture' is one of a number of interrelated expressions which Munz deploys in the development of an intriguing, but in some points fairly obscure, argument. Some of the other expressions are: 'the Positive picture of the world,' 'myth,' 'eternity,' '*salus*,' 'doctrine,' 'theology,' and 'feeling states.' The usage of each of these expressions is fixed partly by reference to one or more of the others. Some of the expressions are poorly developed, and in many places one is not sure exactly what Munz is driving at. His crucial distinction, for example, is a three-pronged distinction between "feeling-states," "symbols," and "theology." But Munz is himself uncertain as to how to make a clear cleavage between "feeling-states" and "symbols." He writes, "... A feeling state without a symbol is so opaque that it cannot really be said to have a separate existence at all" (56), and again, "... I am not in a position to offer a positive description of the relationship between the two." (57) He is equally uncertain about how to draw the distinction between "symbols" and "theology". He remarks, "... It is in practice impossible to say where symbolic perception ends and theological specification begins" (151), and again, "There is, in practice, no hard and fast distinction between the symbol picture and a theory about the symbol picture." (171) I shall try to summarize the main features of Munz's argument, omitting as many of its perplexing elements as possible.

The intent of the book as a whole is clear. Munz sets out to "justify" religious knowledge, an enterprise which, in his case, takes the form of assuming that there is religious knowledge of some sort, and then proceeding to explain just what religious knowledge is knowledge of. The book is conceived as a justification of *religious* knowledge or *religious* belief—the argument is quite general—although Munz obviously intends what he writes to be true of Christianity as well as of other religions. He draws his illustrations from the writings of a number of different religious traditions: Buddhist, Hindu, Egyptian, Babylonian, Greek, Jewish, and Christian. The view he forwards makes only indirect reference to the doctrines of Positivism, but they are there in the background; he exhibits his argument against a backdrop of what he calls "the Positive picture of the world."

Philosophy of religion, according to Munz, is frankly normative in its judgments about religion: "The upshot of the whole matter is that the philosophy of religion imposes its own criterion of what is good theological reasoning and what is bad theological reasoning. And in doing this, it ceases to be purely descriptive of religious knowledge and begins to be normative. There is no denying this fact; and it is just as well to bring it out clearly, lest anyone think that a philosophical treatment of religious knowledge is no more than a roundabout way of justifying the traditional forms of theological speculation." (28-29) Munz's position, accordingly, is an amalgam of what he thinks religion is, and what he thinks religion ought to be. Munz entertains a threefold persuasion about religion. First, religion deals, or it ought to deal, with a particular human problem, a particular "disease." Second, for that disease religion offers, or it ought to offer, a certain sort of cure. Third, this cure is effected, or it ought to be effected, in a particular manner.

The particular problem or "disease" with which Munz thinks that religion deals, or ought to deal, is man's consciousness of transience. "Man's greatest disease is the consciousness of transience." (129) Everywhere men face change, transience, and death. "All we can ever discern [through the natural channels of communication] ... is an everlasting flux—a continuous time series in which everything that is, is transient. A picture where death stands at the end of every individual life; and final annihilation at the end of the universe." (33-34) According to Munz, consciousness of transience is a burden, something unwelcome, something to be got rid of, if possible. "Nothing is so likely to produce despair as the awareness of the contigency [transience] ... of life." (129) Religion is principally concerned with man's "search for *salus*, with the quest for the transcension of transience." (24) When Munz contends that "religious knowledge is, in one way or another, concerned with man's quest for redemption," (7) it must not be overlooked that the redemption in question is a redemption from the awareness of transience, not a redemption from "sin" or "guilt."

That is Munz's persuasion about the nature of the problem with which religion deals, or should deal. It is important to note where he begins. since it will shape where he comes out. A writer's initial assessment of the sort of problem he is dealing with determines to a large extent the sort of resolution that seems appropriate for it. Had Munz decided initially, for example, that religion is principally concerned to "solve" some other basic human problem than that of "transience"—say problems of "guilt" or, following Tillich, "meaninglessness"—his "cure" might have been couched very differently. Munz's notion of "eternity," which will be discussed presently, seems a suitable sort of cure for "transience," but quite an unsuitable sort of cure for Tillich's problem of meaninglessness or the Reformation theologians' concern with sin and guilt. Munz might concede that religion deals with the other problems mentioned, too, since he allows a general medical analogy to dominate his analysis of the function of religion. "The theologian is the great physician." (133) Also he makes use of the imagery of therapy. So his position is adaptable, to some extent, to problems not directly discussed. But his explicit judgment is that religion deals mainly with the consciousness of transience.

Given this initial assessment of the character of man's basic disease, and given the supposition that religion is principally concerned to cure that disease, Munz holds that religion offers, or ought to offer, a particular sort of cure. Religion makes it possible for one to acquire what he calls an intuition of eternity. "A powerful and time-honored cure [for the consciousness of transience] is to seek a perception of eternity. ... The perception of eternity is our greatest consolation and solace. The theologian who helps us to this perception is the great physician." (129) The "intuition of eternity" which Munz thinks religion at its best offers, however, is not an intuition which somehow empowers one to escape transience *itself*; it is an intuition which empowers one to escape the *awareness* of transience. One finds *salus* in a form of faith, a form described as "self-surrender [in which] time is transfigured into the eternal present." (215) Munz calls this concept of eternity, eternity as transfiguration:

> Faith ... is a form of trust. It is not a kind of belief, for there are, in the theology of transfiguration, no propositions about the other world or about Being or beings. Faith is a trust directly generated by the moment of complete self-surrender. With the disappearance of past and future, one lives in the present. And that means in complete trust; for all care and worry have become superfluous. For this reason stories about eschatological behavior and the injunction to live like the lilies of the fields, are cultivated with particular care by the theology of transfiguration. To live eschatologically means to live from moment to moment, to live not in the realm of means, but in the realm of ends, in which every act is an end in itself and has no purpose beyond itself. (215-216)

The theology of transfiguration does not maintain that one might somehow *avoid* living in time and space, and thus not be subject to transience. But "it does maintain that time and space can be capable of realizing eternity. If an unconditional command has been heard or if we have performed an act of self-sacrifice or partaken of more love than we deserve, the theology of transfiguration suggests that in the instant in which any of these ... have taken place, is eternity." (218)

Religion's cure for the disease of transience is effected, or it ought to be effected, in a particular manner. A religious man cultivates, or should cultivate, a certain "symbol picture." According to Munz, a characteristic activity of the human animal is to "create" or to "cultivate" a symbol picture of some sort. A religious man will cultivate, and will devote his principal energies *as* a religious man to cultivating, a particular symbol picture, a picture especially selected to help him to live with the kind of trust and self-surrender involved in the intuition of eternity.

A symbol picture is the composite of the religious man's "symbols." Symbols are objects, natural events, or human actions which are "meaningfully related to us." (54) Objects[12] become meaningfully related to us when we "look at them" under the influence of our "feeling-states." (54-55) Feeling-states themselves are a more or less undifferentiated "opaque [psychic] mass ... ill-defined, tenuous, vague, and fluid". (54, 55) But feeling-states are "symbolized" by objects. Feeling-states somehow become *associated with* objects and in the process the confused mass of feeling-states somehow become differentiated, "shaped" and "formed" into particular feelings on the part of the person making the association. A genetic image which appears to be at work in the argument here prompts one to say that feeling-states become *mated*, so to speak, to objects, to the mutual enrichment of both. A symbol is an object thus mated to a feeling-state. *Before* the mating, so to speak, a person observes, on the outside, "mere" objects, and a person carries inside, subliminally, unformed feeling-states; but *after* the mating, a person no longer observes mere objects and no longer bears unformed feeling-states. He observes *symbols*, that is, objects colored by a person's emotional response of one sort or another.

> For a tree in the sunshine may be there without a feeling-state. But without the feeling-state it is just a tree in the sunshine: it is not suffused with the emotional warmth and perceptive urgency that results from its observation *sub specie essentiae*. In short without the feeling-state (even though that feeling-state may be opaque and receive its clarity and definition only from the way in which it is linked to the tree in sunshine) an object is just only an object. It is not a symbol (56).[13]
>
> Without the symbol, our psychic energy is nothing but an opaque urge. With the symbol, it becomes shaped and formed as a particular kind of consciousness. The first result of designating an event or action as a symbol is therefore an enlarged state of lucidity. After such designation we know exactly how we feel, how we feel ourselves to be (54-55).

The exact nature of symbols and of feeling-states, and of the relationship between the two, is by no means clear. Munz has admitted as much. One must proceed with the rather vague notion of symbols as objects, events, or human actions—perhaps even *persons*—which strike a person in such a

[12] For simplicity, "objects, natural events, or human actions" will be abbreviated here, and subsequently, to simply "objects."

[13] Munz never defines *sub specie essentiae*. *Essentia*, however, is defined as "the way in which we feel ourselves to be." (51)

manner that they develop associative ties with a person's emotional response of one sort or another. According to Munz, people characteristically develop for themselves such symbols, symbols which give expression and form to the way in which they feel themselves to be. Munz does not make it clear how intense a feeling or, for that matter, what *sort* of feeling must come into play and become associated with an object in order for that object to *count* as a symbol. It is quite certain that the detonation of an atomic device would count as a symbol. But would looking with pangs of hunger at a bowl of fresh fruit involve converting them, as it were, into a symbol? Quite possibly. What about looking with cool indifference at a withered, refrigerator-spent artichoke?

At any rate, certain objects or events appear to be "pregnant with deep meaning," (109) and some have this appearance much more strongly than others. "In the symbol picture," Munz writes, "almost all events—and certainly some more than others—strike the observer as possessing a unique emotional significance." (109) The peculiar intensity of some of these symbols sometimes suggests to the persons who develop them the presence of some great mystery, perhaps the workings of an unknown force or supernatural agency. Such symbols seem to "stand for" something other than themselves, something only dimly adumbrated through them; they seem to indicate the presence or activity of some quite extraordinary agency. They "invite," as it were, an explanation of their emergence by claiming the incursion here of special powers or forces. Such symbols appear to invite an interpretation of a very special sort, such as that they are the occasion of God's revelation. Many have so interpreted them. But according to Munz, the symbols themselves are one thing, and the interpretation of the symbols is quite another thing. *Having* a symbol, that is, and *interpreting* a symbol are two quite different sorts of human activity. Munz admits that someone who has a symbol need not *resist* the temptation to interpret it and to explain it, say, in the fashion mentioned. Religious men, in fact, characteristically interpret their symbols in such a manner as this. But one should keep in mind, Munz encourages, that even when one has a symbol, the symbol *itself* does not "stand for" anything mysterious or mystical. Symbols do not stand for the workings of an unknown force or agency; nor do symbosl themselves even *indicate* the workings of an unknown force or agency. Symbols do not stand for anything whatsoever! A symbol's referent, insofar as it may be said to have any referent at all, is to the feeling-states with which it is associated. Symbols function "to bestow meaning upon feeling-states" (62) and for this alone. "According to the view taken in this study," Munz writes, "... the symbols do not stand for a transcendent

Reality. They do not stand for anything at all. They mean something; but what they mean and how they mean it, is something ... we can afford to ignore." (99)

Munz maintains that the typical activity of a religious man, *as* religious man, is his entertaining of a particular symbol picture.

> The symbol picture is composed of both deeds and stories. The first are commonly known as rites and the second as myths. If the preceding account of the nature of symbols is correct, the symbol picture [of the religious man] must be (a) prior to all religious thought and (b) the spontaneous and immediate consequence of our having any feeling-states at all. Ritual and myth are, according to the present theory, the primary data of all religious thought. They precede religious theories. They are the inevitable and essential consequences of feeling-states (65).

The religious man will discover that certain objects, events, and human actions, as well as stories about them, strike him with more emotional force than others. They symbolize *his* feeling-states: "... each of us, sooner or later, tends to create around himself the kind of world that is most apt to symbolize his feeling-states. We return to these worlds, with their events and situations, colors and shapes, tones and nuances, like homing-pigeons." (55) A religious man's symbol picture, accordingly, is composed of symbols which have special significance for him. On Munz's theory, the religious man sets as his principal goal the contemplation and cultivation of that symbol picture. He proceeds to contemplate that picture, not as a means to something else, but because the activity of contemplating it bestows meaning on states of feeling. The contemplation of the symbol picture is therefore not a means to a further end, but a highly satisfying and illuminating activity." (63)

Munz concedes that entertaining a symbol picture will naturally give rise to reflecting about it. Accordingly, a religious man will find himself normally engaged in a second-order activity. Side by side with cultivating his symbol picture, he will also be involved in describing it, in clarifying it, and especially in interpreting it. "We perceive ... things symbolically ... and then proceed to speculate about them and to interpret them." (78) When a religious man engages in speculative activity about his symbol picture, he engages in *theology*; he produces "theological theory." Theological reflection has two functions. First, it helps a religious man to become clear about what symbol picture, or what features of a symbol picture, most adequately symbolize *his* feeling-states. Second, it provides an interpretation, or interpretations, of the symbol picture which he finds himself cultivating. Thus, a religious man might come up with the theory about his symbol picture, for instance, that there is a God who reveals Himself in those events which constitute his symbol picture. "Religious speculation begins," Munz writes, "when an event that is experienced *sub specie essentia* is *interpreted* as the direct effect of a divine agent, or when a forest of awe-inspiring sombreness is interpreted as the abode of God." (71) But the religious man who develops this theory must not, or should not, confuse the symbol picture itself with his interpretation of that symbol picture. He must keep the two distinct for the reason that his *loyalty*, as it were, belongs directly to the symbol picture; the interpretation of that picture which he finds attractive for one reason or another is of secondary importance. The principal activity of a religious man, as religious man, is the cultivation of his symbol picture, the cultivation of it, moreover, without his taking more than a *tentative* stand on the interpretation of that picture. The entire view is nicely summarized in a single passage. Note, near the end, that Munz shifts his writing style: he switches from the impersonal-expository to the first person plural. This confers a strong "confessional" tone on this part of the argument, a colors-to-the-mast feel which should not be overlooked in weighing this aspect of his argument:

A religious community is a group of people who espouse a number of ... symbols and decide to abide by them and to cultivate their practice and their tradition. A confession of faith, in every religious community, should therefore be strictly confined to the declaration of adherence to a symbol picture cultivated by that community. And if it does include matters of doctrine, it should include them as hypothetical doctrine and not as dogma.... The element of certainty that is characteristic of religious faith is connected with the symbol picture. We cling with direct trust to the symbols. Our faith is concerned with the symbolisation of our feeling-states; it is concerned with what we see and hear; with what we see *sub specie essentiae*. The question as to whether the symbol exhibits one god or many, whether it exhibits a transcendent or an immanent godhead, whether it enjoins asceticism or the practice of worldly activity, must always remain open. At best such questions can be decided hypothetically by speculation. But there can never be a final or definite answer to them. Our faith is the quality of our perception of the symbol. It would be wrong to transfer the sense of certainty engendered by the perception of the symbol to our interpretation of the symbol. The interpretation must always remain a hypothesis.... When we say our prayers we say them with complete inward trust, but there is no equal certainty to be had as to whether we are addressing one God or many gods; whether we are begging for supernatural mercy or are surrendering our will.... A religious community exists primarily for the cultivation of the symbol picture, and is concerned with a certain interpretation of that picture only in a secondary sense (175-176).

DISCUSSION. Only one of the three views examined is advanced by its author as a direct attempt to vindicate Christianity in the face of the Positivist attack. Only T. R. Miles explicitly claims that his argument threatens nothing that belongs to the central truths of Christianity. Miles' book contains the clearest example of that type of "analysis" which was classified above as, first, occasioned by the Positivist attack; second, couched as an investigation into the use or function of the language or religion; and third, offered in support of a claim to the effect that Christianity does not necessarily involve that sort of religious belief which the Positivists claimed to be unintelligible. Braithwaite's study is similar to Miles' on all three counts, except that Braithwaite assimilates Christian belief to religious belief in general. Munz's approach is more indirect. His book does not seem to have been occasioned by the Positivist attack, and it contains no explicit discussion of Positivist doctrine, as do Braithwaite's and Miles' works. Nevertheless, "The Positive picture of the world" makes fairly unambiguous reference to Logical Positivism, albeit an indirect one. "The Positive picture of the world is the picture that is drawn when one makes use of none but empirically verifiable observation," Munz writes. (45) Admittedly, he develops his "positive picture by reference to Plato, Jaspers, Russell, and Whitehead. But *those* philosophers do not champion "empirically verifiable observation"; the Positivists do. Similarly, Munz's book is not couched as a linguistic study, a study of the language of religion. Yet Munz does offer an interpretation of what a religious man is doing, or ought to be doing, when he makes this or that religious utterance—that is, he is either expressing his symbol picture, describing it, or interpreting it. Again, Munz does not attempt to "justify" Christianity alone, although he obviously thinks that his view is true of Christianity as well as of other religions. Hence, each of these writers bounces his view of the nature of religious belief off the backboard of Positivism, and each appears persuaded that his view is compatible with Christianity, or compatible at least with what is fundamental to Christianity. Ronald Hepburn alone is exempted, since he is not disposed to think that his view is a viable description of Christianity. The critical remarks offered here concerning quasi-ritualism apply to Miles, not to Hepburn.

Each view has a certain *prima-facie* attractiveness, but each is open to some fairly obvious objections. Braithwaite's view, for example, looks appealing for the reason that it underscores the behavioral implications of being a Christian, Muslim, etc. One would like to know, however, whether the "mood" created by entertaining Christian stories is in fact likely to affect a "Christian's" behavior appreciably, in the sense of making it "easier to resolve upon and to carry through a course of action which is contrary to [his] natural inclinations" in view of the fact that he does not *believe* the stories. Is "entertaining" sufficiently like believing that entertaining a story might colorably promote one's behaving in a particular manner, especially one's behaving in a manner which is contrary to one's natural propensities? It is difficult even to think up examples that illustrate the way in which entertaining a story could influence anyone's behavior. Could a boy, for instance, be induced to eat spinach, which he detests, by hearing stories of the sort which say, in effect, that most boys eat spinach? Presumably not, because the boy is not obliged, on Braithwaite's account, to believe that most boys do eat spinach. But wouldn't entertaining of such stories somehow plant the belief that most boys do eat spinach? Not necessarily. Braithwaite's contention that the entertaining of stories "imposes no restriction whatever upon the empirical interpretation which can be put upon the stories" (29) has the consequence that one who entertains a story, rather than believes it, has no assurance that anyone ever behaved in the manner in which the story reports. Besides, even if most boys, conceivably, do eat spinach, and even if he believes it to be so, whether it is so or not, why should *he* eat it? A more tempting illustration of Braithwaite's thesis, perhaps, might be what happens in the case of the boy's watching a *Popeye* cartoon: marvelous adventures, failure and ignominy when spinach is withheld, success unto glory when spinach is ingested. Adventures!—Spinach! Now the boy need not believe the Popeye stories; yet a connection is formed in the boy's mind between adventure, which he desires, and the eating of spinach, which is "contrary to his natural inclination." Even here, however, Braithwaite's account seems incorrect. It is hard to see how the connection would be made in the boy's mind independently of his *believing* that eating spinach makes one strong, courageous, handsome, etc. And that belief is precisely what Braithwaite's "entertaining "of stories denies.

Miles' view appears attractive expressly because it stresses that aspect of traditional Christian moral instruction which enjoins a Christian to treat other persons as his brothers. It is sometimes said that a Christian is admonished to love his fellow men even though he does not like them; that is, he is exhorted to treat another person as he would treat him if that person were his brother—the supposition being that one loves one's brother. But Miles ought to explain why it is, on his analysis, that a Christian would or should treat others as his brothers, or why, more generally, a Christian would or should, as it were, play the religious game. The traditional Christian answer would be something to the effect that other people *are* one's brothers, one's spiritual brothers because God is the (Spiritual) father of all. But if a Christian were to regard his belief as a slant, would he continue to attend church, to pray, to take Communion, or to request Last Rites? Supposing, that is, that a slant is not a belief, and that a Christian consciously construes his Christianity as a slant, what would prompt a Christian to continue to do the things he does? What justification might there be for adopting a religious slant at all?

At first glance Munz's view looks very inviting. It looks sophisticated, too, principally for the reason that his distinction between the symbol picture and the interpretation of the symbol picture—theology—appears to resemble an important distinction which has often been made by Christian theologians, a distinction between Great Events and men's interpretation of the Great Events. There is no standard expression to designate those events in which Christians understand God to be and to have been revealing Himself. In some Christian theological schools the expression "the locus of Revelation" is popular. "Great Events" is here offered as a name for those events which Christians normally take to constitute the occasions on which God reveals Himself, makes Himself known, acts in history, and so forth. Christians are sometimes disposed to overlook *de facto* doctrinal disagreements, for certain purposes, and call attention, rather, to a larger and more pervasive loyalty that underlies such disagreements:

> The unity of the Christian church is not a uniformity in doctrine. The Gospel is the unifying factor of the church, but it is not a finally formulated, doctrinal authority. If a finally and irrevocably fixed system of doctrine were proposed as the basis of unity, it would lead to an intellectualized orthodoxy and a false objectivity.[14]
>
> The Word as a means of grace signifies for the Christian faith the self-impartation of divine love in the form of a *message*. It is not simply a question of the impartation of a doctrine which man could theoretically appropriate, or that certain subjective "religious experiences" are induced by the Word. The Word appears as a divine message. It is important to emphasize this point of view in contrast both to an intellectualized interpretation of the Word and to a psychological dissolution of it.[15]

Munz appears to be in substantial agreement with Aulén and other men of like mind when Munz writes: "A religious community exists primarily for the cultivation of the symbol picture, and is concerned with a certain interpretation of that picture only in a secondary sense." That agreement appears all the more striking when Munz adds, "The symbol picture coincides more or less roughly with all those actions and stories and thoughts that are said to be known by revelation." (71) But Munz's agreement with Aulén

[14] Gustav Aulén, *The Faith of the Christian Church* (Philadelphia: The Muhlenberg Press, 1948), p. 341.

[15] *Ibid.*, p. 361.

might be only an apparent one. For if a religious man might cultivate his symbol picture, or ought so to cultivate it, without taking any non-tentative, non-provisional stand on "the question as to whether the symbol [the symbol picture] exhibits one god or many", then a religious man might conceivably cultivate his symbol picture without taking any definite stand on the question as to whether it exhibits any God *at all.* Might a religious man, on Munz's account, cultivate his symbol picture and yet not believe in God? Presumably he might. Munz is not explicit about this point, but he certainly does not rule out the possibility. Indeed, if his theory purports to be true of Buddhism, it must allow for that possibility. But might a *Christian* cultivate his symbol picture without believing in God? Might a Christian remain *neutral* with respect to the question of the existence of God? If "the interpretation [of the symbol picture] must always remain a hypothesis" carries the implication merely that a Christian does not *know* that there is a God in the same sense in which he *knows* that there are more than ten people living in New York City, then most Christians, including Aulén, would surely concur. But if "the interpretation must always remain a hypothesis" carries the implication, as I believe it does, that a Christian might go on cultivating his symbol picture and not even *commit* himself to the "hypothesis," that is, not even *believe* that there is a God, then most Christians, including Aulén, would surely disagree.

When Howard Root writes that "The fundamental claim of the Hebrew-Christian tradition is that the God who is utterly transcendent and beyond the world nevertheless acts in the world," [16] he implies that someone who subscribes to Christianity must believe *at least* that there is a God, and that he must at least *believe that.* I. M. Crombie puts the same point more directly:

> Christianity, as a human activity, involves much more than simply believing certain propositions about matters of fact, such as that there is a God, that He created this world, that He is our judge. But it does involve believing these things, and this believing is, in a sense, fundamental; not that it matters more than the other things that a Christian does, but that it is presupposed in the other things that he does, or the manner in which he does them.[17]

[16] Howard Root, "Metaphysics and Religious Belief," *Prospect for Metaphysics*, ed. by I. T. Ramsey (London: George Allen & Unwin, Ltd., 1961), p. 70. The quotation commits Christians to holding that God is utterly transcendent. This crucial claim will be discussed further, notably in chapter four, sections B and C, and again in chapter five, section 6.

[17] I. M. Crombie, "The Possibility of Theological Statements," *Faith and Logic*, ed. by Basil Mitchell (Boston: The Beacon Press, 1957), p. 31.

The striking feature of the views examined in this chapter is that, in one way or another, each challenges the contention that believing in the existence of God is fundamental to Christianity, in Crombie's sense of being presupposed by the other things that a Christian does or the manner in which he does them. The proponents of these views suggest, in effect, that "religious belief" need not involve the belief that there is a God. And that is true. But each of the three views makes the further, stronger claim that such "religious belief" might be Christian belief, or may, at any rate, include every belief that is fundamental to Christianity, while excluding, at the same time, the belief that there is a God. Is that true?

If the decision as to whether those religious views which are maintainable in the absence of a belief that there is a God are *Christian* views should be adjudicated by reference to what Christians by and large have considered as fundamental to Christianity, then there is ample warrant for saying, with alacrity and vigor, "No!" To some extent, admittedly, the question is like the question as to whether being a Christian is compatible with not being a member of the Roman Catholic church. At one time it would have been plainly shocking to hold that one might be a Christian without belonging to the Roman church. That view is generally not so shocking as it once was. So, too, the views examined in this chapter appear shocking; shocking, that is, as views that purport to be compatible with what is essential to Christianity. E. L. Mascall calls Braithwaite's view of the nature of religious belief an "astounding theory."[18] Christianity without God is presumably not preposterous to some. The notion might even be widely endorsed some day. But Christianity without God is arguably *not* Christianity, at least not traditional or classical Christianity.

Transition to Chapters III and IV

I have suggested that a minimal condition for being a Christian is believing that there is a God. I mean that belief in God is a necessary condition for being a Christian though not, of course, a sufficient condition. But from the Positivist's point of view, a Christian who expresses the belief that there is a God, thereby purporting to *state* that there is a God, cannot really be stating anything, cannot be asserting anything true *or* false. He cannot because, first, a genuine factual statement must be testable, and second, the putative statement that there is a God is not testable. If either of these theses can be convincingly overthrown, the Positivist argument collapses. Most of the Positivists' formulations of the first thesis have been subjected

[18] E. L. Mascall, *Words and Images* (London: Longmans, Green, and Co., 1957), p. 55.

to powerful, critical scrutiny. If it turns out that *all* the formulations of the first thesis have not been refuted, if there is a viable version of that thesis, then everything turns upon the strength of the second. Chapter three, accordingly, will try to determine whether the various objections that have been raised against the first thesis have in fact nullified it. It will be suggested that they have not, thus necessitating an examination of the second thesis, which is carried out in chapter four.

CHAPTER III

TESTABILITY AND FACTUAL SIGNIFICANCE

We must now attempt to assess the force of various objections that have been raised against the principal classical formulations of the Positivist criterion of factual significance. In part, no doubt, because of errors involved in its early formulation, many philosophers have recently shown a tendency, almost a predisposition, to reject *all* formulations of a criterion of factual significance fashioned along lines of testability, and perhaps all general formulations of a criterion of factual significance whatsoever. The dominant empirical temper of the age notwithstanding, there has never been less professional sympathy with the attempt, characteristic of the Positivists, to fashion a viable formulation of the quite possibly widely held intuition that meaningfulness and testability are two sides of the same coin. If all such formulations are deficient or, more gravely, misguided from the start, then the principal weapon of the Positivist attack upon metaphysics is disarmed. It is crucial, then, to examine those serious attempts to remove the stinger from the bee, or rather, to discover whether it had one in the first place.

The procedure will be as follows. *Section A* will explore some of the considerations that seem to have induced the Positivists to look for a *criterion* of factual significance, and to have suggested, moreover, that it should be modeled along the lines of testability—that is, along lines of verifiability or falsifiability. *Section B* will examine some of the difficulties that necessitated repeated reformulations of a criterion of this type, together with a recent hybrid formulation combining verifiability and falsifiability into one criterion, as suggested by David Rynin. Although this formulation, as Rynin claimed, is immune from the major objections to which earlier versions were open, there are some difficulties remaining still, some of which Rynin himself recognizes. *Section C*, accordingly, will examine some plausible counter-examples, sentences which are arguably genuine factual statements but which appear, at the same time, not to satisfy Rynin's criterion. It will be argued that the force of the objections which such examples pose for

Rynin's criterion can be substantially mitigated. Rynin's criterion, I will argue, stands as a viable, although not altogether trouble-free, criterion of factual significance.

It is true, of course, that Positivist writings present us not simply with one criterion formulated in various ways but with a number of different criteria. There is no such thing as *the* Positivist criterion of factual significance. However, I think it will be helpful in the handling of certain expository and critical questions to speak, quasi-Platonistically, perhaps, of *the* Positivist criterion of factual significance, as if there were *one* criterion of which the Positivists individually tried to give less and less crude formulations. This way of speaking may suggest that there was more unity among Positivist thinkers on the matter of a given formulation of a criterion of factual significance than was in fact the case. The advantage gained is that it portrays each formulation of such a criterion offered by a particular Positivist as an individual *version* of the shared intuition which gave unity to the entire Positivist movement, namely, the intuition that factual meaningfulness and testability are coextensive. What is mainly at stake in the discussion between Positivists and non-Positivists is the soundness of that general intuition, as well as the acceptability of particular articulations of it.

A. THE SEARCH FOR A CRITERION OF FACTUAL SIGNIFICANCE

The purpose of proposing a *criterion* of factual significance, Herbert Feigl writes, "is to delimit the type of expression which has possible reference to fact from other types which do not have this kind of significance: the emotive, the logico-mathematical, the purely formal, and—if there should be such—the completely non-significant."[1] What would induce the Positivist to urge that *testability* might constitute a satisfactory criterion of factual significance? This is the guiding question for this section.

One possible answer is that *by* adopting a testability criterion, one could *thereby* deny factual significance to that class of sentences whose factual significance the Positivist disputed (hereafter referred to, following their idiom, simply as 'metaphysics'). Were Positivists proposing the testability criterion simply in order to rule out metaphysics? Probably not, at least not most Positivists. Sometimes it looked as if the denial of factual significance to metaphysics was a paramount objective, especially when the Positivists displayed such zeal to revise—and, in fact, did revise—any criterion of

[1] Herbert Feigl, "Logical Empiricism," reprinted, with omissions, from *Twentieth Century Philosophy*, ed. by D. D. Runes, (1943) in *Readings in Philosophical Analysis* [pp. 3-26], p. 9.

factual significance which failed to rule out metaphysics. The testability criterion was not advanced, however, either as an *arbitrary* criterion—e.g., that sentences more than nine words long are meaningless—nor as a tool designed to weed out metaphysics. The Positivists had reasons in mind for their criterion, reasons which even the metaphysician, presumably, ought to accept. The point comes out clearly in the famous 1949 B.B.C. radio debate between Ayer and Copleston. Copleston remarks to Ayer:

> All that is shown, it seems to me, is that metaphysical propositions do not satisfy a definite assumed criterion of meaning. But it does not follow that one must accept that criterion of meaning. You may legitimately say, if you like, "I will accept as significant factual statements only those statements which satisfy these particular demands"; but it does not follow that I, or anyone else, has to make those particular demands before we are prepared to accept a statement as meaningful.[2]

Ayer replies:

> What I do is to give a definition of certain related terms: understanding, meaningful, and so on. I can't force you to accept them, but I can perhaps make you unhappy about the consequences of not accepting them.[3]

What might make a metaphysician unhappy about the consequences of not accepting the testability criterion? Carl Hempel uncovers the root of the claim in his discussion of what he calls the logical status of the empiricist criterion of meaning. The Positivist proposed the testability requirement, Hempel writes, "to provide a clarification and *explication* of the idea of a sentence which makes an intelligible assertion."[4] On the assumption that the authors of metaphysical sentences supposed themselves to be making intelligible assertions, their "assertions," judged by the criterion, emerge as unintelligible.

Copleston asks, in effect, "Why accept the testability criterion?" The Positivist replies, "Because the testability criterion provides an analysis and

[2] A. J. Ayer and Father F. C. Copleston, "Logical Positivism—A Debate." This debate took place on the Third Program of the British Broadcasting Corporation, June 13, 1949; published in *A Modern Introduction to Philosophy*, second edition [pp. 726-756], p. 745.

[3] *Ibid.*

[4] Carl Hempel, "Problems and Changes in the Empiricist Criterion of Meaning," *Revue Internationale de Philosophie*, vol. 4 (1950): reprinted, with an important footnote written by the author in 1958, under the title "The Empiricist Criterion of Meaning," in *Logical Positivism* [pp. 108-129], p. 124. Subsequently the reference to this article will be given as "Problems and Changes. ..."

explication of the logical requirement of a sentence's having factual significance. If you wish to claim that theological sentences, for example, make intelligible assertions about matters of fact, then you must submit this claim to the standard of intelligibility formulated by the testability criterion." One point here requires further emphasis. The Positivist thought that he was attacking the metaphysician on grounds that were, or ought to be, common to both Positivist and metaphysician. What induced the Positivist to advance testability as the weight-bearing notion in an adequate criterion of factual significance was not simply that by adopting it one might thereby disallow factual significance to metaphysics. For in that event the metaphysician, fonder of metaphysics than of a criterion which disallows it, would simply reject the criterion. The justification which the Positivist had to articulate would have to be one whose credentials would claim the loyalty of even the metaphysican. Hempel remarks that the criterion was intended to provide "clarification" and "explication" of the idea of a sentence that makes an intelligible assertion. Metaphysical sentences, adjudged by that criterion, are unintelligible. But unintelligible by contrast to *what*? Obviously, by contrast to some *standard* of intelligibility. Which sentences satisfy that standard?

Where would we look to discover perfectly clear and intelligible sentences by which men unquestionably communicate about matters of fact? Where shall we look to find exemplary assertions "describing the world in which we live and move and have our being"?[5] If someone advances a criterion which purports to distinguish sentences which make intelligible reference to fact from those which do not, then to what kinds of sentences shall we attend in order to assay the criterion's adequacy? The Positivist answer was: Look to commonsense statements and look to scientific statements; the latter, they thought, are special cases of the former. Ayer writes, "I should claim that the account I've given ... is the account that does apply to ordinary common-sense statements, and to scientific statements. ... I then say that statements which don't satisfy these conditions are not significant, not to be understood. ..."[6]

The standard cases of sentences which are generally acknowledged to make intelligible assertions about matters of fact, then, are those by contrast to which the sentences comprising metaphysics are judged as unintelligible. Now questions about matters of fact, the Positivist maintained, are not only *characteristically* empirical questions; questions of fact are

[5] A. J. Ayer, "The Vienna Circle," *The Revolution in Philosophy*, ed. by A. J. Ayer *et al.* (London: Macmillan & Co., Ltd., [pp. 70-87], 1957), p. 75.

[6] Ayer and Copleston, "Logical Positivism—A Debate," p. 744.

always empirical questions. In an article entitled "The Nature of Facts," Peter Herbst also claims that "If, as I have suggested, it must always make sense in factual questions for there to be or to have been a (more or less infinitely observant) observer or witness to obtain the answer, then for all factual questions what somebody saw, heard, or felt, the outcome of some experiment, or what he measured or counted, etc., must always be relevant."[7] Accordingly, factual questions fall to the purview of the empirical sciences. "Whatever question is a question of fact," Victor Kraft writes, "must be answered by some one of the special sciences ... [and] science, as we come down to its empirical basis, presupposes ordinary everyday knowledge. ..."[8]

The reason, then, which the Positivist offered for accepting the testability criterion was that it is faithful to the accepted, standard cases of fact-stating discourse—those sentences which, as they were wont to express it, constitute empirical knowledge. Putative fact-stating sentences are genuine fact-stating sentences if and only if they measure up to the standard, only if they turn out, upon inspection, to be sufficiently like the accredited fact-stating paradigms of commonsense and science.

Suppose that the Positivist could show that the sentences of metaphysics are really quite different in the respect in question from those sentences of science and everyday discourse which are taken by most people as standard instances—paradigms—of fact-stating discourse. Suppose, that is, that statements drawn from science and commonsense, whatever diversity they might display when compared with one another, should all satisfy the testability criterion while none of the sentences of metaphysics should satisfy it. Would that be sufficient reason to doubt the factual significance of the sentences of metaphysics? The Positivist answer, in a word, was "Yes." If the Positivist had indeed managed, as he alleged, to note that condition satisfied by all scientific and commonsense statements, but not satisfied by "metaphysical statements," then there is strong support for a decision unfavorable to the latter—the combined weight of commonsense and science. For if the testability criterion countenances, without exception, the fact-stating paradigms, then testability could plausibly be employed as a necessary and sufficient condition—that is to say, as a *criterion*—of factual significance in at least one creditable and important sense of "factual significance."

[7] Peter Herbst, "The Nature of Facts," *Australasian Journal of Philosophy* (1952); reprinted in *Essays in Conceptual Analysis*, ed. by Antony Flew (London: Macmillan & Co., Inc. [pp. 134-156], 1956), p. 139.

[8] Kraft, *The Vienna Circle*, pp. 25-26.

To the Positivist eye, putatively fact-stating sentences fell rather readily into two classes. Some sentences were clear enough, but there were others which bore surface resemblance to those they found intelligible and yet failed to yield any clear meaning. The closer they looked, the more sentences of the first class appeared to differ in one recurrent fashion from sentences of the second. If a generalization could be framed which expressed the characteristic common to sentences of the first, but absent from sentences of the second, then that generalization might stand as a criterion for distinguishing one group from the other. That generalization, the Positivist alleged, is the testability criterion.

Everything depended, however, upon the testability criterion's fitting the fact-stating paradigms. This turned out to be a point of crucial importance. It seemed evident that before anyone would be prepared to adopt testability as the weight-bearing notion in a general *criterion* of factual significance, that criterion must first commend itself by its ability to discriminate between obviously significant and obviously nonsensical sentences and must be satisfied by all acknowledged factual statements. In other words, the reasonable test of the adequacy of the testability criterion was that it would *rule in* "a large class of sentences which are rather generally recognized as making intelligible assertions"[9] and that it *rule out* "another large class of which this is more or less generally denied."[10] Ayer writes that "There are some *prima facie* propositions which by universal agreement are given as significant and some expressions which are agreed to be meaningless."[11] If the testability criterion proves sufficient to cleave cleanly between the two classes, it commends itself as an adequate criterion of factual significance. "Trusting our criterion," Ayer continues, "if it accepts the former class and rejects the latter, we apply it to such doubtful cases as that of the propositions of metaphysics, and if they fail to satisfy it we pronounce them nonsensical."[12] The Positivists were confident that within the first class, the class of sentences which "are rather generally recognized as making intelligible assertions" would fall all the sentences of commonsense and science. They were equally confident that within the second class, "the class of which this is more or less generally denied," would fall the sentences of metaphysics.

[9] Hempel, "Problems and Changes ...," p. 124.

[10] *Ibid.*

[11] Ayer, "Demonstration of the Impossibility of Metaphysics," p. 768.

[12] *Ibid.*

B. FORMULATIONS AND DIFFICULTIES

The principal vehicle of the Positivist attack upon metaphysics was the doctrine that a sentence has factual meaning (hereafter designated Meaning) if and only if it is empirically testable. There is no standard Positivist expression for the kind of "meaning" that empirical sentences were credited with having and metaphysical sentences accused of not having. The expression "Meaning" as here adopted and employed, covers what the Positivists also called indifferently "factual meaning," "factual content," factual significance," "literal meaning," "literal content," "literal significance," "cognitive meaning," and "cognitive significance." These expressions are used interchangeably in Positivist writings except that "cognitive meaning" and "cognitive significance" are often broadened to cover what has been called "analytic" sentences as well. In what follows, the variant terms "Meaningful," "Meaningfulness" and their contraries will also be utilized.

Positivists were puzzled and annoyed with sentences which purport to be true or false, but for which there seems to be no test for deciding their truth-value. Sentences which purported to be true or false divided into two classes, the non-perplexing and the perplexing. Non-perplexing are those sentences for which one knows what would count as finding them true or false. But if one is unable to state the conditions under which an assertion could be judged true or false, it makes no sense, the Positivist maintained, to claim that the assertion *is* true or false. Of the sentence "Reality is the Absolute expressing itself," Ayer writes, "... I don't know what it would be like for such a proposition to be true."[13] In that event such an "assertion" is no assertion at all; it is a nonsense-utterance masquerading as an assertion.

If testability and Meaningfulness are related in the way the Positivists thought, then it should turn out that every sentence which is Meaningful should be testable, and vice-versa. Most of the difficulties which critics spotted in the various formulations of the criterion arose because this symmetry between testability and Meaningfulness is broken by plausible counter-examples. A number of reformulations of the criterion have been proposed to meet various kinds of objections. With the help of illustrative examples, some of the more important formulations and difficulties will now be examined.[14]

[13] Ayer and Copleston, "Logical Positivism—A Debate," p. 734.

[14] Sections one, two, and three examine various attempts to formulate the testability criterion in terms of verifiability. Analogous formulations requiring falsifiability, rather than verifiability, are also possible. In order to avoid unnecessary repetition only one such formulation is discussed, in section four.

1. The paradigm case: The criterion of verifiability

Consider the following sentences: "Assisi is built of pink stone." "The Campanile of the Pisa Cathedral is tilted 23° to the southwest." "The *S. S. France* is 1034 feet long." These sentences are true; that is, persons uttering these sentences are typically making true statements. Furthermore, they are paradigms of sentences customarily considered to be understandably, intelligibly true or false. While not without their conceptual difficulties,[15] such sentences are safe, stable sentences, if any are. Almost everyone employs sentences such as these without misgivings. Their use, under normal conditions, does not elicit the suspicion that people should not talk in this manner. Under what conditions? The conditions mentioned will be delimited by the problem at hand. Many important topics in the theory of knowledge will be left untouched, but not, it is hoped, much which is crucial to understanding the Positivist criterion of factual significance and the objections which it has been progressively tailored to meet.

In the following example the pertinent conditions are satisfied. In the course of a discussion of Renaissance painting, it happens that I mislocate the *Mona Lisa*. I say, or imply, that it hangs in the Uffizi Gallery in Florence. You correct me, rightly, saying that you think it hangs permanently in the Louvre. "Of course", I readily agree, "I remember now; you're right." "But I thought it was in the British Museum", someone remarks. "No," I say, "The *Mona Lisa* is in the Louvre."

Thus used, let the sentence 'The *Mona Lisa* is in the Louvre' be called a standard empirical sentence, or a sentence which is typically used to make an assertion. It is standard in that, in the example given, it is used in a standard assertive way; it states a matter of fact. This is not to say that standard discourse is always fact-stating discourse; there are other standard locutionary acts. It is only to say that "The *Mona Lisa* is in the Louvre" looks like an ordinary fact-stating sentence, and it is. In saying "The *Mona Lisa* is in the Louvre" I am not joking, speaking ironically, raising my voice at the end and putting a question, babbling to keep up conversation, reciting something, speaking in code, or the like. In uttering this sentence, I make a point of fact, assert something about a current state of affairs. I say something about the location of the *Mona Lisa* and I mean what I say. I use the sentence to make a statement, to say something true or false, true in this

[15] See, for example, F. Waismann's discussion of "open texture" in "Verifiability," *Aristotelian Society Supplementary Volume XIX* (1945): reprinted in *Logic and Language* I [pp. 117-144]. Also see below, chapter five, section B, 1.

instance. And the sentence I speak is an empirical sentence in that the truth or falsity of the statement it formulates is testable by observation.

Sentences of the type illustrated by "The *Mona Lisa* is in the Louvre" stand as models of one type of clear utterance. What are the minimal pertinent conditions that govern the intelligible functioning of this type of sentence in the manner illustrated? First, their use-in-context specifies, or helps to specify, the speaker's intention: in this case, it is to make a statement. In judging a speaker's intention by the context of his utterance one might, of course, be mistaken. Is he joking or not? There's nothing here to indicate one way or the other. Contextual settings provide no certain guide to discerning a speaker's intention; but from the context of a remark we sometimes get important clues as to what a speaker is intending to express. A speaker contextually suggests so-and-so rather than such-and-such. Second, there are agreed criteria for deciding whether the statement the sentence makes is true or false, in this case (a) a criterion for something's being the *Mona Lisa*; knowing when it is satisfied might require calling in experts; (b) a criterion for something's being the Louvre; and (c) a criterion for determining the spatial relations of each. Associated with such sentences, then, are certain operations which the hearer may perform, in light of the conditions mentioned, in order to verify the statement made. Sentences like "The *Mona Lisa* is in the Louvre" have empirical cash-value.[16]

As employed here, "The *Mona Lisa* is in the Louvre" is an instance of one intelligible use to which a sentence may be put. The sentence makes a statement. The statement is true or false; true, in this case. The statement makes a declaration of fact about definite, easily recognizable, enduring public objects. By giving information about a matter of public fact, the sentence is open to verification or falsification by observational procedures available to anyone who wishes to settle the question as to whether or not the *Mona Lisa* hangs in the Louvre. Go to the Louvre and look; *that* will settle the question. The sentence is intelligibly used, is Meaningful, and can be currently verified on the condition that one goes to the Louvre and looks. The sentence is "verifiable" in that it can be shown, more or less conclusively, to be true or false. "The *Mona Lisa* is in the Louvre" illustrates what

[16] The term "cash-value," in contemporary discussion, appears calculated to provide a rough-and-ready way of talking about the standard use of empirical sentences without entering into the intricacies of the question as to whether the meaning of an empirical sentence *is* the method of its verification. The typical use of the expression, however, does adumbrate a judgment on that question: we cannot explicate the meaning of an empirical statement without at the same time specifying, or being able to specify, the criteria by which it could be verified if it were true.

C. I. Lewis has called the simplest case of verifiability, that is, "observability at will."[17]

Suppose that someone tried to formulate a criterion of factual significance which would cover the case just considered, as well as the other sample sentences mentioned as they might be spoken in appropriate fact-stating contexts. Suppose that the suggested criterion of factual significance were formulated as follows : Any sentence, *S*, is Meaningful if and only if observational evidence might currently be obtained which would conclusively establish the truth of *S*. Let this be called the criterion of verifiability. Hempel reports that some of the early Positivists restricted the permissible evidence to what might be observed "by the speaker and perhaps his fellow beings during their lifetimes."[18] Would the criterion of verifiability be a satisfactory criterion of factual significance? Obviously not, since it would deny Meaningfulness to sentences about the past and the future, and to sentences for which it is currently impossible, technically, to make the relevant verifying observations. This will be clear in the following examples.

2. *The criterion of verifiability-in-principle*

A great many sentences are sufficiently similar to the paradigm assertions such as "The *Mona Lisa* is in the Louvre" to justify grouping them in a single class, but differ from these assertions in one awkward respect. Such sentences include : "The *Bismark* was sunk by British warships on May 27, 1941", "The 1988 Democratic Convention will meet in Honolulu", "There are trees on Mars", etc. The peculiar feature of such sentences is that none of them can be verified now, directly, by anyone. No one can go-and-verify them now, for the state of affairs they describe is such that it is too late, too early, or too difficult, in the sense of being technically impracticable now, to make the observations requisite to satisfying the criterion of verifiability. And yet these sentences are clearly Meaningful: They are ordinarily used to do the same kind of job as that done by the paradigm assertion, although they may be used to do different jobs as well. The sentences describe this or that state of affairs, albeit not a state of affairs that we are in a position to observe currently either because the state of affairs has already passed, or because the state of affairs has not yet occurred, or because we currently lack the technical means of putting anyone in a position to ascertain whether or not the state of affairs does obtain. Except for the fact that "There are

[17] C. I. Lewis, "Experience and Meaning," *The Philosophical Review*, 43 (1934); reprinted in *Readings in Philosophical Analysis* [pp. 128-145], pp. 137-138.

[18] Hempel, "Problems and Changes ...," p. 110, n. 5.

trees on Capri" satisfies the verifiability criterion while "There are trees on Mars" does not, the sentences look in other respects very much alike. A satisfactory criterion of factual significance would surely include the latter as well as the former.

The standard Positivist adjustment was to distinguish between verifiability-in-practice and verifiability-in-principle, and to include in the class of Meaningful sentences also those which are verifiable-in-principle. There are many assertions, Ayer writes, whose Meaningfulness no one seriously questions even though we could not verify them if we tried, "simply because we lack the practical means of placing ourselves in the situation where the relevant observations could be made."[19] This is the case with the assertion that there are trees on Mars. And there are other assertions whose Meaningfulness no one seriously questions even though we could not verify them now, but for a different reason: they are about past or future states of affairs, the difficulty being one of temporal, rather than practical, limitation. Such is the case with "There were trees on ancient Capri." Yet surely a sentence is not deprived of Meaningfulness when, in all respects save that of not being open to verification currently, it conforms to the logic of the paradigm assertion. After all, *someone saw* the *Bismark* go down under the fire of ships flying the Union Jack. Someone could, and will, attend the convention in Honolulu if it meets there several years hence. And someone might, and conceivably may, photograph trees on Mars if he were transported to that planet. As Ayer remarks, "... I am unable to decide the matter by actual observation. But I do know what observations would decide it for me, if, as is theoretically conceivable, I were once in a position to make them. And therefore I say that the proposition is verifiable in principle, if not in practice, and is accordingly significant."[20]

A statement is verifiable-in-principle, then, when we know what observations someone might have made at time T^{-n} (past), might now make at time T (present), or might be in a position to make at time T^{+n} (future) in order to determine whether the statement is true. A sentence is Meaningful not only if its truth-value is actually discoverable by a living man, but also if someone might conceivably have discovered its truth-value in the past, or might conceivably do so in the future, or might conceivably, though no one can actually, discover it now.

Let the criterion of factual significance formulable to cover the cases

[19] *Language, Truth, and Logic*, p. 36.
[20] *Ibid.*

considered be called the criterion of verifiability-in-principle. According to this criterion, any sentence, *S*, is Meaningful if and only if observational evidence (1) might at some time have been obtained by someone, (2) might now be obtained by someone if it were not for technical limitations, or (3) might be obtained in the future by someone, which would conclusively establish the truth of *S*. Would the criterion of verifiability-in-principle suffice as a satisfactory formulation of a criterion of factual significance? Obviously not, for it would deny Meaningfulness to some clearly Meaningful sentences of a different sort than those mentioned so far. This will emerge in the following examples.

3. *The extended criterion of verifiability-in-principle*

A word or two of review might be in order at this point. Attempting to reconstruct the Positivist rationale for a testability criterion for Meaningfulness, the first task was to isolate certain pertinent logical features of a class of relatively trouble-free sentences exemplified by "The *Mona Lisa* is in the Louvre." These sentences, it was said, (a) make statements or assertions, that is to say, say something true or false, (b) have truth-conditions which are easily ascertainable by the application of tests implicit in the tacitly agreed-upon criterion for the application of their constituent terms, (c) are verifiable in the safest and surest sense of "verifiable," namely, observability-at-will, and (d) are aptly dubbed "empirical" because their truth or falsity is ascertainable by an empirical operation, by observation. No independent analysis of "observation" will be here attempted. It is hoped that the relevant kind of observation is implicit in each example discussed. Next, we considered a much larger class of sentences which shared with those of the first class all the relevant characteristics save that they cannot be verified now, either for reasons of temporal or of practical limitation. But such sentences do satisfy the criterion of verifiability-in-principle since they could have been or might be shown to be true by someone living at some time in the past or future, or they might conceivably be shown to be true by someone living now, though not actually so, because of current technical limitations.

Certain sentences, however, do not satisfy the criterion of verifiability-in-principle either; yet, at the same time, they appear quite clearly to be Meaningful. Consider, for example, "Atomic warfare will kill all men on earth." Such a sentence satisfies neither the criterion of verifiability nor that of verifiability-in-principle. But the sentence describes a state of affairs very much like that described by "Atomic warfare will kill all men on earth *save one*". The latter is verifiable-in-principle, since the remaining man might conceivably do the verifying. Since the former is not verifiable-in-principle, at least not in the sense thus far specified, are we to say that it is not Meaningful?

There is no good reason to accept a criterion of factual significance which allows Meaning to "Atomic warfare will kill all men on earth save one" and denies Meaning to "Atomic warfare will kill all men on earth." For the former clearly does not have a kind of "significance" or "factual meaning" which the latter lacks, in spite of the former's being open to verification by the surviving man, while the latter is closed to verification by anyone, ever. Accepting the requirement of verifiability-in-principle, as construed so far, would also oblige us to disallow the Meaningfulness of many quite obviously Meaningful statements, for example, most of those made by paleontologists. For the criterion, as it stands, allows Meaning only to those statements which might have been found true by someone in the past, which might conceivably be found true by someone currently, though not actually, for technical reasons, or which might conceivably be found true by someone in the future. "At time T^{-n} there were no men" is admittedly different from "At time T there were men" in the respect that one is verifiable in principle and one is not. But is it not the case that *both* statements, not the latter only, can significantly be said to be true or false, and hence Meaningful?

Ayer has said that sentences of the type in question are still *understandable*, "understandable" in the sense that we know what observations *would* settle the question of their truth or falsity *if*, contrary to fact, someone were in a position to carry them out.

> ... I should try to derive this principle [the verifiability principle] from an analysis of understanding. I should say that understanding a statement meant knowing what would be the case if it were true. Knowing what would be the case if it were true means knowing what observations would verify it, and that in turn means being disposed to accept certain situations as warranting the acceptance or rejection of the statement in question.[21]

Ayer here declares, in effect, that the Positivist criterion of factual significance, at least as he interprets it, derives from an analysis of what we mean when we say that we understand a statement of fact. Much earlier, Moritz Schlick wrote in a similar vein: "... according to our opinion, 'verbal' and 'logical' understanding *consists in* knowing how the proposition in question

[21] Ayer and Copleston, "Logical Positivism—A Debate," pp. 742-743.

could be verified.... Thus knowledge of how a proposition is verified is not anything over and above its verbal and logical understanding, but is identical with it. It seems to me, therefore, that when we demand that a proposition be verifiable we are not adding a new requirement but are simply formulating the conditions which have actually always been acknowledged as necessary for meaning and intelligibility."[22] Similarly, for Ayer, understanding a statement of fact means knowing what would be the case if it were true, which means knowing what observations *would* verify it. Do we not know what observations would verify "Atomic warfare will kill all men on earth"? If we understand that statement in the sense indicated, and surely we do, then if the criterion of verifiability-in-principle disallows it, there is an exception to the criterion. Some emendation of the principle is required.

The more or less official Positivist emendation was that of extending the notion of verifiability-in-principle to cover the cases disallowed by the more narrow reading of that notion. Ayer, for example, claimed that the statement "Atomic warfare will take place and it will blot out the whole human race" is verifiable in principle:

> ... it describes a possible situation ... one knows quite well what it would be like to observe devastation, and fail to observe any men. Now it wouldn't necessarily be the case that, in order to do that, one has to observe oneself. Just as, to take the case of the past, there were dinosaurs before there were men. Clearly, no man saw that, and clearly I, if I am the speaker, can't myself verify it; but one knows what it would be like to have observed animals and not to have observed men.[23]

The Meaningfulness-requirement which Copleston credits to Ayer in their debate is the requirement of one's being able to "imagine the state of affairs that would verify [a statement]."[24] 'Imagine' is Copleston's term; Ayer does not use the word himself. Nor, however, does he protest Copleston's using it in connection with the point under discussion. Speaking to a similar point, C. I. Lewis has also appealed to "imagination" in like fashion. "If all minds should disappear from the universe, the stars will still go on in their courses. This hypothesis is humanly unverifiable. That, however, is merely a pre-

[22] Schlick, "Meaning and Verification," p. 150.

[23] Ayer and Copleston, "Logical Positivism—A Debate," p. 746. For a much earlier statement and discussion of this extension, see M. Schlick, "Meaning and Verification," pp. 150-157 and 168-170.

[24] Ayer and Copleston, "Logical Positivism—A Debate," p. 746.

dicament which prevents assurance of truth but does not affect meaning. We can only express or envisage this hypothesis by means of imagination, and hence in terms of what any mind like ours *would* experience if, contrary to hypothesis, any mind *should* be there."[25] Accordingly, if it is possible to imagine the state of affairs that would verify a statement, that statement is Meaningful. Atomic ruin is a possible situation, observers or not. Dinosaurs and no men is also a possible situation. We know what it would be like to observe that situation. On the extendeed usage, then, sentences like "Atomic ruin will occur and blot out the whole human race" and "There were dinosaurs before there were men" are verifiable in principle, not in the sense that they are verifiable earlier-or-later-than-now, nor in the sense that they are possibly verifiable though not actually so because of technical limitations, but in the sense that one can imagine—describe, conceive—what *would* verify them, whether now or at any other time. We do not expect that any living man has ever made or will ever make the requisite verifying observations; but we can conceive what it would be like to find these statements true if, contrary to hypothesis, any person were in a position to make an observational test. Carl Hempel writes:

> ... If the concept of *verifiability in principle* and the more general concept of *confirmability in principle* ... are construed as referring to *logically possible evidence* as expressed by observation sentences, then it follows ... that the class of statements which are verifiable, or at least confirmable, in principle includes such assertions as that the planet Neptune and the Antarctic Continent existed before they were discovered, and that atomic warfare, if not checked, may lead to the extermination of this planet.[26]
>
> As has frequently been emphasized in empiricist literature, the term "verifiability" is to indicate, of course, the conceivability, or better, the logical possibility of evidence of an observational kind which, if actually encountered, would constitute conclusive evidence for the given sentence; it is not intended to mean the technical possibility of performing the tests needed to obtain such evidence, and even less does it mean the possibility of actually finding directly observable phenomena which constitute conclusive evidence for that sentence.... Analogous remarks apply to the terms "falsifiability" and "confirmability."[27]

Consistent with the spirit of these remarks, let us call the criterion of factual significance formulable for the extended range of cases just considered "the extended criterion of verifiability-in-principle" or, more simply—

[25] Lewis, "Experience and Meaning," pp. 142-143.

[26] Hempel, "Problems and Changes ...," pp. 110-111, n. 5.

[27] *Ibid.*, p. 111, n. 6.

since the handle is getting fairly ponderous—let us continue to call it the criterion of verifiability-in-principle but let every further reference to verifiability-in-principle be construed in the extended, rather than the narrow, sense. One formulation of this new extended criterion would run as follows: Any sentence, *S*, is Meaningful if and only if it is possible to describe a set of observational data which, if actually encountered, would conclusively establish the truth of *S*. In order to facilitate elucidation of the principal objections to this formulation, let us adopt a simplified version of Hempel's formulation: A sentence, *S*, is Meaningful if and only if it follows logically from some finite class of observation sentences.[28]

Objections to the criterion of verifiability-in-principle

Several objections to this criterion have been voiced.[29] The criterion would rule out, it is claimed, sentences of universal form, many of which are quite arguably Meaningful in spite of the fact that they cannot be verified conclusively. That all observed ravens have been black does not rule out the possibility that the next observed raven, and all ravens from now on, will be not-black. No *finite* set of observations, therefore, could conclusively establish the truth of "All ravens are black" and other sentences of this form. Yet such a sentence clearly makes a statement that might be true or false, hence Meaningful. Analogous remarks apply to sentences whose formulation involves mixed quantification, that is, which contain both universal and existential quantifiers: "For every substance there exists some solvent" could not be shown true from any finite set of observation sentences; yet that sentence, too, seems quite clearly to be Meaningful anyway.

Second, the criterion would rule out the denial of purely existential statements, since such denials are logically equivalent to sentences of universal form. As Hempel points out, this generates an annoying asymmetry, which

[28] Hempel's exact formulation is: "A sentence has empirical meaning if and only if it is not analytic and follows logically from some finite and logically consistent class of observation sentences." (*Ibid.*, p. 111) In this formulation, and in those which follow, an "observation sentence" is "any sentence which—correctly or incorrectly—asserts of one or more specifically named objects that they have, or that they lack, some specifically observable characteristic"; an "observable characteristic," which is designated by a term called an "observation predicate," is any property or relation of specifically named objects whose presence or absence in a given instance "can be ascertained through direct observation." (*Ibid.*, pp. 109-110.)

[29] For a thorough discussion of these objections, see Hempel's "Problems and Changes ...," pp. 111-116.

takes the form of a dilemma: either we must relinquish the view that the denial of *p*—"There exists at least one unicorn"—where *p* is verifiable in principle, is logically equivalent to "Nothing has the property of being a unicorn," which is not verifiable in principle; or we must relinquish the view that *if* "There exists at least one unicorn" were conceivably true, hence Meaningful, then its denial—"Nothing has the property of being a unicorn"—must surely be, correspondingly, false, hence Meaningful too.

A third objection has also been alleged. The criterion *appears* to have the consequence of allowing Meaningfulness to any sentence whatsoever. For if *S* is some sentence which satisfies the criterion of verifiability-in-principle—for example, "Assisi is built of pink stone"—then if *S* follows logically from some finite set of observation data, then the (non-exclusive) alternation *S or P* follows from the same set, where *P* is any sentence at all, such as "There's a drogulus over there." Whatever observations were to have established the truth of "Assisi is built of pink stone" would also have established, *ipso facto*, the truth—hence the Meaningfulness—of the compound statement " 'Assisi is built of pink stone' *or* 'There's a drogulus over there.' "

4. The criterion of falsifiability-in-principle

Analogous objections are said to apply to a criterion of factual significance which takes the testability-requirement for Meaningful sentences to be one of falsifiability-in-principle rather than verifiability-in-principle. A general formulation of such a criterion would run as follows: Any sentence, *S*, is Meaningful if and only if it is possible to describe a set of observational data which, if actually encountered, would conclusively establish the falsity of *S*. Let us again adopt a shorter rendering: A sentence, *S*, is Meaningful if and only if its falsity follows logically from some finite class of observation sentences.[30]

The objections would parallel those mentioned above, point for point. First, allowing that sentences of universal form are Meaningful, the criterion of falsifiability-in-principle disallows all purely existential assertions. The falsity of *S*—"Nothing has the property of being a unicorn"—would follow logically from some finite class of observation sentences: we might conceivably *find* a unicorn. But the falsity of the denial of *S*—"There exists at least

[30] This, again, is a simplified version of Hempel's formulation: "A sentence has empirical meaning if and only if its denial is not analytic and follows logically from some finite logically consistent class of observation sentences." *Ibid.*, p. 113.

one unicorn"—would not follow from any finite class of observation sentences: not-finding a unicorn does not guarantee that we will not find one. For the same reason, the criterion of falsifiability-in-principle also disqualifies sentences which involve mixed quantification. Not finding an insoluble substance does not guarantee that we will not; yet it is surely intelligible to wonder whether "For every substance there exists some solvent" is false. Nevertheless, that sentence would come out as Meaningless on the criterion in question since there is no finite set of observational data which, if actually encountered, would establish its falsity.

Furthermore, the criterion of falsifiability-in-principle would indeed, as just noted, allow the Meaningfulness of sentences of universal form: "All swans are white" might be falsified by finding a non-white swan. But then it disallows the Meaningfulness of their denials, which would be logically equivalent to purely existential assertions: "There exists at least one non-white swan" could not be falsified by not-finding any non-white swan, for failing to find one does not guarantee that we will never find one. Thus, the criterion of falsifiability-in-principle generates the same annoying asymmetry generated by the criterion of verifiability-in-principle and thereby necessitates our choosing between the two equally unwelcome alternatives described above.

Third, the criterion of falsifiability-in-principle also appears to have the consequence of allowing significance to any sentence whatsoever. For if *S* is a sentence which satisfies the criterion of falsifiability-in-principle—for example, "Assisi is built of lime jello"—and *P* is any other sentence whatsoever—"There's a drogulus over there"—then if the falsity of *S* follows logically from some finite set of observation data, then the falsity of the conjunction of *S and P* follows from the same set. Thus, if observations would have established the falsity of "Assisi is built of lime jello" then the same observations would also have established, *ipso facto*, the falsity—hence the Meaningfulness—of the compound statement " 'Assisi is built of lime jello' *and* 'There's a drogulus over there.' "

5. *The criterion of partial verifiability*

Ayer attempted to meet the objections mentioned above by proposing a criterion of factual significance requiring only what he called weak or partial verifiability for Meaningful sentences. According to Ayer's criterion, any sentence, *S*, is Meaningful if and only if from *S*, in conjunction with certain subsidiary hypotheses, it is possible to deduce some observation sentences which are not deducible from the subsidiary hypotheses alone. But in response to an objection noted by Isaiah Berlin, Ayer conceded that his criterion is too weak. It appears to allow that any and every sentence is Meaningful:

> For, given any statement "S" and an observation-statement "O", "O" follows from "S" and "if S then O" without following from "if S then O" alone. Thus, the statements "The Absolute is lazy" and "if the Absolute is lazy, this is white" jointly entail the observation-statement "this is white", and since "this is white" does not follow from either of these premises, taken by itself, both of them satisfy my criterion of meaning.[31]

To meet Berlin's objection, Ayer amended his criterion as follows: A statement is Meaningful if and only if it is either directly or indirectly verifiable. These expressions are defined as follows:

> I propose to say that a statement is *directly verifiable* if it is either itself an observation-statement, or is such that in conjunction with one or more observation-statements it entails at least one observation-statement which is not deducible from these other premises alone: ... a statement is indirectly verifiable if it satisfies the following conditions: first, that in conjunction with certain other premises it entails one or more directly verifiable statements which are not deducible from these other premises alone; and secondly, that these premises do not include any statement that is not either analytic, or directly verifiable, or capable of being independently established as indirectly verifiable.[32]

Hempel maintains, however, that Ayer's criterion is still too weak. For if *S* is a sentence which satisfies the criterion, and *N* is any other sentence whatsoever, then Ayer's criterion allows that the compound sentence formed by conjoining *S and N* is also Meaningful.

> Indeed: whatever consequences can be deduced from S with the help of permissible subsidiary hypotheses can also be deduced from *S* . *N* by means of the same subsidiary hypotheses, and as Ayer's new criterion is formulated essentially in terms of the deducibility of a certain type of consequence from the given sentence, it countenances *S* . *N* together with *S*.[33]

6. The criterion of Verifiability: verifiability-or-falsifiability-in-principle

In 1956 David Rynin proposed a modified criterion of factual significance which states that a sentence is Meaningful if and only if it is *either* verifiable *or* falsifiable.[34] The advantage of Rynin's criterion, which will be called the

[31] *Language, Truth, and Logic*, second edition preface, pp. 11-12.

[32] *Ibid.*, p. 13.

[33] Hempel, "Problems and Changes ...," pp. 115-116.

[34] David Rynin, "Vindication of L*G*C*L*P*S*T*V*SM," hereafter designated as

criterion of Verifiability in what follows, is that when supplemented by certain other recommendations Rynin makes, it appears to be virtually immune from the criticisms brought against the formulations discussed above.

Rynin sets up his criterion as follows: Any sentence, *S*, is Meaningful if and only if it is Verifiable (note the upper-case 'V'). *S* is Verifiable if and only if *S* is either verifiable or falsifiable, or both. *S* is verifiable if and only if *S* has at least one ascertainable sufficient truth-condition. *S* is falsifiable if and only if *S* has at least one ascertainable necessary truth-condition. *S* has one sufficient truth-condition if and only if there is a "contingent state of affairs that entails the truth of that statement"; *S* has one necessary truth-condition if and only if there is a "contingent state of affairs whose non-existence entails the falsity of that statement."[35] Rynin observes that "... it *is* sufficient to establish the meaningfulness of a statement to state some way in which it can be verified or falsified, for if either can be done then the statement can be true or false, and hence meaningful."[36]

By allowing *either* verifiability *or* falsifiability as sufficient to establish the Meaningfulness of a sentence, Rynin's formulation avoids certain difficulties which attach to formulations built upon verifiability or falsifiability exclusively. For example, sentences of universal form, which are not verifiable-in-principle are countenanced by Rynin's formulation, since they *are* falsifiable-in-principle. "All giraffes are herbivorous" could not be verified, but it might conceivably be falsified: we might find a carnivorous giraffe. Uniquely existential statements, which are not falsifiable-in-principle, *are* countenanced by Rynin's formulation, since they are verifiable-in-principle. "There exists at least one man ten feet tall" could not be falsified, but it might conceivably be verified: we might find a man that tall. Moreover, since Rynin's formulation countenances the Meaningfulness of both universal and existential statements, it does not generate the objectionable logical asymmetry generated by both the criteria of verifiability-in-principle and falsifiability-in-principle taken by themselves.

To meet the objection, proleptically, that Rynin's formulation might allow Meaningfulness to any sentence whatsoever—provided that the sentence is made a conjunct or a disjunct with a verifiable of falsifiable conjunct or disjunct in a compound statement, Rynin stipulates that "the components of a

"Vindication...." Professor Rynin's article was originally delivered as the presidential address before the Pacific Division of the American Philosophical Association and is printed in their *Proceedings* for 1956.

35 *Ibid.*, pp. 53-54.

36 *Ibid.*, pp. 52-53.

disjunction [or conjunction] must *all* be genuine statements, i.e., sentences possessed of a truth-value."[37] In order for a compound statement to have a truth-value, each component must have a truth-value. Consider the alternation ' "The sun is shining" (uttered when the sun is shining) or "There's a drogulus over there." ' Now, as to the question of truth-value, if it were to be suggested that the truth-value of "true" should be assigned to the alternation as a whole, it could only be because "The sun is shining" is true. The truth-value of the whole is an outright steal, so to speak, from the truth-value of the first component. The same consideration applies to the question as to the *intelligibility* of the compound. Whatever meaning or meaningfulness the compound as a whole may be said to have derives from its first component alone. Are we to countenance what might be called a logical laying on of hands, such that one patently meaningless expression is judged to be accreditably emplaced in a compound and the compound as a whole is to enjoy the benediction of "true" merely because one component is true? Surely the muddle arises because "There's a drogulus over there" is *not* accreditably emplaced in the compound. If one component is a genuine statement and one is not, then in combining them we achieve no genuine compound statement at all to which the logical rules for conjunction or disjunction would be applicable, although the sentence admittedly contains one statement-component.

> No one supposes that the sentence "There are some people in this room or please pass the spaghetti" is completely verifiable just because "There are some people in this room" is.... Similarly, the expression "There are some people in this room or all blaps are draps" does not become a disjunction to which the truth rule for disjunctions is applicable simply because it contains a meaningful and furthermore true component. It is simply not the case that this compound is a statement at all, and *a fortiori* not one that follows logically from its meaningful component.[38]

Rynin urges, in other words, that each component of a compound statement must first independently *qualify* as a legitimate statement by satisfying the requirements of either verifiability or falsifiability. Thus, the inference alleged by Hempel from the Meaningfulness of sentence S to the Meaningfulness of the sentence $S \vee N$ (where N is any sentence whatever) fails. Hempel, incidentally, has since conceded the force of Rynin's reply.[39]

Rynin has more difficulty, however, with sentences containing mixed quantification. Since such sentences are disallowed by a criterion of factual

[37] *Ibid.*, p. 57. Italics mine.

[38] *Ibid.*

[39] See Hempel's footnote, written in 1958, to the reprinting of "Problems and Changes ...," in *Logical Positivism*, pp. 127-128.

significance requiring verifiability and by one requiring falsifiability, it follows that they would also be disallowed by one requiring, as does Rynin's, either verifiability *or* falsifiability. For some sentences involving mixed quantification, although presumably not all of them,[40] have no "ascertainable truth-conditions" in the sense of that expression which Rynin requires for a statement's Meaningfulness, namely, a contingent state of affairs that "entails" or "necessitates" the truth or falsity of the statement in question. There is no set of observation-statements [41] that entails the truth or falsity of the sentence *S*: "For every substance there exists some solvent." Finding thus far only soluble substances does not prove the truth of *S*, since we might conceivably find a substance tomorrow for which we would never subsequently find a solvent. Nor, on the other hand, would finding a thus-far insoluble substance prove the falsity of *S*, since tomorrow we might conceivably find a solvent for that substance. The sentence—being an unrestricted universal statement *and* an existential statement—is unverifiable by virtue of its universal component and unfalsifiable by virtue of its existential component. If by 'verifiable' one means, as Rynin apparently means, "capable of being proved true" and by 'falsifiable' one means "capable of being proved false," then *S* appears to be neither verifiable nor falsifiable. Sentences like *S*, Rynin concedes, "are admittedly such that we could never hope to *determine* their truth or falsity." Yet, in spite of the fact that *S* is untestable, hence disallowed by a strict reading of Rynin's formulation, it appears intelligible to suppose, doubt, wonder about, even to assert that *S* is true or that it is false. But if *S* is true or false, albeit not *ascertainably* so, then surely *S* is Meaningful, since by Rynin's admission, "... it is a sufficient condition for a statement to be meaningful, that it be true, and likewise sufficient provided it be false.... If the empiricist or any other criterion of meaning knows its business it would do well to countenance the meaningfulness of true statements; if not I, and I suppose, everyone interested in a criterion of cognitive meaningfulness, will willingly part company with it."[42]

[40] "Every man is in love with a woman at some time in his life" is clearly unverifiable since it makes reference to an indeterminate number of men. But the statement is arguably falsifiable; if even one man were to live and to die without being in love with a woman—presumably this could be ascertained—the statement is false.

[41] Rynin stipulates a rough equivalence between what Hempel calls "observation sentences" and what Rynin himself calls "true statements affirming the occurrence of ascertainable states of affairs." Rynin remarks that "the difference in manner of formulation seems to me to be non-essential." *Ibid.*, p. 54.

[42] *Ibid.*, pp. 60 and 55-56, respectively.

Unwilling, on the one hand, to give up the conception of a criterion of factual significance resting upon the notion of ascertainable truth-conditions, and unable, on the other hand, to rest fully content with a formulation which, regardless of its other advantages, disallows sentences like "For every substance there exists some solvent," Rynin concludes with the abrupt and obscure observation that such sentences might perhaps be viewed as "quasi-cognitively meaningful." "On the one hand," he writes, "one would like to include them in the class of cognitively meaningful statements in terms of the criterion of possessing truth conditions; on the other hand they seem not to qualify fully. Might one call them 'quasi-cognitively meaningful'? This doesn't seem to be very elegant, and I am at a loss as to how to make the decision."[43]

The exact import of that remark is not entirely clear. The safest presumption, perhaps, is that Rynin has simply not made up his mind about whether to go on record as allowing or disallowing the Meaningfulness of sentences like *S*. A more interesting presumption, strengthened by those things he says in favor of viewing them as Meaningful, is that Rynin here gently opts for the view that sentences like "For every substance there exists some solvent" are Meaningful in spite of not satisfying the Verifiability criterion. This need not constrain him to give up the Verifiability criterion in general; it would constrain him only to allow for a certain class of exceptions and for a specific reason. Let this view, then, be ascribed to him, remembering, however, that Rynin also inclines somewhat to disallowing such sentences altogether.[44] In sum, let us attribute to Rynin the position that the Verifiability criterion is an adequate criterion except in those cases where verification or falsification is denied us because of a statement's making reference to an inexhaustible number of cases, every one of which would have to be checked, *per impossibile*, to ascertain the statement's truth-value; in those cases, and in those alone, the Verifiability criterion should be relaxed.

C. FURTHER PROBLEMS

1. Statements about other minds

There is a large class of statements whose Meaningfulness might at first appear to be denied by the Verifiability criterion. Statements about other minds seem to be true or false, but at the same time highly resistant to

[43] *Ibid.*, p. 62.

[44] Rynin's more recent thinking about statements containing mixed quantification may be found in "Cognitive Meaning and Cognitive Use," *Inquiry*, Vol. 9 (1960), pp. 109-131.

public verification or falsification. Very often we want to attribute to other people experiences—pain, for example—to which we are not privy. If we were philosophically very cautious we might declare, rather tentatively, that we observe signs, evidences, indications of another person's having such-and-such experiences. More typically, perhaps, after giving due attention to his behavior we would straightforwardly declare—whether with sufficient philosophical warrant or not—that we *know* that someone else is experiencing, say, pain or elation; and we would declare this on the basis of inspecting what he says and does. But if, on either formulation, we mean to attribute to other persons, as most of us typically do, experiences which are different from and beyond either their physical states or their behavior as manifest to us—on the basis of which we feel justified in making our claim to know what experiences they are having—then there arise a number of problems, among which is the problem of the testability of sentences making such attributions.

If we are prepared to accept a behavioristic analysis of psychological expressions, then the problem of testing sentences containing such words is substantially eased. If we hold, for example, that to "have a headache" *is* to display behavior of such-and-such an intersubjectively observable sort, or that sentences about headaches, whether my own or someone else's, are translatable without loss of meaning into sentences about publicly observable behavior of a certain sort, then there appear to be no special problems about verifying or falsifying statements of the form 'X has a headache.' Behaviorism is by no means exclusively Positivistically inspired, but some of the early Positivists, or some attracted to their way of thinking, adopted such a position. Carl Hempel's essay, "The Logical Analysis of Psychology," is a case in point, although Hempel later recanted the argument contained in that atricle.[45] One fairly main-line Positivist example, several years earlier, was Rudolf Carnap's "Psychology in Physical Language,"[46] in which he claims that statements about other persons' minds are logically equivalent to statements about their publicly observable responses, or their tendencies to respond, to certain physical stimuli.

However, if when we ascribe to a person the having of a headache, we mean to attribute to him something internal and at least partially private,

[45] Carl Hempel, "The Logical Analysis of Psychology," trans. by Wilfrid Sellars from *Revue de Synthèse* (1935) and reprinted in *Readings in Philosophical Analysis* [pp. 373-384]. For the recantation, see footnote 1, written in 1947, of the reprint cited, p. 373.

[46] Rudolf Carnap, "Psychology in Physical Language," trans. by George Schick from *Erkenntnis*, II (1931) and reprinted in *Logical Positivism* [pp. 165-198]; see pp. 170ff, especially p. 172.

then the question of the testability of statements comprising such ascriptions becomes more problematic. For in the case of statements about other minds there sometimes arises the irrepressible suspicion that perhaps things are not as they appear to be on the surface. It is sometimes true that I, and presumably others as well, *have* such-and-such an experience without *showing* that I have it. In consequence, it is plausible to hold that statements about other minds, at least some of them, are not conclusively verifiable. It would appear, for example, that we could never *verify* "John has a headache," and that the most we could ever verify is "John acts as if he has a headache," while John might nevertheless not have a headache all the while.

Two questions, then, should be explored here: Are statements about other minds Meaningful? Can statements about other minds plausibly be held to be Verifiable?

"*All the dons want to murder me.*" An example introduced by R. M. Hare serves to highlight these problems. Consider the case described by Hare:

> A certain lunatic is convinced that all the dons want to murder him. His friends introduce him to all the mildest and most respectable dons that they can find, and after each of them has retired, they say, 'You see, he doesn't really want to murder you; he spoke to you in a most cordial manner; surely you are convinced now?' But the lunatic replies 'Yes, but that was only his diabolical cunning; he's really plotting against me the whole time, like the rest of them; I know it I tell you'. However many kindly dons are produced, the reaction is still the same.... There is no behavior of dons that can be enacted which he will accept as counting against his theory; and therefore his theory ... asserts nothing.[47]

Presumably Hare is conceding that "All the dons want to murder me" asserts nothing because nothing the dons can do will dissuade the lunatic from his persuasion about the dons. If this is Hare's claim it is surely mistaken. Even though nothing the dons can do will satisfy the lunatic that he is wrong about the dons, the lunatic *is wrong* about the dons, and asserts something incorrect about them, namely, that they all want to murder him. Hare's confusion arises, perhaps, from his not noting the fact, or from not appreciating its importance, that "want to murder me" covers, for the lunatic, both (1) thinking murderous thoughts and (2) actually planning the murder in secret sessions behind closed doors, etc. The reason why "All the dons want to murder me" is unfalsified, and in a sense unfalsifiable, is that although there is, or might be, conclusive evidence against "All the dons want to murder me" in the second sense, there is and can be no con-

[47] Hare, "Theology and Falsification," pp. 99-100.

clusive evidence against it in the first. I do not mean to argue that the dons' behavior is not evidence for their state of mind. Nor need the lunatic. The dons' kindly behavior provides considerable evidence against (1); considerable, but not conclusive. If by "All the dons want to murder me" the lunatic means to assert principally that which is covered by (2) then he might eventually be persuaded to abandon his worry. Certain behavior on the part of the dons is incompatible with the truth of "All the dons want to murder me" if that statement asserts nothing more than that the dons are indulging in certain murder-planning behavior: meeting, secretly purchasing weapons, drafting threatening letters, planning when to strike, etc. A complete photographic and phonographic record of the dons' waking behavior would falsify "All the dons want to murder me" if *that* were what the statement principally asserts. But such a record would not quiet the lunatic's unrest. When the lunatic says "All the dons want to murder me" he means, or has come gradually to mean, that the dons have murderous thoughts about him regardless of how they behave. No observable don-behavior is logically incompatible with their thinking murderous thoughts. It is conceivable, even by a non-lunatic, that the dons should go on indefinitely thinking murderous thoughts, but always smile, wait for another time to strangle their victim, never meet together, and never tip their hand, even under sodium pentothal. Either Hare has not seen that his lunatic must mean (1) and not (2), or he contends that murderously inclined dons must slip sometime and, so to speak, show their mind. The former is unlikely. The latter is false.

The lunatic believes that the dons want to murder him; in believing this the lunatic believes, *ipso facto*, that the dons have seriously murderous thoughts about him, thoughts which will eventuate—unless they change their minds—in the action of attempting to kill him. The lunatic's belief, which takes the form of an assertion, gains immunity from falsification not, as Hare in effect alleges, from its being no assertion at all, but from the *prima facie* inherent unfalsifiability, and unverifiability, of statements about other minds. For it very often makes sense, in the case of statements about other minds, to wonder whether things are as they seem; for that reason even someone considerably short of lunacy might well wonder about any given case that has special importance for him. But whatever difficulties there might be about Verifying statements about other minds, it surely does not follow that such statements are Meaningless.

For example, if "Don-A wants to murder me" makes the same predication of Don-A as is made of me in "Kenneth Klein wants to murder me"—and why shouldn't it?—then I know roughly what it would be like for the lunatic's assertion about the don(s) to be true. I have had murderous thoughts about someone without showing them; I know what it would be like for the dons to have murderous thoughts about the lunatic without showing them. It would be very much like *my* having them, say, about the lunatic, if I had them. It would be very much like the lunatic's having them about the dons, if *he* had them. The lunatic himself knows, presumably, what it would be like for the dons to have or not to have murderous thoughts about him; it would be like his having or not having murderous thoughts about them or about someone else. It is simply not the case that there is no difference between the truth of the lunatic's assertion and the truth of its contradictory; it amounts to the difference between the dons' having or not having murderous thoughts. It is not, therefore, as Hare seemingly alleges, that "All the dons want to murder me" rules out nothing: it rules out the dons' not having murderous thoughts. Not being able to find out whether the dons have or do not have murderous thoughts—and *we* cannot find that out, although we may have excellent reasons for thinking we know their homicidal intentions about a given person—does not evacuate the assertion. Hare is surely wrong if he is arguing, as he seems to be, that an untestable assertion about another man's mind is not really an assertion at all. C. I. Lewis writes, "We can envisage the conscious experience of another, by empathy, in terms of our own. And we do. Any denial of that would be too egregious for consideration."[48]

The difficulty that presents itself with respect to Verifying statements about other minds is different in one important respect from the difficulties discussed so far. Speaking very generally, the difficulties of Verifying this or that arguably Meaningful statement are those of envisioning some observer appropriately *placed* in time, space, or duration, to confront the fact or facts asserted by the statement, *S*, in question. In light of the Verifiability criterion's requirement that a bona fide statement must be testable, it is always appropriate to ask not only, first, under what conditions might *S* be Verified, but also, second, *by whom* is *S* supposed to be Verifiable. Thus far the difficulties which the Verifiability criterion was designed to meet pertain largely to the first set of considerations: the difficulties of envisioning an observer sufficiently projected into the remote past or the distant future to Verify statements about events occurring at those times, or the difficulties of an observer's procuring sufficient evidence to Verify statements involving existential, mixed, or universal quantification. With respect to

[48] C. I. Lewis, "Some Logical Considerations Concerning the Mental," reprinted from *The Journal of Philosophy*, 38 (1941) in *Readings in Philosophical Analysis* [pp. 385-392], pp. 391-392.

statements involving these complication, *any* more or less normal observer would suffice to do the Verifying. But with respect to statements about other minds, the question "By whom is *S* supposed to be Verifiable?" becomes crucial, since *not* any observer will suffice. The only person in a position to confront the fact asserted by "John has a headache" is John himself, no one else. John alone is in a position to Verify that assertion. Even Ayer would seem to agree with such a conclusion:

> ... If the words "I am angry" are used to say that I am angry, then it does not seem in any way mysterious that my being angry should verify the proposition that they express. But how do I know that I am angry? I feel it.... If this answer is not regarded as satisfactory, I do not know what other can be given. ... When I say "I am in pain" I mean that I am in pain, and if *p* then *p*. But how do I establish *p*? How do I know that I am really in pain? Again the answer can only be "I feel it."[49]

Does this mean that statements about other minds, psychological propositions, are not Verifiable? Of course not. Rynin does not consider the question as to the Verifiability of statements about other minds. What he might say is conjecture. But there is nothing in the general line of argument that would preclude the claim that psychological propositions satisfy the Verifiability criterion.

This judgment is both textually sound and, in my opinion, plausible, at least with respect to the conditions requisite for establishing the *Meaningfulness* of psychological propositions, if not their truth or falsity in particular cases. There is nothing in Rynin's view which requires that the "ascertainable truth-conditions" requisite for the Meaningfulness of a statement must be ascertainable by anybody and everybody. If Rynin, or anyone, should argue that Meaningful sentences must be Verifiable *by anyone*, that would present serious trouble for psychological propositions. But surely all that should be required, so far as Meaningfulness is concerned, is that a bona fide statement must be Verifiable by *someone*. The truth conditions essential to Verifying psychological propositions are presumably ascertainable by the person or persons to whom they refer. Such propositions are obviously not Verifiable by just anyone; but they are Verifiable by those to whom they pertain.[50] And *that* much Verifiability, one would think, is sufficient for establishing their Meaningfulness.

[49] A. J. Ayer, "Verification and Experience," *Proceedings of the Aristotelian Society*, 37 (1933-1937); reprinted in *Logical Positivism* [pp. 228-246], pp. 241-242.

[50] Analytic philosophers sometimes find this point attractive even when they are chary of endorsing a Verifiability theory of Meaning. See John Hospers, *An Introduction to Philosophical Analysis* (Englewood Cliffs, New Jersey: Prentice-Hall, 1967), p. 265.

There is some appeal, to be sure, in the less troublesome view that psychological propositions, while not *translatable* into sentences describing the physical condition and behavior of the persons to whom they refer, are at least *testable* by virtue of the *de facto* connections which ordinarily obtain between a person's state of mind and his physical and behavioral responses. It is surely true that we ordinarily consider psychological propositions to be "verified," or at least reliably confirmed, whether we should do so or not, by ascertaining the truth of what Hempel calls "physical test sentences."[51] In many cases, however, it is difficult to quiet the lurking suspicion that while the former might be true, the latter might be false, or vice versa. We can have excellent reasons for thinking that another person, say, is in pain, while all the while he may not be in pain at all.

There is also some appeal in the claim that psychological propositions fit the testability condition required by the criterion of verifiability-in-principle, namely, that we know what experiences would verify statements about other minds if, contrary to hypothesis, we were in a position to have direct access to such minds. A temptation to argue in that fashion once occurred to Ayer: he once held the position that although the experiences of other persons are in fact inaccessible to my purview, "it is not logically inconceivable that I should have an experience that is in fact owned by someone else."[52] Ayer has since abandoned this view.[53]

Let us allow, then, that statements about other minds are not, perhaps, publicly or intersubjectively Verifiable, since no one except the persons to whom such propositions pertain is privy to the facts which they assert. If intersubjective Verifiability were required for Meaningfulness this would indeed constitute a telling difficulty for the Meaningfulness of psychological propositions and, consequently, at least for most of us, would redound to the unacceptability of the Verifiability criterion. But Rynin's understanding of the criterion does not explicitly make this requirement; nor, so far as I can see, is there any reason to construe any of his remarks as implicitly requiring it. Nor, for that matter, would it be required by the position Ayer endorsed in 1949:

[51] Hempel, "The Logical Analysis of Psychology," p. 377.

[52] A. J. Ayer, *Foundations of Empirical Knowledge* (London: Macmillan & Co., Ltd., 1940), p. 169.

[53] Introduction to the 1946 edition of *Language, Truth, and Logic*, pp. 19-20. More recently Arthur Pap has flirted with a different form of the claim that we might have direct access to other minds. See his *An Introduction to the Philosophy of Science* (Glencoe, Illinois: The Free Press, 1962), pp. 21-22.

> ... I [do not] wish to restrict experience to sense experience; I should not at all mind counting what might be called introspectible experiences, or feelings, mystical experiences if you like. It would be true, then, that people who haven't had certain experiences won't understand propositions which refer to them; but that I don't mind either. I can quite well believe that you have experiences different from mine.... I should be in the position of the blind man, and then I should admit that statements which are unintelligible to me might be meaningful to you. But I should then go on to say that the factual content of your statements *was* determined by the experiences which counted as their verifiers or falsifiers.[54]

We do not, in practice, assume that all the facts, so to speak, are accessible to everyone. Nor should we. We readily concede, for example, that there is a certain set of facts about color-blindness—the visual experiences of a color-blind person—of which only a color-blind person is cognizant, and about which, consequently, only such a person is in a position to report. Information so acquired does not constitute a small, unimportant part of our body of factual knowledge. When we want to know certain select facts about color-blindness, perfect pitch, synesthesia, etc., we consult not just anyone, but rather those persons who possess, or claim to possess, these modes of perception. If you state that whenever you hear middle-C played on a cello, your visual field is suffused with yellow, your statement is surely Meaningful to me, even though you, and only you, are in a position to Verify that statement.

Intersubjective Verifiability for every bona fide statement, then, would surely be an excessively rigid Meaningfulness-requirement. Since the truth-conditions for psychological propositions are presumably ascertainable by those persons to whom these propositions refer, and may, in consequence, be plausibly construed as Verifiable *by them*, the Verifiability criterion may plausibly be taken to countenance the Meaningfulness of statements about other minds.

2. Statements about "unobservables" in science

There is another important class of statements whose Meaningfulness the Verifiability criterion might at first be thought to disallow, namely, statements which refer to unobservables in science. In advanced physical science, we increasingly find statements containing terms which, it is often maintained, cannot be defined in terms of, or reduced to, observational sentences. The terms 'absolute temperature,' 'gravitational potential,' 'electric field,' 'psi-function,' 'gene,' 'atom,' and the several sub-atomic particles have been

[54] Ayer and Copleston, "Logical Positivism—A Debate," p. 743.

mentioned in this connection. "The electron," MacCorquodale and Meehl write, "... is supposedly an *entity* of some sort. Statements about the electron are, to be sure, supported by means of observational sentences. Nevertheless, it is no longer maintained ... that this set of supporting sentences exhaust the entire meaning of a sentence about the electron."[55] Judged by the early Positivist slogan that the meaning of a statement is the method of its verification, "clearly meaningless terms seem to be required," Scheffler asserts, "for adequate expression of our scientific beliefs."[56] A significant number of scientists no longer hold to the view that all the key expressions in science—and particularly the theoretical constructs [57]—are synonymous, as P. W. Bridgman suggested in *The Logic of Modern Physics*,[58] with a set of operations or, in Hempel's idiom, "are explicitly definable by means of observation predicates."[59] Sentences containing theoretical constructs are commonly taken as *hypothesizing* the existence of entities, processes, or relations between entities and processes, which are not themselves reducible to observation predicates or sets of observation sentences. S. F. Barker writes, "It looks as though there is no way of dispensing with these hypotheses which imply the existence of unobserved things; we need to retain them as essential elements in our empirical knowledge."[60] Again, Herbert Feigl reports:

[55] Kenneth MacCorquodale and Paul E. Meehl, "Hypothetical Constructs and Intervening Variables." reprinted from *Psychological Review*, 55 (1948) in *Readings in Philosophy of Science* [pp. 596-611], p. 597.

[56] Israel Scheffler, "Prospects of a Modest Empiricism," *The Review of Metaphysics*, Vol. X, Nos. 3-4 (1957); reprinted, in part (under the title "Theoretical Terms and a Modest Empiricism"), in *Philosophy of Science*, ed. by Arthur Danto and Sidney Morgenbesser (Cleveland, Ohio: The World Publishing Company, 1960 [pp. 159-173]), p. 164. For a typical early Positivist response, see Schlick's discussion of electrons in "Positivism and Realism", pp. 88-89 and *passim.*

[57] Israel Scheffler is of the opinion, however, that the "dispositional terms" such as "irritable," "flexible," "brittle," etc., are not as problematic as is sometimes thought (e.g., by Hempel, "Problems and Changes ...", pp. 118-120). Scheffler holds that dispositional terms might conceivably be shown to bear a "sufficiently determinate application to chosen observable entities [to] qualify as ... clearly observational predicate[s].... The problem is to define the relationship between dispositional terms and what are customarily taken as their respective non-dispositional counterparts in specific contexts." "Prospects of a Modest Empiricism," *The Review of Metaphysics*, vol. X, Nos. 3-4 (1957), pp. 608-609.

[58] P. W. Bridgman, *The Logic of Modern Physics* (New York: The Macmillan Co., 1928), p. 2.

[59] Hempel, "Problems and Changes ...," p. 118; also p. 121.

[60] S. F. Barker, *Induction and Hypothesis* (Ithaca, New York: Cornell University Press, 1957), p. 152.

Generally, the "theoretical constructs", i.e., the hypothetically assumed entities of the sciences cannot be identified with (i.e., explicitly defined in terms of) concepts which apply to the directly perceptible facts as they are manifest in the contexts of ordinary observation or of experimental operations.[61]

Advanced scientific theories which contain theoretical terms tend to assume the form of what Hempel calls "hypothetical-deductive systems," the characteristic feature of which is this: observation sentences are logical consequences of one or more interlocking scientific hypotheses, but not vice versa:

Thus, beginning with the hypothesis that gases are made up of small particles which obey the laws of mechanics, plus certain approximating assumptions about the relation of their sizes to their mutual distances, their perfect elasticity, and their lack of mutual attraction, one can apply mathematical rules and eventually, by direct substitution and equation, lead without arbitrariness to the empirical equation $PV = K$. However, one cannot rigorously reverse the process. That is, one cannot commence with the empirical gas law $PV = K$ and arrive at the full kinetic theory.[62]

The problem, then, with ascertaining the truth-value of a scientific hypothesis characteristic of such hypothetico-deductive systems, is twofold. First, certain key sentences that figure centrally in the system cannot be directly verified, since they contain terms which refer to unobservable entities or processes. Second, and perhaps more significant, although one can deduce verifiable observation sentences from an hypothesis, or set of hypotheses, containing theoretical terms—let us call such a set a "theory"—*the converse does not hold.* The reason that the converse does not hold is that a *different* theory, or a set of theories, might conceivably be devised from which the very same observational consequences, statable by observation sentences, would follow. Cohen and Nagel write, "The hypothesis is only probable on the evidence because it is always logically possible to find some other hypothesis from which all the verified propositions are consequences."[63] Suppose, for example, that P and R are rival, perhaps incompatible, theories, and that O is a set of observation sentences which follow from

[61] Herbert Feigl, "The Mind-Body Problem in the Development of Logical Empiricism," reprinted from *Revue Internationale de Philosophie*, 4 (1950) in *Readings in the Philosophy of Science* [pp. 612-626], p. 618.

[62] MacCorquodale and Meehl, "Hypothetical Constructs and Intervening Variables," p. 599.

[63] Morris Cohen and Ernest Nagel, *An Introduction to Logic and Scientific Method* (New York: Harcourt & Co., 1934), p. 205.

both theories. Obviously, the truth of theory-*P* cannot be said to be established by " 'If *P* then *O*' and '*O*' " any more than the truth of theory-*R* could be said to be established by " 'If *R* then *O*' and '*O*' ". This is not to say, of course, that theory-*P* cannot be true, or that theory-*R* cannot be true. It is only to say that in those areas of inquiry where rival theories might be devised to account for *O*, then the truth of theory-*P*, which accounts for *O*, no more can be said to follow from or to be conclusively established by the evidence, *O*, than could the truth of theory-*R*, which accounts for the same evidence be said to follow from that "evidence." In short, the truth of any theory is not proved by determining the truth of any "evidence" which it implies. To claim the reverse would involve what is commonly called the fallacy of affirming the consequent: "If *P*, then *Q*; *Q*; therefore, *P*" is an invalid inference-form. Cohen and Nagel describe the bearing of this fallacy upon scientific reasoning as follows : "... the hypothetical simply asserts that if the antecedent is true, the consequent must also be true; it does not assert that the consequent is true *only on the condition* that the antecedent is true.... For example, if the theory of organic evolution is true, we should find fossil remains of extinct animal forms; but the discovery of such remains is not a proof, is not conclusive evidence, for the theory.[64] If any theory, then, is itself unverifiable by virtue of terms it includes which refer to unobservable entities or processes, that theory cannot be said to be verified by the verification of *O* which it implies. Accordingly, the satisfactory determination of the truth of a set of observation sentences cannot be said to constitute a sufficient truth-condition for any theory which implies them. Theories are characteristically said not to be more or less *verified* but to be more or less *confirmed* by their supportive evidence.

From some writers, to be sure, the cognitive significance of sentences employing theoretical terms is a moot point. Many writers dealing with this question hold that theories are not, properly speaking, true or false at all; theories function rather as conceptual "instruments" for resolving specific problems of control, explanation, and prediction. Scheffler labels this view "instrumentalistic fictionalism"[65] and Nagel discusses the view sympathetically in *The Structure of Science*.[66] As early as 1939 Nagel had written of this view as follows:

[64] *Ibid.*, pp. 98-99.

[65] Scheffler, "Prospects of a Modest Empiricism," pp. 164-166.

[66] Ernest Nagel, *The Structure of Science* (New York: Harcourt, Brace & World, Inc., 1961), Chapter VI: "The Cognitive Status of Theories," pp. 129-140.

... questions of the *truth* of theories ... are of little concern to those who actually use theories. Reflective inquiry is instituted for the sake of settling a *specific* problem, whether it be practical or theoretical, and inquiry terminates when a resolution of the problem is obtained. The various procedures distinguishable in inquiry (such as observation, operation upon subject matter including the manipulation of instruments, symbolic representation of properties of subject matter, symbolic transformation and calculation, etc.) are to be viewed as instrumental to its end product. The use of theories is one patent factor in reflective inquiry. They function primarily as means for effecting transitions from one set of statements to other sets, with the intent of controlling natural changes and of supplying predictions capable of being checked through manipulating directly experienceable subject matter. Accordingly, in their actual use in science, theories serve as *instruments* in specific context, and in this capacity are to be characterized as good or bad, effective or ineffective, rather than true or false or probable. Those who stress the instrumental function of theories are not necessarily committed to identifying truth with effectiveness and falsity with uselessness.[67]

In contrast to this position, however, many writers hold that theories are really composed of bona fide *statements* of which truth and falsity are properly applicable. It is for those who endorse this latter, "realistic" view of theories[68] that the specification of the truth-conditions for theoretical statements becomes problematic.

Although Professor Rynin does not offer a full discussion of the question of the Meaningfulness of theoretical statements, he does sketch a position in some brief remarks he makes at the end of "Vindication of L*G*C*L*P* S*V*T*SM," and by his general argument in "The Dogma of Logical Pragmatism."[69] The position, in brief, is this: Since scientific theories are set up in such a manner that testable deductions can be derived from them, it is plausible to hold that theories have ascertainable *necessary* truth-conditions; if so, the Verifiability criterion countenances their Meaningfulness. A theory which makes reference to unobservables may not perhaps be verifiable, but such a theory, or set of interrelated theories, is presumably *falsifiable* since, as Cohen and Nagel state, "its implications can be clearly traced, and then subjected to experimental confirmation."[70] If the observation sentences or empirical laws deducible from a given theory, or set of interlocking theories, turn out to be false, then the *theory-complex* implying

[67] Excerpted from Ernest Nagel's "Principles of the Theory of Probability," vol. I, No. 6 (1939) of *The International Encyclopedia of Unified Science*; reprinted in *Philosophy of Science* [pp. 235-265] under the title "Probability and Degree of Confirmation," pp. 264-265.

[68] See Nagel, *The Structure of Science*, pp,. 141-145.

[69] David Rynin, "The Dogma of Logical Pragmatism," *Mind* (July, 1956).

[70] Cohen and Nagel, *An Introduction to Logic and Scientific Method*, p. 207.

them cannot be true, which is to say, is false.[71] Sentences employing theoretical terms, by virtue of their placement within hypothetico-deductive systems, bear a relation to the states of affairs which can conceivably serve as *evidence* for their truth such that if the latter do not obtain, then the theory is judged incorrect. "The empirical laws are necessary for the truth of hypothetical sentences, since the latter imply them.... In the statement of a hypothetical construction ... there occur words ... which are not explicitly defined by (or reduced to) the empirical relations. Once having set up sentences (postulates) containing these hypothetical words, we can arrive by deduction at empirical sentences which can themselves be tested."[72]

The reply here attributed to Rynin is not offered here mainly as an argument, either in his behalf or independently, for the Meaningfulness of scientific theories.[73] In light of the fact, however, that many have argued for their Meaningfulness, it has been the concern here to decide whether the Verifiability criterion, if adopted, would exclude theories from the class of Meaningful statements. If one were disposed to hold that theories are Meaningful, would theories, so contrued, constitute an exception to the Verifiability criterion? If the account given above of the relation between theory and observation stipulated by the procedures of advanced scientific theorizing is correct, it is plausible to hold that theories are falsifiable, even though they may not be verifiable. Hence, the Verifiability criterion countenances their Meaningfulness.

One further note about falsifiability in connection with scientific theories.

[71] If *P*, then *Q*; not-*Q*; therefore not-*P*.

[72] MacCorquodale and Meehl, "Hypothetical Constructs and Intervening Variables", p. 598.

[73] Ernest Nagel makes the following informative comments about the ongoing disagreement among philosophers of science concerning the relative viability of the realistic or the instrumentalistic view of theories: "Indeed, those who differ in their answers to it frequently disagree neither on matters falling into the province of experimental inquiry nor on points of formal logic nor on the facts of scientific procedure. What often divides them are, in part, loyalties to different intellectual traditions, in part inarbitratable preferences concerning the appropriate way of accommodating our language to the generally admitted facts. It is a matter of historical record that, while many distinguished figures in both science and philosophy have adopted as uniquely adequate the characterization of theories as true or false statements, a no less distinguished group of other scientists and philosophers has made a similar claim for the description of theories as instruments of inquiry. However, a defender of either view cannot only cite eminent authority to support his position; with a little dialectical ingenuity he can usually remove the sting from apparently grave objections to his position. In consequence, the already long controversy as to which of the two is the proper way of construing theories can be prolonged indefinitely." *The Structure of Science*, p. 14.

In 1934, Karl Popper noted a difficulty about the contention that scientific theories are falsifiable,[74] a difficulty which Professor W. V. O. Quine has recently re-emphasized in "Two Dogmas of Empiricism."[75] A scientific theory is a conjunction of a *number* of hypotheses. In consequence, the falsity of a *particular* hypothesis is not always conceded in light of observations that run contrary to the observational expectations logically associated with that hypothesis. A simple example might illustrate the point. For simplicity, an example is selected which does not involve reference to unobservables. The hypothesis of the continued existence of the stars that form the constellation *Orion* is not falsified by the disappearance of that constellation from the skies of the far-northern hemisphere during the summer months; for that disappearance is accommodated by the hypothesis of the earth's axial tilt. The latter hypothesis, in turn, yields the prediction that *Orion* will appear in the skies of the southern hemisphere during the summer months, an hypothesis which is verifiable and true. However, the latter hypothesis yields this prediction only with the help of yet another hypothesis, namely, the heliocentric hypothesis. Scientific hypotheses thus intermesh with one another to form theories, and experiences which run counter to expectation necessitate changes in one or more of the many hypotheses amalgamated into a theory. The problem with holding that scientific hypotheses are falsifiable, is that the falsification of a *particular* hypothesis is sometimes avoided, in actual scientific practice, by re-evaluating the acceptability of *other* hypotheses that bear upon the specific question being investigated. Recalcitrant experimental experiences, in other words, show that the conjunction of a *given set of hypotheses* is false, but do not show with *which* constituent hypothesis the trouble lies. But this point about scientific method does not abrogate the claim that theories are falsifiable, provided that one understands by "theory" the conjunction of the full set of relevant hypotheses constituting it. Far from showing that theories are not falsifiable, Quine's remarks, supposing him to be correct in his description of *de facto* scientific procedures, actually support the claim that theories are falsifiable. For why should experiences that run counter to the empirical expectations based upon a given conjunction of hypotheses occasion readjustment of certain of these hypotheses *unless* it be that the conjunction of hypotheses constituting the theory has more or less fixed logical interrelations with statements that describe human experiences, however the latter might be

[74] Popper, *The Logic of Scientific Discovery*, p. 42.

[75] W. V. O. Quine, "Two Dogmas of Empiricism," *Philosophical Review* (January, 1951); reprinted in Quine, *From a Logical Point of View* (Cambridge: Harvard University Press [pp. 20-46], 1953).

formulated, and under whatever stipulable experimental conditions they would be expected as forthcoming? Surely it is only because theories *are* logically incompatible with the advent of certain experiences, or with statements reporting their occurrence, that one or more of the hypotheses constituting the theory must be readjusted upon receipt of such experiences. Indeed, it would seem that the principal reason that Quine describes certain experiences as "recalcitrant" is that statements reporting their occurrence *are* logically incompatible with a given theory. "Reevaluation of some statements entails reevaluation of others, because of their logical interconnections...."[76] It is because there are stipulated connections between theory and observation that theories may plausibly be regarded as falsifiable. "Any scientist," John Hospers writes, "can tell you, if you understand his vocabulary, the observable difference between his hypothesls [where "hypothesis" = "theory"] being true and its not being true."[77]

RETROSPECT. In denying factual significance to a large number of sentences which many people thought to possess that status, the Positivists were employing a criterion of factual significance tailored to their understanding of the conditions under which a sentence may be used to make an intelligible assertion. Their view was both animated and dominated by the intuition that Meaningfulness and testability are two sides of the same coin. The general doctrine which they advanced was that the factual significance of an intelligible assertion—its true-or-falseness—is a function of its being such that some experience or set of experiences could conceivably show it to be true or show it to be false. Of this general doctrine the Positivists gave various, progressively less crude formulations. The position taken in this chapter is twofold: first, that the search for a criterion of factual significance formulated in terms of verifiability or falsifiability, or a combination thereof, is not misguided; second, that David Rynin's formulation of the Positivist criterion of factual significance is substantially acceptable. Rynin's formulation requires that a Meaningful statement must have associated with it either an ascertainable truth-condition or an ascertainable falsity-condition. The Verifiability principle thus restricts the range of Meaningful propositions to those for which it is possible to imagine—conceive, describe —what it would be like to Verify them. The Verifiability principle is not open to the lethal objections to which earlier versions of the principle were

[76] *Ibid.*, p. 42.

[77] Hospers, *An Introduction to Philosophical Analysis* [first edition, 1953], p. 361. This topic is discussed further, and from a slightly different point of view, in chapter 5 *infra*: "The translatability criterion," pp. 161-166.

open, and if the argument contained in Section C of this chapter is essentially correct, the Verifiability principle also countenances the Meaningfulness of statements about other minds and statements about unobservables in science. Rynin's formulation of the Verifiability principle stands as a correct, or at least plausible, criterion of factual significance.

It is not easy to assess the weight and importance of the difficulty posed for the Verifiability principle by those cases of mixed quantification which make reference to an inexhaustible number of cases. It is true that we could never *actually* verify or falsify an assertion such as "For every substance there exists some solvent" in the sense of *finishing* the job. But surely we are not confused about what we would count as the verification-condition or the falsification-condition for any particular case covered by such an assertion. The difficulty arises from the quantificational aspect of the sentence(s) in question, from their unrestricted generality, not from either any inherent obscurity in what they are used to assert, or from any inherent disengagement of what we *would* expect to find as the case in any instance—and, by extension, in all instances—covered by such sentences if we *were* in a position to make the requisite verifying or falsifying observations.[78]

If the argument is correct thus far, its weight comes to rest on the third, theological issue; everything depends on an answer to the question as to whether the statement that God exists is or is not Verifiable. Do theological sentences, at least those which make putative statements, satisfy the Verifiability criterion? This question is investigated in the next chapter.

[78] For further discussion of this matter see chapter 5 *infra*: "*Ad hoc* exceptions," pp. 159-161.

CHAPTER IV

ARE THEOLOGICAL SENTENCES TESTABLE?

> A gardener may be elusive, an architect retiring, a watchmaker hard to find, but we know what it would be to see them and so confirm the guesses that it is they who are responsible for what we see before us. Now what would it be like to see God? Suppose some seer were to see, imagine all saw, move upwards from the ocean to the sky some prodigious figure which declared in dreadful tones the moral law or phophesied most truly—our fate. Would this be to see God?
>
> Wouldn't it just be a phenomenon which later we were able to explain or not able to explain but in neither case the proof of a living God? The logic of God if there is such a logic isn't like that.
>
> —John Wisdom, "The Logic of God," 1950.

The Positivist attack upon theism turns, in part, upon the contention that the *prima-facie* statement that God exists is not testable. Responding *directly* to Positivism, certain contemporary apologists for Christianity have denied this contention, have maintained, contrariwise, that the statement that God exists *is* testable. The purpose of this chapter is to examine several typical and influential forms which this denial has taken and to assess their plausibility. And the purpose of this analysis, in turn, is to highlight the feature of "transcendence" in the logic of "God" as "God" figures in classical Christianity, a feature which, in my opinion, is indispensable to the Christian concept of God. It will be argued that by virtue of this feature each of the views of the type under consideration fails to meet the Positivist attack. None of the views, in short, satisfies the Verifiability requirement. Accordingly, the problem posed for Christianity by Positivism is neither nullified nor solved; the discussion must continue.

The formulation of the guiding question for this chapter by reference to sentences rather than to statements is perhaps overly cautious. Properly speaking, testability pertains not to sentences but to statements, or to sentences which people use to make statements. "Let us serve the Lord with gladness" is a theological sentence, but the question as to its testability does not arise since the sentence does not make a statement. Those theological sentences whose testability is in question, of course, are only those which are typically used to make (putative) statements, such as "God exists," "God loves us," "For God so loved the world that He gave His only begotten Son ...," "God was in Christ reconciling the world unto Himself," etc. The guarded formulation of the question is meant to ward off the savor of question-begging which might be suggested by the formulation "Are theological *statements* testable?" At this stage of the argument 'testable' is used interchangeably with "Verifiable," that is, either verifable or falsifiable, or both.

Generally speaking, the counter-contention to be explored is that the sentences containing the word 'God' which Christians use to express their religious beliefs, make statements, are true or false, and that these statements, or some crucial ones among them, *are* testable. Given the traditional Christian distinction between "this life" and "life after death," and given the stipulation, according to the Verifiability principle, that a genuine statement must be either verifiable or falsifiable, four types of test-situation might be envisioned for theological sentences: (1) terrestrial verifiability, (2) eschatological verifiability, (3) terrestrial falsifiability, and (4) eschatological falsifiability. Within the first three categories fall the views of those who, by way of explicitly attempting to reply to the Positivists directly and on their own terms have maintained that certain crucial theological sentences are testable. To my knowledge, no one has explicitly proposed a view of the fourth type although certain suggestions, which will be examined presently, adumbrate such a view. The cross-classification mentioned accommodates a number of different theoretical positions, only some of which have thus far been defended. One could hold, for example, that *all* theological sentences, or that only *some* of them, are verifiable but not falsifiable, are falsifiable but not verifiable, are both verifiable and falsifiable, terrestrially or eschatologically, terrestrially-and-eschatologically taken conjointly, eschatologically but not terrestrially (or conversely), and so on. My purpose here is to discuss only those positions that have in fact been maintained by certain contemporary Christian apologists, not those which might be. The views to be examined do not always fit this classification precisely, inasmuch as the defenders of Christian theism, particularly those who advocate views classified under "terrestrial falsifiability," sometimes offer no clear indication as to whether the test-situations which they envision occur within this life or within some life beyond. The points at which the schema fails to fit a particular view should be evident to the reader, and no great violence will be inflicted by employing it for the purposes of rough classification.

For reasons which will become clear presently, it will be appropriate to look, first, at certain writings which appear to suggest that theological sentences might be falsified in this life; second, at one attempt to describe how theological sentences might be verified eschatologically; and third, at an attempt to show how theological sentences might be verified here and now, in this life.

A. TERRESTRIAL FALSIFIABILITY: MIGHT THEOLOGICAL SENTENCES BE FALSIFIED DURING THIS LIFE?

In response to the streamlined neopositivist view put forth by Antony Flew, certain contemporary writers have maintained that some crucial theological sentences are falsifiable, and seem to have maintained, moreover, that they might be falsified at some point in this life. Alasdair MacIntyre, for example, adumbrates this line of argument. The argument is essentially that the "facts of evil" *count against* the Christian claim that there is a God who is both good and omnipotent. Since the facts of evil count against this claim, it is right and fitting to regard the claim as "falsifiable." The objection that will be invoked against this argument is the following: *counting against* is not the same as *falsifying*, as some of those who have been attracted by this line of argument admit. There are good reasons, theologically speaking, to maintain that nothing which this life could present would sufficiently count against theological sentences to falsify them.

Consider, first, the position of Alasdair MacIntyre in his book, *Difficulties in Christian Belief.* MacIntyre observes that "either the facts of evil are admitted to be inconsistent with belief in God or they are not. If they are not admitted to be inconsistent, then there are good grounds for saying that belief in God is unfalsifiable...."[1] He maintains, however, that the facts of evil indeed do count against belief in the existence of a good, omnipotent God, and since they do, he reasons, the assertion that there is a God is properly regarded as falsifiable. MacIntyre claims that "... the believer does ... both see that the facts of evil are as they are and that there is an

[1] Alasdair MacIntyre, *Difficulties in Christian Belief* (London: SCM Press, Ltd., 1959), p. 33.

inconsistency between admitting this and avowing belief in a good God. So that his assertions are not unfalsifiable."[2] Now it is unlikely that MacIntyre is simply *equating* "counting against" with "falsifying," for he also holds, as he surely would not if he made this equation, that a Christian may not-irrationally hold to his beliefs in spite of some occurrences which constitute grave difficulties for such beliefs.[3] MacIntyre would appear to be arguing that at *some* point, although he does not describe that point, the facts of evil might become so severe and dramatic as to falsify the theistic claim that the universe is governed by a good, omnipotent God.

Certain other writers argue in like fashion. They, like MacIntyre, acknowledge that "counting against" is not equivalent to "falsifying," but they also, like MacIntyre, do not appear to have appreciated the importance of this non-equivalence to their argument. Consider the responses of I. M. Crombie and Basil Mitchell to Flew's article. Both couch their remarks in the idiom Flew initiated, namely in terms of seeking something which will "count against" the truth of an assertion like "God loves us" or "God is merciful." Both hold that pain and evil count against the truth of such assertions, but both also maintain that pain and evil do not count *decisively* against them. In making the first point, they would presumably claim to be meeting the force of Flew's attack squarely, but in making the second point, and in failing to give an acceptable account of what *would* count decisively against "God loves us," that is, falsify it, they nullify their replies as viable rejoinders to Flew's argument. The point merits closer scrutiny.

Crombie's first comment. Crombie's reply to Flew, for example, is substantially contained in two comments, the first concerning "God loves us," and the second, "God is merciful." He claims, first, that "God loves us" obliges us to believe that "whatever is allowed to happen to us can be turned to our own well-being."[4] Second, he claims that suffering which was "utterly, eternally, and irredeemably pointless" would not merely count against the truth of "God is merciful," but would count decisively against it.[5] But note how each comment nullifies the force of the other. The first remark in effect posts a peculiar sort of operational caveat which in fact drains the second of its seeming significance. For to say that "God loves us" obliges us to believe that whatever is allowed to happen to us can be turned to our own well-being, is to show in effect how thoroughly that assertion is

[2] *Ibid.*, p. 32.

[3] *Ibid.*

[4] I. M. Crombie, "The Possibility of Theological Statements," in *Faith and Logic*, ed. by Basil Mitchell (Boston: The Beacon Press, 1957), p. 70.

[5] Crombie, "Theology and Falsification," p. 124.

insulated against falsification. The comment suggests that what is in fact being tested is not the truth of the assertion that God loves us but the *character*, so to speak, of the person making and believing it. Any putative test of the assertion would always turn into a test of the person making the test. Can we or can we not succeed in meeting adversity with courage, hope, and gratitude? If we fail, we can always be advised to persevere, to endure with trust, patience, and obedience. God will turn things to our *eventual* well-being, it will be said, even if we cannot understand how and when it is to be so. God's wisdom is operative, by hypothesis, and will eventually be made manifest. The *locus classicus*, of course, is the *Book of Job*. But this transforms a test of the proposition into a test of character. We can fail the test, but the assertion cannot fail. Following the dialectical spirit of Crombie's first comment, we could *never* get into a position fairly to judge that God does not love us, for although pain and evil, it is claimed, "count against" the truth of "God loves us," since they do not count decisively against it, pain and evil are not really excluded from the state of affairs covered by the assertion—their non-occurrence is not a necessary condition for its truth—hence are not falsifers. Crombie has surely not met the force of the question Flew asks: What could count decisively against it? What would not only make us *suspect* that God does not love us? Pain and evil do that. What would *show* it? If pain and evil are counters, though not falsifiers, what would be a falsifier? What is the criterion for saying it, or for denying it? If one recognizes nothing as falsifying "God loves us" then one admits no criterion for asserting it. The assertion thus fails to declare that things stand thus-and-so and not otherwise. It declares that *however* things stand, "God loves us."

Mitchell's parable of the Stranger. Before turning to Crombie's second comment it will be well to consider a parable which Basil Mitchell has fashioned which attempts to mitigate the force of this objection. What the parable actually does, however, is to underscore the problem. Mitchell likens the Christian's terrestrial situation to that of a member of the Resistance during time of war. The difficulty with "God loves us," the parable suggests, is not, as Flew alleges, that we are perplexed as to what is asserted. It is rather that there is merely some special difficulty in finding out whether or not the assertion is true. The parable goes as follows: In time of war, a member of the Resistance is puzzled by the ambiguous behavior of a Stranger he once met secretly by night. At that time the Stranger declared himself to be not merely a supporter of the Resistance movement, but the leader of it. He urged the partisan to trust him and the cause of the movement which both shared, whatever happens. The Stranger is seen subsequently befriending members of the Resistance. But sometimes he is also seen in the uniform of the Occupation army, betraying the members of the Resistance, or so it would appear. However, in spite of appearances, the partisan urges his doubting comrades, the Stranger spoke the truth. Perhaps he has a complicated plan to help the cause of the Resistance that involves temporary, strategic conciliations with the enemy; some members of the Resistance will have to be sacrified for the sake of the overarching strategy. But do not despair. "Whatever happens, remember that the Stranger is on our side."[6]

Is "Whatever happens, remember that God loves us" analogous, as Mitchell suggests, to "Whatever happens, remember that the Stranger is on our side"? I think not. The partisan is never confused about what "The Stranger is on our side" asserts. The goal of the Resistance movement is the eventual defeat of the enemy and the liberation of the country from the Occupation forces. "Being on our side" is working to that end. Certain things "count against" the partisan's belief about the Stranger, such as the Stranger's betraying members of the Resistance. But occasional "betrayals" do not count *decisively* against the truth of "The Stranger is on our side." For the partisan knows that liberation is bought at a price. What looks like betrayal might be, in fact, expedient forfeiture furthering the cause, although admittedly, the reverse is true as well. The surface behavior of the Stranger is ambiguous because it fits, alternatively, either of two descriptions: either sacrificing for the cause, which does not "count against," or betrayal to the Occupation, which does. That is why belief that the Stranger is on our side can be shaken but seems to be able to withstand falsification indefinitely.

Yet there is one feature about the parable which Mitchell appears not to have noticed. "The Stranger is on our side" could not withstand every conceivable contingency. The assertion is falsifiable in principle. Since the partisan is never in doubt about the difference between what "being on our side" and "not being on our side" means, he could surely envision a contingency which would falsify his belief. Something could let the cat out of the bag. The partisan would surely recognize either of two contingencies as settling the question: (a) a complete victory of the Resistance, with the Stranger discovered as having played a crucial role in the overthrow of the Occupation; or (b) a complete rout of the Resistance, with the Stranger discovered as having effected that rout by turning over to the Occupation-police the names of all the Resistance members which he learned while

[6] Mitchell, "Theology and Falsification," pp. 103-105.

pretending to be one of them. The point is sometimes exploited in films about World War II. Contingency-(a) would verify the assertion; contingency-(b) would falsify it. Since the argument in question seeks to establish the falsifiability of theological sentences, let us overlook the first and pursue the analogy in terms of the second.

"The Stranger is on our side" excludes the Stranger's turning in all the patriots. If that happens, the jig is up; the Stranger's loyalty is decided. The state of affairs covered by the assertion is limited. The partisan knows what would falsify it if, heaven forbid, *that* happened! Mitchell's parable suggests this analogy: Just as the Stranger's plan involves occasional acts of sacrifice of members of the Resistance to the Occupation, so too pain and evil cannot falsify "God loves us," since pain and evil, however unwelcome they are, are part of, or at least not inconsistent with, the governance God is taken to exercise over the world. But since "The Stranger is on our side" is falsifiable in principle, the analogy would require the same of "God loves us." Accordingly, the implication of the parable for dealing with the *prima facie* unfalsifiability of "God loves us" is that *if* certain key pieces of evidence were to come in, then the Christian would be in a position to decide whether God loves us or not, just as the partisan would be able to decide, given certain imaginable developments, whether the Stranger is really loyal to the one side or to the other. What analogous developments might obtain in the case of "God loves us"? What foreseeable contingency would settle the question? We are now in a position to examine Crombie's second comment, together with one by John Hick.

Crombie's second comment. Crombie claims that suffering which is "utterly, eternally, and irredeemably pointless" would count decisively against "God is merciful." Similarly, John Hick alleges that conclusive refutation of Christianity would be provided by a Satanic Vision, "a direct confrontation with an all-powerful and wholly evil being whose existence precluded the possibility that a God should exist as described by Christianity."[7] In making these remarks, both Crombie and Hick appear to be saying that something might falsify the theistic claim, namely, the discvery of either of the states of affairs they mention. But the difficulty with these envisioned states of affairs which allegedly would falsify the theistic claim if either obtained is that in both cases there appear to be no circumstances which this life might present which a dedicated Christian would be justified in judging to be the state of affairs in question.

[7] John Hick, *Faith and Knowledge* (New York: Cornell University Press, 1957), revised edition, 1966, p. 156. Unless otherwise indicated references are to the first edition.

What would show, for example, that suffering is utterly, eternally and irredeemably pointless? Could anything conceivably bring a theist like Crombie, *remembering the force of his first comment*, to that conclusion? Could a Christian ever conclude that occasional or even prolonged suffering is utterly pointless? At what point would a theist of Crombie's persuasion *justifiably* abandon his disposition to put the best construction upon his troubles—a forward-looking response—or else to regard them as just recompense for sin—a backward-looking response—or both? Could anything ever constitute that evidential crux Crombie seems to envision; could there be any point at which a Christian would be not merely tempted, but justified in moving from saying "We can never see all of the picture"[8] to saying "We see enough of it now to know"? It would seem that no state of affairs could involve suffering sufficient to bring a dedicated, earnest Christian theist to conclude that God does not love us. I do not mean to deny that in point of fact a Christian *can* forfeit his faith in response to the advent in his life of extreme, extensive, prolonged suffering. Many surely do so. But the logic of his faith is such that a Christian could never be sure that the suffering *warranted*, rather than merely *occasioned*, his failure of faith. If this is so, then Crombie's adumbration of some alleged falsification-condition characterized as "suffering which was utterly, eternally, and irredeemably pointless" is an adumbration of a condition of which nothing could ever count as an example.[9]

Hick's claim is open to a similar objection. Can one conceive what it would be like to have a Satanic Vision such as he describes? One could surely have a vision of a being so hideous that one would be disposed to call it Satan. But Satan's existence, as evidenced by Christian theology, is clearly compatible with God's existence. How could one possibly tell whether it is or is not the Satan which Hick mentions? How, that is, could one ever know that the being one confronts in a vision is an all-powerful and wholly evil being whose existence precludes the possibility that a God should exist as described by Christianity? [10] In the face of some possible "Satanic Vision" a Christian would probably be disposed to say that the being in question is the Antichrist who will have his period of *seeming* triumph, but who will be overthrown when Christ returns to subdue him.

[8] Crombie, "Theology and Falsification," p. 124.

[9] For further discussion of this point see *infra*, Chapter 5: "Falsifiability and theological statements," pp. 166-169.

[10] Alasdair MacIntyre raises a similar objection in his "Visions", *New Essays in Philosophical Theology*, p. 256, although the objection is directed against a somewhat different claim.

Surely no "vision" that one might have in this life would suffice to establish the falsity of "God loves us." No terrestrial exposure to the "forces of evil," however severe and prolonged it might be, could entitle a dedicated Christian to abandon his belief that God has a plan, of which everything that happens, even sustained calamity, is a part. No "vision" would constitute warrant for the dispelling or defeat of the Christian's belief about God's overarching providence. And that conclusion should hardly be surprising; it is a matter of relevant historical fact that Christianity has usually flourished during periods of extreme persecution and hardship.

B. ESCHATOLOGICAL VERIFIABILITY: MIGHT THEOLOGICAL SENTENCES BE VERIFIED DURING THE LIFE BEYOND?

Professor John Hick has repeatedly claimed that the statement that God exists is verifiable, not in this life but in a life after death.[11] I shall argue that this view fails. Its failure has already been forceably argued, notably by Kai Nielsen,[12] but without apparent success; Hick's views remain substantially unchanged in his reply to his critics.[13] So I shall advance what I

[11] John Hick, *Faith and Knowledge*, hereafter designated "FK"; "Theology and Verification," *Theology Today* (April, 1960), hereafter designated "TV"; and *Philosophy of Religion* (New York: Prentice-Hall, Inc., 1963 [revised ed., 1973]), hereafter designated "PR." Page numbers of simple quotations are indicated, in accordance with the convention introduced in chapter two, immediately after the citation, in parentheses.

Hick was not the first to invoke eschatological existence as a possible reply to the Positivists, although he was the first to work it out in any detail. I. M. Crombie adumbrated something of the same sort two years before Hick wrote on the subject, but Crombie's remarks are sketchy. At the end of his contribution to "Theology and Falsification," Crombie remarks that the Christian has certain "prepared positions on to which he retreats" by way of answering the Positivists. Two of the three positions he mentions are relevant here: "... first, he [the Christian] looks for the resurrection of the dead, and the life of the world to come; he believes, that is, that we do not see all of the picture, and that the parts which we do not see are precisely the parts which determine the design of the whole.... Second, he claims that he sees in Christ the verification, and to some extent also the specification, of the divine love. That is to say, he finds in Christ not only convincing evidence of God's concern for us, but also what sort of love the divine love is, what sort of benefits God is concerned to give us." ("Theology and Falsification," p. 129.) Incidentally, Crombie's article, published in 1955, is not mentioned in Hick's book, published in 1957, although Hick does mention it in his later article, published in 1960.

[12] Kai Nielsen, "Eschatological Verification," *Canadian Journal of Theology*, IX, No. 4 (1963), pp. 271-281.

[13] Hick's views remain substantially unchanged in the second edition of *Faith and Knowledge* (1966), Chapter 8, "Faith and Verification," pp. 169-199. See also his most

believe to be the most crucial objection in as strong a form as possible; I shall argue that Hick holds contradictory views.

First, consider Hick's position on each of the theses constitutive of the Positivist attack. These theses were: (1) The statement that God exists, or any statement of the fundamental claim or claims of Christianity, is, at least putatively, a genuine statement of fact. (2) A necessary condition of something's being a genuine statement of fact is that it is testable, and (3) The statement that God exists—etc.—is not testable.

Hick wishes to vindicate the factual character of theism by denying thesis-(3). His argument, in brief, is that "... the central religious claim, 'God exists' " (TV 17) might be verified posthumously by confronting Christ. "The possibility of experimental confirmation is thus built into the Christian concept of God" (TV 18). As we have already seen, one might try to nullify the Positivist attack by denying either thesis-(1) or thesis-(2) as well. But if one affirms those theses, as does Hick, then everything depends upon successfully refuting the third. Otherwise one lands in a contradiction. My argument against Hick will be that his form of denying thesis-(3) fails. He actually winds up *defending* thesis-(3); accordingly, he falls into the position of holding contradictory views.

Thesis-(1) Hick stoutly rejects any position which construes sentences containing the word 'God' as variant ways of speaking about something other than God. One might urge, for example, that such sentences are really sentences which pertain in an indirect fashion to people wishing, resolving, or choosing to live or to feel in this or that specified way. Several such views have been examined in chapter two. Even on these views, to be sure, it might be maintained that "God exists" makes a factual claim, for "facts about God," it might be suggested, are really facts about people. But such an analysis of theological sentences, on Hick's account, misses the distinctive element in a Christian's use of them, and that is to express beliefs about God. "... Theistic religion", he writes, "in claiming that the world mediates a divine activity, must also claim that God exists as a real Being, transcending our world as well as meeting us in and through it.... For the theist, the word 'God' does not designate a logical construction, nor is it simply a poetic term for the world as a whole; it refers to the unique transcendent personal creator of the Universe" (FK 188-189). What a Christian's use of 'God exists' asserts, then, is that there is a "real Being" of some sort, a "Supernatural" being (FK 181-184), a Creator "lying behind" the

---

recent, albeit abbreviated statement of the position in the third edition (1973) of his *Philosophy of Religion*, pp. 90-92.

world (FK 185). When Hick maintains that "God exists," as spoken by a theist or as presupposed by a theist in the things he characteristically says and does, expresses a "factual assertion," it is *that* sort of factual assertion he has in mind.

Thesis-(2) Hick subscribes to verifiability as a necessary condition of something's being a genuine statement of fact. "To say that a proposition has meaning, or, more strictly ... that it has factual or cognitive meaning, is to say that it is in principle verifiable, or at least 'probabilifiable,' by reference to human experience. This means, in effect, that its truth or falsity must make some possible experienceable difference. If its truth or falsity makes no difference that could possibly be observed, the proposition is cognitively meaningless; it does not embody a factual assertion" (PR 95). Note that "factual assertions," for Hick, clearly must assert *experienceable* differences in the state of the universe: "... An indicative sentence expresses a factual assertion if and only if the state in which the universe would be if the putative assertion could correctly be said to be true differs in some experienceable way from the state in which the universe would be if the putative assertion could correctly be said to be false, all aspects of the universe other than that referred to in the putative assertion being the same in either case."[14] Any statement asserting a "public fact"[15] will yield, to properly placed observers, experiences different from those it would yield if the statement were false. Every genuine factual assertion must be settleable, at least in principle, by appeal to some experience which someone undergoes or might undergo. The latter qualification covers assertions which are predictive in the sense that they cannot be verified now but might be verified at some time in the future. "If a proposition contains or entails predictions which can be verified or falsified, its character as an assertion ... is thereby guaranteed."[16] To *verify* proposition *p* is not, for Hick, to show

[14] TV 12, n. 1. This formulation accords with one given in *Faith and Knowledge*, although there is one noteworthy formulation in that book which makes no explicit reference to *experience* at all: "If a proposition *p* is to constitute a (true or false) assertion, the state of the universe which satisfies *p* must differ, other than in the fact of including this assertion, from any state of the universe that satisfies not-p" (FK 147).

[15] Hick contrasts public facts with private facts. " 'Experienceable' ... means, in the case of alleged subjective or private facts (e.g., pains, dreams, after-images, etc.), 'experienceable by the subject in question' and, in the case of alleged objective or public facts, 'capable in principle of being experienced by anyone.' My contention is going to be that 'God exists' asserts a matter of objective fact" (TV 12, n. 1).

[16] TV 14. Hick appears to hold that a sentence's character as an assertion is guaranteed if it can be *either* verified *or* falsified. His later remarks about the asymmetry of verification and falsification in some cases—used in connection with the claim that the hypothesis

that *p* is logically necessary; nor is it to rule out the possibility of perceptual illusion. Yet this possibility, Hick suggests, should not dispose us to doubt the veracity of our experience in disclosing matters of fact. To verify *p*, then, is to gather such weight of evidence as would suffice, for the sort of case in question, to exclude rational doubt about *p*. "... Something happens which makes it clear that *p* is true. A question is settled so that there is no longer room for rational doubt concerning it". (TV 12)

The following six conditions, then, fix Hick's notion of verification:

1) ... Verification consists in the exclusion of grounds for rational doubt concerning the truth of some proposition.

2) ... this means its exclusion from particular minds.

3) ... verification is often related to predictions and ... such predictions are often conditional.

4) ... verification of a factual proposition is not equivalent to logical certification.

5) ... the nature of the experience which serves to exclude grounds for rational doubt depends upon the particular subject-matter.

6) ... verification and falsification may be asymmetrically related (TV 17).

Thesis-(3) There are two steps to Hick's argument pertaining to this thesis, both trading on predictions he believes to be contained in the Christian view of the universe. The first argues that we might survive death and be raised again, with celestial bodies closely resembling our terrestrial bodies, into a post-mortem world located somewhere in "celestial space." The second argues that our surviving of death might put us in a position to verify theism. If the first step fails, so does the second. But I propose to pass over the first step entirely, without commenting on any of the intriguing notions employed there, because even if the first step were to succeed, the second does not. Hick's principal announced objective is to show how survival, if it were to come to pass, might establish the factual character of theism. What features of post-mortem existence, were it to obtain, would allegedly verify "God exists"?

Mere survival, Hick concedes, would not suffice. The next life might be no less ambiguous with respect to God's existence than is this one. "For survival, simply as such ... would not necessarily be a state of affairs which is manifestly incompatible with the non-existence of God. It might just be

of continued personal existence after death is verifiable if it is true but not falsifiable if it is false—bear this out too.

taken as a surprising natural fact. The atheist, in his resurrection body, and able to remember his life on earth, might say that the universe has turned out to be more complex, and perhaps more to be approved of, than he had realized. But the mere fact of survival, with a new body in a new environment, would not demonstrate to him that there is a God" (TV 25-26).

But two conditions obtaining together *would* jointly suffice. The first is that the resurrection-state will confer, in some currently unspecifiable sense, "an experience of the fulfillment of God's purpose for ourselves ..." (TV 26-27). The second is that such fulfillment will be accompanied by a direct confrontation of "Christ reigning as Lord of the New Aeon" (TV 29). A certain set of felicific experiences, plus a confrontation with the person of Christ; these two conditions allegedly constitute a *situation* which "points unambiguously to the existence of a loving God" (TV 26). Again, I propose to say little about the first condition; the difficulty I want to emphasize pertains to the second.

What induces Professor Hick to bring Christ into the argument? The chief difficulty with verifying theism is that a theist is strongly inclined to think of God in such a way that nothing could ever count as having "observed" or "directly confronted" God. Consider the following passage:

> God is described in Christian theology in terms of various absolute qualities, such as omnipotence, omnipresence, perfect goodness, infinite love, etc., which cannot as such be observed by us, as can their finite analogues, limited power, local presence, finite goodness, and human love.... One might claim, then, to have encountered a Being whom one presumed, or trusts or hopes to be God; but one cannot claim to have encountered a Being whom one recognizes to be the infinite, almighty, eternal Creator (TV 28).

Apparently Hick finds himself in the following dilemma: Either God is as He is traditionally described, a transcendent Being, that is, a being characterized by "certain absolute qualities which, by their very nature, transcend human experience" (TV 28), or "God" turns out to be a visible, perhaps tangible being, in which case one would seriously doubt that *this* being is God. This way of expressing the alternatives, however, suggests a more far-reaching dilemma in Christian thinking about God. It is in this more general dilemma, I believe, that Hick is increasingly involved.

It would appear that a theist is obliged to take either, but not both, of two positions. Either he must allow that what "God" refers to transcends human experience, which has the consequence that no experience could be an experience of God; or he must allow that what "God" refers to does not transcend human experience, which seems to have the consequence that certain features of the traditional concept of God must be abandoned. Maintaining, as he does, that the possibility of experimental confirmation is built into the Christian concept of God, one would expect that Hick would choose the second. But he selects the first. Actually he wants both, as will be shown presently, but he wants to disallow the consequence of each. "God is the transcendent Creator." "Only God himself knows his own infinite nature." "Our beliefs about God's infinite being are not capable of observational verification, being beyond the scope of human experience," etc. Accordingly, it is not surprising to find Hick chary about the contention that one might enjoy a post-mortem Beatific Vision of God. He avoids building his case on that notion—a notion which might conceivably be employed for just such purposes as Hick undertakes—for several reasons. First, he cannot decide what it really means (FK 158; TV 26). Second, he wonders whether the notion is anything more than picture-language and questions whether it is "sufficiently explicit or explicable to be of service to Christian theology."[17] Third, and most important, Hick appears increasingly inclined to hold that God is not the sort of Being whom man could *ever* confront directly, not even post-mortem.[18]

Still, after death *something* will be importantly different from the way it was on earth and therein, he maintains, is all the experiential difference one needs to establish the existence of God. Hick has provided us with not one, but with two accounts of this difference. It is important to understand not

[17] FK 158. Hick says some favorable things about the notion of the Beatific vision in *Faith and Knowledge* (pp. 158-162), but in the later reworkings of the argument he no longer finds the notion attractive. Even in the book his concluding remarks suggest this direction in his thinking: "... we have not seen any sufficient reason to adopt the doctrine of the Beatific Vision, and therefore we are not obliged to shoulder its attendant difficulties". (pp. 159-160)

[18] There are many small evidences for this claim. See FK 159-160 and *passim*; TV 28-29 and *passim*; PR 103. Ponder, for example, the disclaimers contained in the following striking quotation from "Theology and Verification" and particularly the italicized (italics there mine) dependent clause contained in the concluding sentence: "The important question ... is ... whether one can conceive of after-life experiences which *would* serve to verify theism. I think that we can. In trying to do so I shall not appeal to the traditional doctrine, which figures especially in Catholic and mystical theology, of the Beatific Vision of God. The difficulty presented by this doctrine is not so much that of deciding whether there are grounds for believing it, as of deciding what it means. I shall not, however, elaborate this difficulty, but pass directly to the investigation of a different and, as it seems to me, more intelligible possibility. This is the possibility not of a direct vision of God, *whatever that might mean*, but of a *situation* which points unambiguously to the existence of a loving God" (TV 26).

only that they vary but why they do. In *Faith and Knowledge* he entertains the supposition that we might enjoy corporate communion with *God* in the afterlife. There will be something about people's relations with one another that enables us to "see all things as God sees them, apprehending at last their full significance and nature" (FK 160). God will be seen "in all things" and people will live consciously in His presence. "For we are supposing the divine purpose of the perfecting of human personality to have reached its fulfillment. There will thus be a complete conformity of the subjective to the objective, of man's cognitive powers to his environment as being wholly of God and as serving solely the divine purpose" (FK 160).

But Hick changed his view significantly three years later. There is still the stress on "corporate well-being," the "bringing of the human person, in society with his fellows, to enjoy a certain valuable quality of personal life" (TV 27). But there is a new element; personal communion with *Christ*. In the book the argument is explicated in terms of communion with *God*; the absence of references to Christ is conspicuous. In the article, and subsequently, the argument is explicated by reference to Christ. The entire view is now Christologically focused. Why?

This move has perhaps two sources. First, there is the difficulty of explaining his earlier notions of "communion with God," "seeing things as God sees them," and so forth. Second, there seems to be a growing appreciation in Hick's argument for the doctrine of God's transcendence, with its consequence that no experience could be an experience of God, not even in the resurrection-world. The problems are easier, Hick presumably thinks, if the argument is titled in such a way as to continue to assert God's transcendence and, at the same time, claim "indirect" verification of God's existence by appealing to a conceivable confrontation with Jesus of Nazareth, who is, according to Christian doctrine, the incarnate Son of God (FK 199). It might be possible, Hick thinks, to confront, even to identify, Jesus posthumously. Accordingly, it is easier to give empirical cash-value to "communion with Christ" than to "communion with God."

The movement in Hick's thinking about God is clearly away from the undifferentiated "God" of the first version of the argument, and toward a view which is conceptually more complicated but which gives clearer promise of delivering the *experienceable* yield necessary to establish that "God exists" is indeed a genuine statement. In traditional terms, the move is away from the first person of the Trinity and toward the second person. The Kingdom of God is Christologically shaped. In the resurrection-world we will live under the reign of *Christ* and thereby enjoy communion with God "as he has made himself known to men in Christ." Living under *that* reign people will know that this is no mere natural state of affairs. "Our beliefs about God's infinite being are not capable of observational verification, being beyond the scope of human experience, but they are susceptible of indirect verification by the removal of rational doubt concerning the authority of Christ. An experience of the reign of the Son in the Kingdom of the Father would confirm that authority, and therewith, indirectly, the validity of Jesus' teaching concerning the character of God in his infinite transcendent nature" (TV 29).

If Hick were to claim that Jesus of Nazareth *is God, simpliciter*, then his view might possibly succeed. For then one might conceivably *point out* God in the resurrection-world: *he* is God, Jesus of Nazareth. But Hick does not claim that Jesus is God *simpliciter*. Yet he clearly wishes to preserve for his claim—that Jesus is the Incarnation of God—the advantages which the former claim would provide for solving the problem of reference attendant upon the claim that God exists. Hick's argument that a posthumous confrontation with Jesus of Nazareth, even under the extraordinary conditions he adumbrates, surely begs the very question he has tried to answer.

Admittedly, if one could without doubt confront *Christ*, the problem would be solved *by definition*, for by "Christ" Hick clearly means not only (a) Jesus of Nazareth, but also (b) the Incarnation of God. Perhaps one might intelligibly claim to be able to identify Jesus in the resurrection world. But the claim that there is a God of whom Jesus is the incarnation is a different claim, a claim whose meaning is avowedly *not defined* by reference to the eschatological expectations whose fulfillment Hick envisions, hence a claim not even indirectly verified by their fulfillment. However felicific they might be, the eschatological events are beside the point they were advanced to establish; they are uninformative with respect to the question of the existence or the non-existence of God. Hence, the notion of eschatological verification cannot establish the statement-status of "God exists."

Hick realizes, of course, that the verification of a statement asserting the existence of God presents special difficulties since God, on his view, as it is on the classical view, is a transcendent Being. For the special case in question, however, he avers that receipt of the eschatological experiences mentioned would "confirm ... indirectly, the validity of Jesus' teaching concerning the character of God in His infinite transcendent nature." But is it not possible that an inhabitant of the post-mortem world might find himself, perhaps with enormous surprise, delight, and gratitude, accepting the "authority" of Christ and *still* wonder whether God exists, and would not the reason be that an eschatological assertion of God's existence, even one uttered there by Jesus, is fully as problematic in its *purport* as is a terrestrial one? Hick writes, in answer to his critics, "... It is not suggested that the fulfillment of these [eschatological] expectations, by participating in the ultimate Kingdom of God, defines the *meaning* of 'God exists.' In trying to describe a situation in which it would be irrational for a human being to doubt the reality of God, as allegedly revealed in Christ, one is not undertaking to define exhaustively the nature of God or, therefore, the truth-conditions of 'God exists.' "[19] But if the fulfillment of the specified eschatological expectations would not satisfy the truth-conditions of "God exists" then, by virtue of that fact, it would not verify it. It would certainly *not* constitute a situation in which it would be irrational for a human being to doubt the reality of God, since an inhabitant of the post-mortem world, on Hick's view, would know nothing more eschatologically about what the "reality of God" *comes to* than he knew terrestrially. There would be no experienceable difference on the relevant point at issue as between the two estates, terrestrial and eschatological experience, although presumably he would have vastly different experiences in other respects which do not bear on the disputed point. Accordingly, he would have neither direct nor indirect verification that God exists. As Nielsen has urged against Hick: "... If we have no idea of what it would be like to experience that which we *supposedly* have indirect evidence for, then we in fact do not understand what it would be like to have evidence (direct or indirect) for it. We do not even understand what it could *mean* to say that there is a so-and-so such that we have no idea at all of what it would be like to experience it, but something else can be experienced which is evidence for it. The 'it' here cannot refer to anything, for in such a case how could we *possibly understand* what it is that our putative 'evidence' is supposed to be evidence for? That is just the difficulty we have in using Jesus as the evidence for God."[20]

Hick's argument is important not merely as an item in a growing body of Positivistically-oriented Christian apologetics, but because it highlights the conceptual implications of two doctrines which many still regard as indispensable to Christianity, the Incarnation and the Trinity. Hick is no less explicit about maintaining a distinction between the first and the second persons of the Trinity than he is about maintaining that Jesus is God-Incarnate. "In Christianity God is known as 'the God and Father *of* our Lord

[19] Hick, *Faith and Knowledge*, second edition (1966), pp. 197-198.

[20] Nielsen, "Eschatological Verification," pp. 279-280. Nielsen's criticism of Hick is one item in a growing body of literature on this issue, very much of it critical of Hick. Rem B. Edwards' recent book, *Religion and Reason* (New York: Harcourt Brace Jovanovich, Inc., 1972) contains an interesting discussion (pp. 358-367). Mr. Edwards also gives some helpful bibliographical references on this topic.

Jesus Christ.' God is the Being *about whom* Jesus taught; the Being *in relation to whom* Jesus lived, and into a relationship with whom he brought his disciples; the Being whose *agape* toward men was seen on earth in the life of Jesus. In short, God is *the transcendent Creator* who has revealed himself in Christ.... Only God himself knows his own infinite nature...."[21] What Hick does not seem to realize, however, is that the post-mortem experiences he mentions would not constitute verification for the very special sort of thing he takes "God exists" to assert, while it might yield verification, to be sure, for some of the Christian beliefs traditionally *associated* with that theistic claim. Hick is assuredly not guilty of failing to distinguish the *general* Christian expectations concerning the future—the "Christian picture of the universe, entailing as it does certain distinctive expectations concerning the future" (TV 18)—from the *specific*, *different* claim that there is a God. Otherwise he would not have claimed that the former constitutes *indirect* verification for the latter. But the distinction is fatal to the argument. Instead of refuting thesis-(3), Hick's argument supports it.

To this objection Hick will reply by re-emphasizing the force of the doctrine of the Incarnation: all that the Christian *means* by 'God,' he might urge, is given in Jesus Christ. Hick concurs with Karl Barth: "Jesus Christ is the knowability of God". Yet if Hick heeds certain other themes within classical Christian doctrine, as most appropriately he seems to want to do, then the doctrine of the Incarnation cannot do the job Hick assigns to it. While classical doctrine has stressed the Incarnation of God in Jesus, it has, at the same time, indeed by that very emphasis, denied the co-intensiveness and co-extensiveness of "Jesus" and "God." As Ninian Smart observes, "Strictly, incarnation presupposes the existence of a deity to be incarnated."[22] By holding *both* the doctrine of the Incarnation *and* the doctrine of the Trinity, classical Christian theologians have not permitted the principal thrust of the former to override the principal thrust of the latter: although the second person of the Trinity is held to be continuous in some respects with the first person, the second person is eventually *distinguished* from the first. What appears to be a *numerical* distinction between the persons comes out looking very much like a distinction in *kind*, although, of course, the doctrine of the Incarnation is again reinvoked to justify a denial of just such a conclusion.

Christian theologians have laid vigorous stress upon the knowability of

[21] TV 28-29. Italics mine.

[22] Ninian Smart, *Reasons and Faiths* (London: Routledge & Kegan Paul, 1958), p. 154, n. 1.

God. Indeed, the doctrine of the Incarnation is calculated, in part,[23] to make the point that in Jesus, God has declared His will, His heart, His plan for mankind, His disposition toward mankind, or something to that effect. But Christians characteristically hold this doctrine in conjunction with certain other doctrines [24]—the doctrine of the Trinity, for example—which protect the essential characteristic of God's transcendence. Implicit in the doctrine of the Trinity is the claim that the persons of the triune God must not be conflated or confused.[25] Moreover, the traditional doctrines concerning the person and work of Christ, indispensable as they are to the character of Christian belief and practice, have not generally been upheld in any manner which would blunt or nullify the import of the doctrine to the effect that the first person of the Trinity remains essentially transcendent, "His infinite transcendent nature" *hidden behind* His interventions, His revelations, even His incarnation in Jesus Christ. Emil Brunner, for example writes not untypically: "Even the revealed God remains a hidden God and He wills to be worshipped as one who is Hidden and Unfathomable. God dwells in light unapproachable. This applies not only to the time before but to the time after the revelation through Christ, and in spite of it. *Pater est fons totius Trinitatus.* The mystery of God stands at the beginning and at the end of revelation."[26] It is this essentially mysterious, transcendent

[23] The doctrine of the Incarnation functions also, of course, in connection with other theological issues, and particularly, as illustrated by the writings of St. Paul, Athanasius, and Anselm, in connection with the doctrine of the Atonement.

[24] Ninian Smart has labeled this phenomenon the "weaving together of different strands of spiritual discourse." He illustrates this doctrinal weaving principally by reference to non-Christian religions. The strand with which I am mainly concerned here Smart calls the "numinous strand," obviously following Rudolf Otto. Smart shows that the numinous strand is fully developed in non-Christian religions as well as in Christianity; his references draw from scriptural and devotional documents of Buddhism, Hinduism, Islam, and Taoism. See his *Reasons and Faiths*, Chapters I-IV.

[25] There was an early Christian heresy which arose from neglecting this claim. Third century "modalistic monarchianism" blurred the distinctions between the Persons of the Trinity. The teachings of the Modalists—principally Noetus of Smyrna, Cleomenes (a disciple of Noetus), Praxeus (an unknown writer against whom Tertullian directed his *Adversus Praxeum*), and Sabellius—were condemned. See J. N. D. Kelley, *Early Christian Doctrine* (London: Adam & Charles Black, 1958), pp. 120-122.

[26] Emil Brunner, *The Christian Doctrine of God*, trans. by Olive Wyan (London: The Lutterworth Press, 1949), pp. 225-226. It is noteworthy that the distinction between the revealed Christ and the transcendent God is sometimes drawn, perhaps inadvertently, even within theological excursuses devoted somewhat singlemindedly to emphasizing the essential divinity of Christ. Gustav Aulén's chapter on the Incarnation in *The Faith of the Christian Church* provides a case in point. Commenting on Luther's words "We find the heart and will of the Father in Christ," Aulén remarks, "The deed of Christ

God who "*created* the heavens and the earth," "so loved the world that he *gave* His only begotten Son," "*raised* Christ from the dead," "*reconciled* the world unto Himself," etc. If Hick wants to preserve God's transcendence *even in the resurrection world*, as I take it he does, then receipt of the post-mortem experiences he envisions would not constitute verification of the statement that God exists *as* God is conceived in the tradition Hick wants to vindicate.

I am not myself advancing any *argument* to the conclusion that transcendence or hiddenness is an essential feature of the concept of God which has by and large prevailed in the mainstream of Christian doctrine.[27] Nor do I wish to claim that Christians have always and everywhere maintained the essential transcendence of God or, at least, the essential transcendence of the first person of the Trinity. All that is here claimed is that *very often* transcendence is held to be an essential feature of the concept of God as that concept is expressed in the writings of prominent Christian theologians. Hick's views seem to represent this type. If Rudolf Otto's *The Idea of the Holy* fairly portrays the position of the theologians discussed there, the sheer number and influence of classical Christian theologians who may fairly be claimed to subscribe to this kind of theological position is not inconsiderable. Hick's views concerning the transcendence of God are mild, in fact, by contrast to those, say, of a Chrysostom or a Luther, even though, of course, there are contravailing doctrinal themes within their writings, too. Further evidence could be provided by illustrations from the Bible, from the classical creeds, and from many of the devotional works that constitute the history of Christian mysticism and piety.

I have maintained that Hick's views amount to a defense of three mutually inconsistent theses. Notably, he winds up defending, rather than denying, thesis-(3). I have suggested that the reason he does so is because he has construed 'God' in such a way that, when certain crucial qualifications are made, no set of actual or possible experiences could viably be said to verify the statement that God exists. The traditional theological basis for such a view is the doctrine of the transcendence of God or, at least in Christianity,

---

removes the veil and reveals the heart of God. Christ is 'the effulgence of his glory and the very image of his substance'.... *He is not identical with God*, but he and the Father are 'one' ... one in will, in heart, in purpose, and in work." Aulén, *The Faith of the Christian Church* (Philadelphia: The Muhlenberg Press, 1958), pp. 212-213. Italics mine.

[27] Certain writers have attempted to argue that it is an essential feature of the concept of God that God be "hidden" or "screened off." See R. C. Coburn, "The Hiddenness of God ...," and his interesting article "The Concept of God" in *Religious Studies* II, pp. 61-74, and Ninian Smart's *Reasons and Faiths*, Chapter I. Also see *infra*, Chapter 5: "The transcendence of God", pp. 169-174.

of the first "person" of God. However, Hick's subscription to the equally prominent doctrine of the Incarnation seems to lead him to believe that obscurities connected with the former doctrine can be nullified or can somehow be overlooked by stressing the promising empirical cash-value of the latter doctrine and doctrines related to it. Some of the key issues, then, that figure in the ongoing Positivist-Christian discussion are purely theological issues requiring theological resolution. Just what can be made of the distinction between the persons of the Trinity? Are the doctrines of the Trinity and the Incarnation compatible? In just what respect is God transcendent? The centrality of such questions to the question as to whether the statement that God exists is verifiable may be seen more clearly still, perhaps, by examining yet another kindred position concerning thesis-(3), that of John Wilson in his book *Language and Christian belief.*[28]

C. TERRESTRIAL VERIFIABILITY: MIGHT THEOLOGICAL SENTENCES BE VERIFIED DURING THIS LIFE?

John Wilson maintains that "religious statements are informative, and are ultimately verifiable by a special type of experience, namely religious experience or experience of the supernatural...." (60) His argument pertains to Christian belief, as indicated by the title of his book; but he repeatedly speaks, more generally, of "religious belief." He may think that much of what he says is applicable to non-Christian religious beliefs, but he does not so claim. In the summary-statement just quoted Wilson amalgamates four contentions: (1) Sentences expressive of religious belief, especially of Christian belief, make statements. The language of the Christian religion, Wilson writes, "is backed by a number of assertions about the supernatural.... Most Christians ... would surely regard the 'good news' of the gospel as factually informative. To say 'There is a God' is to state a fact...." (5-6) (2) A sentence which makes a statement must be verifiable, at least in principle.[29] (3) Religious statements, accordingly, must be shown to be verifiable in principle if they are to be considered genuine statements. Three citations are relevant: "... saying 'God exists,'" Wilson writes, "is

[28] John Wilson, *Language and Christian Belief* (London: Macmillan & Co., Ltd., 1958). Simple quotation-citations are given in the text, in parentheses. Wilson restated his views several years later in his *Philosophy and Religion* (London: Oxford University Press, 1961), Chapter III. What I call the reductionistic-strain in Wilson's theological views is considerably more muted in the later book, but otherwise the argument is substantially the same.

[29] Wilson, *Language and Christian Belief*, pp. 6ff., especially pp. 9-11.

a particular instance of saying 'Such-and-such is the case': ... Whether it is or not precisely constitutes the test which any informative statement must pass.... Religious believers have to face up to the problem of providing their religious statements with established ... verification" (8-9). "... My contention is that if God is real and exists, the unambiguous logic and language of statements about existence, and the verification needed for these statements, must apply to God as much as to anything else ..." (13). "It is not true, as so many modern writers suggest, that religious believers have simply been mistaken in supposing that religious statements are intended to be informative and verifiable in the same sense that scientific statements are informative and verifiable. On the contrary, if religion is to survive these are precisely the criteria which religious statements have to (and can) satisfy" (65). (4) Religious statements are verified by people having religious experience. The first three contentions have been discussed in sufficient detail previously; the fourth is pleasantly straightforward and new.

Wilson's argument is as follows: "God" typically and presumably *refers* to something or to someone. "God exists" or "There is a God" makes an existential statement. "I begin by assuming ... that religious statements are supposed to be factually informative, like empirical statements: that when we talk of 'God,' we intend to refer to something that really exists" (16). With bold simplicity, Wilson drives straight to his conclusion: religious experience is direct experience of this something-that-really-exists, namely, of God. Religious experience is direct acquaintance with God:

> ... both the statement 'God exists' and the (logically subsequent) statement 'we know God' must be based on certain experiences: experiences which justify the belief that God exists and that we have acquaintance with Him ... we could say something like: 'We have certain experiences (in prayer, worship, confession, etc., perhaps) which justify our belief that God exists; moreover, we are directly acquainted with Him.... There is such a thing as knowing how to get in touch with God, knowing how to worship, pray, behave, and so on: and there is also such a thing as direct acquaintance with God (49).

The prevailing model at work in Wilson's argument is the simple empirical statement. On his view, the question as to how we might verify the statement that there is a God is exactly parallel to the question as to how we might verify the statement that there is a table or an elephant in the next room: first, we put ourselves in a position to observe, and then we observe:

> When I say 'there is a table' [in the next room] I imply that if you do certain things, you will have certain experiences: in other words, that the statement is

verifiable.... I say 'There is a table [in the next room]: by this you are led to expect certain experiences of your own (19, 21).

Suppose I say, 'There is an elephant in the next room'. You say, 'What do you mean by that?' I reply, 'Well, most of what I mean is that if you and other people were to enter the room, you would have such-and-such experiences' (22).

Similarly, Wilson maintains that "There is a God" might be verified, presumably by anyone,[30] by the expedient of performing certain operations and acquiring, in consequence of these operations, certain unique experiences. Wilson devotes considerable space to describing how those who do not currently have religious experiences might come to have them. Three quotations trace and illustrate this theme:

By following Christ, listening to His words, seeing how He acts, praying to Him and so forth, we come to have experiences of an unambiguous and unique character.... All this, however, represents a long and difficult process. First, there is knowing *how*; how to pray, how to allow Christ to speak to us, how to worship, how to behave towards our neighbours. Here we are (to put it at the lowest) 'going through the motions': learning by doing what we are told to do, or by trying to do it ... In the second place, we come as a result of this to have certain experiences (52).

What we need is experience: ... Christ is saying and acting the injunction, 'Try it and see'.... He teaches us the direct acquaintance with God ... (50-51).

If, for instance, we are led by Him [Christ] to pray, worship, contemplate, and so on, we may fin dthat we meet something that we should want to call, and could sensibly call, God.... Following His advice might even entail pretending to beliefs which it would be otherwise irrational to hold: e.g., we might assume the existence of God in order to discover whether we could have genuine experience of the supernatural in prayer and worship. This sort of pretence, undertaken simply for the purposes of trying to have certain experiences and make certain tests, is entirely reasonable (41-42).

DISCUSSION. Wilson's view is difficult to evaluate for the reason that his argument is not entirely perspicuous. Two questions, in particular, might be asked. First, what sort of experience is "religious experience"? Second, what sort of claim does Wilson take "God exists" to make?

Wilson does not indicate what sort of experience counts for him as "religious experience," whether, for example, there is a specific and identifiable sort of experience which is "religious" as distinguished from another which is non-religious. By "religious experience" one might conceivably

[30] "Christians," Wilson remarks, "at least suppose everyone to be capable of religious experience ('knowing God')." *Ibid.*, p. 29.

mean experiences of a number of different types, since the alleged incursion of the Divine into the realm of human experience has taken many different forms. The annals of religious thought contain reports of extraordinary experiences which vary considerably in type and degree of felt intensity. Some of these reports are perhaps spurious, but surely not all of them. Others, but surely not all, contain spurious elements, in the sense that a person might embellish an experience, in the reporting of it, with an interpretation or with the addition of features which were not part of the original experience. Religious experiences might be classified, very generally, as follows: (i) omen-ous experiences, (ii) numinous experiences, and (iii) visitation experiences.

(i) *Omen-ous experiences.* First, there is a comparatively mild variety of religious experiences. Experiences of this sort are characteristically vague, elusive, and inchoate in the sense that the subject of these experiences is not quite sure either how to describe them or how to account for their occurrence. Omen-ous experiences are sufficiently unusual both in quality and in degree of felt intensity to induce the subject to feel warranted in looking for, or wondering whether or not there is, a special factor operating to occasion them; yet they are sufficiently similar to kindred experiences of love, sudden insight, exhibitions of power, and aesthetic experience that the subject is not entirely confident in attributing their occurrence to anything "supernatural." The comparatively mild variety of religious experience is ably discussed in H. D. Lewis' *Our Experience of God*,[31] a recent book written from an English Christian's point of view. Lewis describes "live moments of religious awareness" variously as follows: a consciousness, sometimes sudden and disruptive, of some kind of "power" (123), a "peculiar alertness and heightening of attention" (124), a state of "exaltation and excitement" (123), an "emotional charge and drive which energizes various other propensities of our nature and sets in train various activities" (117), an experience in which we are "more than usually perceptive of certain things in our present environment and responsive to them" (114), a state in which one is "startled into sober and perhaps terrifying realization of the limitations of ... [one's] own existence and activity and ... some dawning ... of this realization ... of the complete but unexpected appropriateness by which the world comes, with a peculiar inevitability of its own, to have a sustaining wholeness ..." (108).

(ii) *Numinous experiences.* Second, there is a variety of religious ex-

[31] H. D. Lewis, *Our Experience of God* (London: George Allen & Unwin, Ltd., 1959). Simple quotation-citations are given in the text, in parentheses.

perience which has in common with omen-ous experience that the subject is characteristically at a loss for words to describe it. The distinctive feature of numinous experiences is that they are extraordinarily vivid and overpowering, as well as different in quality from other kinds of experience which the subject has had. Numinous experiences are experiences of overriding intensity, experiences which, because of their power, blot out everything or almost everything else in one's sense-field at the time of their occurrence, in a way similar, perhaps, to the striking of a bolt of lightning nearby, the scream of a jet poised for take-off, or a flash of severe pain. Because of their overriding intensity, their difference in quality from other sorts of human experiences, and their relative infrequency, numinous experiences are peculiarly susceptible of being interpreted by the subject as special incursions of a supernatural power or spirit into the mundane. Rudolf Otto's *The Idea of the Holy* [32] is perhaps the best known study of experiences of this type. The word 'numinous' was coined by Otto. Some of the features of numinous experience which Otto mentions are these: a feeling of the "uncanny" or the "eerie" (192) accompanied by "horror and shudder and spectral haunting" (193-194); a "devout awe" (199), a "mood of trepidation, awed surmise, the hush of mystery ... strange exultation" (217-218). Numinous experience possesses, so to speak, a seizure-and-shudder quality which is nicely illustrated in one of Otto's comments about a flash of lightning mentioned in a verse of the *Kena-Upanishad*: "The unexpectedness and suddenness of the lightning-flash, its dreadful weirdness, its overpoweringness and dazzling splendour, the fright and the delight of it, gives it an almost numinous impressiveness ..." (192).

(iii) *Visitation experiences.* Third, there is a variety of religious experience which sometimes carries the affective intensity common to the first two varieties, and has in common with experiences of the numinous variety both that it is different in quality from normal kinds of human experiences and that it occurs with relative infrequency. The peculiar feature of visitation experiences is that they are usually not so difficult for the subject to describe as are omen-ous or numinous experiences, largely because visitation experiences contain some fairly vivid and arresting kinesthetic, auditory, or visual "visitation," such as the sensation of certain "touchings" inflicted upon one's body, or the "feeling" of certain floating sensations, the "hearing" of particular sounds such as music or spoken words, or the "seeing" of certain sights such as hands, flowers, lights, persons, and so forth. It is

[32] Rudolf Otto, *The Idea of the Holy*, trans. by John W. Harvey in 1949 from *Das Heilige* and printed, with additions and omissions by Oxford University Press (New York: Galaxy Book GB 14, 1958).)

difficult to tell how similar or dissimilar this "touching," "feeling," "hearing," and "seeing" are to ordinary touching, feeling, hearing, and seeing. No doubt some of the concrete kinesthetic, auditory, and visual details contained in the reports are imagery culled from these respective sense fields. There is no compelling reason to think, however, that it is *all* imagery. Examples of this type of religious experience are fairly easy to find. They bulk large, for example, in two famous twentieth-century studies, William James's *Varieties of Religious Experience* [33] and Evelyn Underhill's *Mysticism*.[34] Visitation experiences are highly susceptible of being interpreted by the subject as incursions of some supernatural power, spirit, or person into the realm of the mundane.

Let us suppose that by "religious experience" Wilson means to designate experiences of any or all the varieties mentioned. Does the occurrence of religious experience, so construed, constitute verification of the statement that there is a God?

The crucial interpretive problem in Wilson's argument is deciding exactly what Wilson takes "God exists" to assert. The argument is not clear as to the nature of the claim which he construes such a sentence, when spoken by a Christian, as making. Perhaps Wilson thought that he could carry through his argument without discussing this crucial question. But the viability of an argument to the effect that "religious statements ... [are] ultimately verified ... by religious experience" depends upon a prior ruling or decision as to what "religious statements" are going to be interpreting as stating. *If* Wilson holds to the kind of claim which the statement that God exists has traditionally been held to make, or at least very often been held by Christians to make, then it is difficult to understand how religious experience, however Wilson might describe it, would verify that statement. In light of his contention that religious experience *does* verify the statement that God exists, the suspicion arises that he has in fact scaled down the traditional claim to manageable, that is, to verifiable, proportions. One begins to suspect, in particular, that insofar as "God" *refers*, it "refers" to a set of experiences in the way, say, that 'toothache,' in "I have a toothache," refers to a set of experiences; and that "God exists," insofar as it *asserts*, "asserts" that people have such-and-such experiences when they prepare themselves in certain preliminary ways. Several of Wilson's remarks encourage this suspicion. Consider, for example, the following passage:

[33] William James, *The Varieties of Religious Experience* (New York: Modern Library edition, n.d.), pp. 60-62, 70-71, 220-222.

[34] Evelyn Underhill, *Mysticism* (New York : Harcourt, Brace & World, Inc.; Meridian Books edition, 1955), pp. 185-186 and Chapter V, "Voices and Visions."

> A says: 'There is a God', B says: 'How do you know?' A says: 'I have had certain experiences: I have seen God, talked with Him, been a changed man ever since, etc.' But this is of merely psychological or autobiographical interest to B: what B wants to know is whether there 'really' is a God, or whether A is just a dreamer. *And the whole question is whether the experiences which A uses to base his assertion upon are available to B also.*[35]

Now whether the experiences which A has are also available to B is surely *not* the whole question at issue between A and B, unless Wilson is taking "There is a God" to assert no more than that B, where B is any person at all, might have such-and-such experiences when he becomes properly penitent, reverent, and so forth. Is "God" a name for a set of human experiences? For Christians generally, surely not. For Wilson? It is hard to ascertain. In a passage likening "religious assertions" to "aesthetic assertions,"[36] Wilson remarks that "both aesthetic and religious assertions *refer to* potential experiences...."[37] Yet in the passage just examined, Wilson said that A *bases* his assertion that there is a God *upon* such-and-such experiences, that *that* seems to be clearly and importantly a different matter from A's assertion *referring* to those experiences. Is Wilson taking "There is a God" to assert that there is a God, a God who stands in a causal or quasi-causal relationship with those experiences, or is he taking the statement that there is a God to assert, or better, to *predict* something to the effect that any person will have such-and-such experiences under such-and-such conditions? In the passage under consideration, one wonders which view Wilson endorses: the reader must balance the import of "the *whole* question" against the import of "to base his assertion *upon*." If one reads the entire passage in light of Wilson's remark, "When we talk of 'God,' we intend to refer to something that really exists" (16), then one is inclined to discount the import of Wilson's remark—or wonder, at least, what its import might be—that the whole question at issue between A and B is the question as to whether experiences such as A has are also available to B. If, instead, one reads the entire passage in light of "Both aesthetic and religious assertions refer to potential experiences," then one is inclined to discount the import of "to base his assertion upon," or wonder, at least, what *its* import might be.

The passage which most strongly suggests that Wilson has scaled down the claim of "There is a God" to something substantially less than traditional

[35] Wilson, *Language and Christian Belief*, p. 23. Italics mine.

[36] According to Wilson, an "aesthetic assertion" is a sentence such as "Beethoven's 'Eroica' is noble, dramatic, and powerful." *Ibid.*, p. 26.

[37] *Ibid.*, p. 27. Italics mine.

Christian dimensions, occurs at the point immediately preceding the citation just examined. Part of the passage has already been quoted; here it stands in its entirety:

Suppose I say, 'There is an elephant in the next room,' You say, 'What do you mean by that?' I reply, 'Well, most of what I mean is that if you and other people were to enter the room, you would have such-and-such sense-experiences.' You check whether these experiences are actually to be had, and find that they are. But you are not content: you say, perhaps, 'Yes, you are right about the experiences; but surely this does not entitle you to make any existential statement: they might be "subjective," or self-induced or non-cognitive.' Then I say: 'Well, I think I can convince you that they are not illusory: I know no scientific tests, but you will find that a large number of people have the experiences, and that they are not drunk, or subject to illusions, or liars.' You say, 'Perhaps so; but I still do not see that any number of experiences entitles you to make this existential assertion.' Then I begin to lose patience : I say, 'My dear fellow, I am no philosopher: if you don't want to call my statement "existential", then don't. *All I really mean to assert is included in the experiences which you have already admitted: this is what I mean by "There is an elephant."* I can't understand what you mean by asking for proof that the experiences are cognitive, or that the existential statement is justified, or that the elephant is "really" there.'[38]

Wilson adds that "this is the point which is surely of the greatest practical importance in discussions between believers and non-believers" (23). And then he proceeds to the passage already discussed ("A says: 'There is ...' ").

The long citation just recorded is perplexing. If Wilson is serious about the exact logical parallel between "There is a God" and "There is a table [in the next room],"[39] then it looks very much as if whatever factual claim Wilson takes "There is a God" to be making, it is assuredly not the claim that Christians have traditionally made. For a Christian would surely *not* maintain that all he really means to assert by "There is a God" is already contained in the experiences which he and others have had when they have had "religious experiences." Nor would a Christian be unable to understand what is worrying someone who might ask for "proof that the experiences are cognitive, or that the existential statement is justified or that the elephant [God] is 'really' there." Most Christians would surely hold that it is of *maximum* importance that religious experiences be experiences *of* something or someone (God), and that this something or someone be, in Wilson's phrase, "really there." Most Christians would probably *not* hold that religious assertions *refer to* "potential experiences." They would hold that

[38] *Ibid.*, pp. 22-23. Italics mine.

[39] For further indications that Wilson indeed means to stand by this logical parallel see *ibid.*, pp. 17-23 and 25.

religious assertions make direct or indirect reference to a unique being or agency, God, as a result of whose existence or "operations" or "free decisions" or "redeeming grace" etc., what is generally called "religious experience" is sometimes made available to people.

It sometimes seems that Wilson is not so much concerned to wrestle with the question as to the Meaningfulness of the statement that God exists as he is with encouraging people to live in a manner, and thereby to enjoy the sort of experiences, calculated to dispose them to *forget about* that issue, or at least to come to regard it as unimportant. There is a perplexing passage, for instance, at the conclusion of Wilson's fourth chapter, "Knowledge of God":

> If we succeed in the discipline and attain the experience, learning both to 'know how' and to know by acquaintance, then there is a sense in which our knowing *that* various Christian statements are true is of secondary importance; just as to the music-lover, rather than a music critic, knowing of facts is less important than enjoying and appreciating the music, and approaching it in the right spirit. The person with true Christian experience knows more about religion, in the most important sense of 'knows', than the most acute philosopher; and that is why—thank goodness—philosophy is not requisite to salvation (54).

It is a little unsettling to find such a passage in a book about which its author declares, in his introduction: "I hope that what follows will go some way towards showing that Christian apologetics can stand on their own feet, can meet the philosopher with his own weapons, and need not cloak any weakness by evasion, ambiguity, or failure to meet the philosophical points, be they never so sharp" (xv).

The strength or weakness of an argument to the effect that terrestrially available "religious experience" constitutes verification of the statement that God exists, depends upon the character of the assertion which that statement is held to make. Thus far it has been indicated that Wilson's book, which contains an argument of the type in question, contains what might be called a reductionistic motif—a tendency to reduce the claim made by the theistic assertion to the claim that under certain conditions men might obtain, and presumably can obtain, a set of unique, desirable devotional experiences. Insofar as Wilson's interpretation of the purport of the theistic assertion is really reductionistic in the way indicated, to that extent his claim that having religious experience verifies the assertion, becomes plausible. For, as in the case of "There is an elephant in the next room," once one has secured the expected relevant experiences—sees the animal with the trunk and the long ears, or analogously, feels the "presence of God" in the celebration of the

Eucharist, etc. [40]—then all that is asserted by "There is an elephant in the next room" ("There is a God") has been verified *ipso facto*. "There is a God" might be verified by having religious experience, on a reductionistic analysis, precisely because its claim has been interpreted as being equivalent to the claim that most everybody might have, can have, certain experiences that many people already have and continue to have. But if this is Wilson's position, then, while he has indeed met the force of the Positivist argument, he has done so in behalf of a claim which few Christian theologians would cheerfully endorse. This is so for two reasons. First, one of the recurrent themes of classical Christianity is a theme which declares that God reveals Himself, so to speak, when and where He chooses. There is no *assurance*—though Wilson suggests the contrary—that a person who attempts ever so dilligently and sincerely, say, to "practice the presence of God" will in fact secure those experiences which he would count as constituting success in the attempt. Second, and more importantly, whatever 'God' refers to in classical Christian thought, sentences about God are not translatable without loss of meaning into sentences descriptive of actual or possible human experiences.

But suppose one overlooks the reductionistic-sounding passages in Wilson's book. He does in fact say that the Christian religion is "backed up by a number of assertions about the supernatural," that "when we talk of 'God' we intend to refer to something that really exists," that a Christian bases his assertions on such-and-such experiences, and that " 'God' ["There is a God"] entails the possibility of a number of experiences." Whatever Wilson might mean here by 'entails,' it is perhaps implausible to suppose that he means merely "names" or "is synonymous with." Perhaps he does after all wish to stand by the traditional claim that there is a God who "really exists." Would having religious experience of one sort or another verify that claim? For one type of claim which "There is a God" might be held to make, perhaps *yes*; for another type of claim, *no*.

The claim, which is also Wilson's claim, that one might have direct acquaintance with God and thus verify the statement that God exists, is

[40] Wilson does not say how many religious experiences, or of what variety, or in what pattern of occurrence, would be required to verify the statement that there is a God. He might perhaps hold that the example given above is one of a number of religious experiences the conjoint occurrence of all or some of which in the life of any one believer would constitute a jointly sufficient condition for verifying the statement that there is a God; e.g., feeling the "presence of God" at the Eucharist *and* enjoying the "guidance of the Holy Spirit" during prayer *and* etc. This is conjectural, however; Wilson does not address himself to this important problem.

an intelligible one *provided* that 'God' names the sort of being, spirit, person, or phenomenon with which one might be directly acquainted. "God" must perforce be analogous in this respect, although not necessarily in all respects, to "the *Mona Lisa*," "the spirits one 'sees' under the influence of a particular drug" (cp. the *delirium tremens* effect), "Winston Churchill," or "the auto-kinetic phenomenon," respectively. What is important is that "God" must be a *confrontable* being (spirit, person, or phenomenon). In the discussion which follows, that parenthesis will be dropped; the qualifications it is designed to convey may henceforth be conveyed by the sufficiently general term 'being.'

Now according to one arguably Christian theological point of view, "God" does name a being with whom one might be directly acquainted. According to another arguably Christian theological point of view, "God" names a being with whom one *cannot* be directly acquainted: "God" names a being which (who) transcends everything with which a person might conceivably be directly acquainted. If one endorses the former theological point of view, Wilson's line of argument is at least plausible. But if one endorses the latter theological point of view, Wilson's argument, together with every argument of this type, fails.

From the beginnings of Christianity there has been a tendency among Christians, particularly among those who are devotionally oriented, to declare that God is immanent in the world, or in the human "soul," or in both. For this strain in Christian thinking and writing, Evelyn Underhill coins the expression "immanence-theory." The principal, although not the sole, thrust of immanence-theory is to declare, first, that "the whole world is full of God," and second, that man and God, during worship, for example, come into some sort of direct contact. Formulated theologically, immanence-theory tends to assume the form of a thesis to the effect that "God" names a being which is at least in principle not inaccessible to human experience. Attached to this thesis there is normally a caveat to the effect that one does not confront God as He is in His essence, or that one can never know all there is to know about God, or something of that sort. But immanence-theory holds, in effect, that God is the sort of being with whom one might be more or less directly acquainted, and, furthermore, that men *do* sometimes, under certain conditions, achieve that relationship of direct acquaintance with God. In one striking passage Miss Underhill writes:

> This discovery of a "divine" essence or substance, dwelling ... at the apex of man's soul is that fundamental experience—found in some form or degree in all genuine mystical religion—which provides the basis of the New Testament doctrine of the indwelling spirit. It is, variously interpreted, the "spark of the soul"

of Eckhart, the "ground" of Tauler, the Inward Light of the Quakers, the "Divine Principle" of some modern transcendentalists: the fount and source of all true life. At this point logical exposition fails mystic and theologian alike. A tangle of metaphors takes its place, We are face to face with the "wonder of wonders"—that most real, yet most mysterious, of all the experiences of religion, the union of human and divine, in a nameless *something* which is "great enough to be God, small enough to be me." In the struggle to describe this experience, the "spark of the soul," the point of juncture, is at one moment presented to us as the divine to which the self attains; at another, as that transcendental aspect of the self which is in contact with God. On either hypothesis, it is here that the mystic encounters Absolute Being. Here is his guarantee of God's immediate presence in the human heart; and, if in the human heart, then in that universe of which man's soul resumes in miniature the essential characteristics.

According to the doctrine of Immanence, creation, the universe, could we see it as it is, would be perceived as the self-development, the self-revelation of this indwelling Deity. The world is not projected from the Absolute, but immersed in God. "I understood," says St. Teresa, "how our Lord was in all things, and how He was in the soul: and the illustration of a sponge filled with water was suggested to me."[41]

There are obvious difficulties connected with the view that religious experience is experience *of* God-immanent-in-the-world, or "encounter with God," "apprehension of God," or the stronger claim of "union with God." One especially worrisome difficulty is that we seem to have no reliable criterion by which to distinguish between delusory and veridical religious experience.[42] But the claim that there might conceivably be non-delusory, veridical religious experiences is at least not incoherent. "God," on this view, names a being which is in principle experienceable, knowable, at least partially, by direct acquaintance. Some men, upon receipt of certain experiences, experiences which are perhaps denied to most people, have been prepared to say that they have had direct acquaintance with such a being. Some have been prepared to say, in short, that a sufficient condition for saying "There is a God" has been satisfied for them at a certain time, and that it was satisfied by their having had such-and-such religious experiences. There are, of course, many problems connected with such a claim, but if "God" is understood to name a being who is immanent in the world, then an argument to the effect, first, that religious experience of some sort might be a medium of acquaintance with such a being, and second, that religious

[41] Underhill, *Mysticism*, p. 100.

[42] See Ronald Hepburn, "Poetry and Religious Belief," *Metaphysical Beliefs*, ed. by Alasdair MacIntyre and Ronald G. Smith (London: SCM Press, Ltd., 1957), pp. 107 and 132; Ronald Hepburn, *Christianity and Paradox*, Chapters III and IV; C. B. Martin, *Religious Belief* (Ithaca, New York: Cornell University Press, 1959), pp. 87-94.

experience might accordingly verify the statement that there is a God—*so construed*—does not appear implausible.

Although it does not bear directly on the theme under study in this book, let me offer one remark about the view just conceded. I do not mean to minimize the difficulties connected with it, and I am not myself proffering it here. I believe, however, that the problems might be largely resolved, although it would take considerable work. It has been noted that if God is immanent in the world, that makes room, logically, for acquaintance with Him. But it might not make room for *knowing*, that is, for *recognizing* that it is *God* whose acquaintance one has made, for *identifying* the being one "encounters" or "confronts" as God, as unlimitedly wise, powerful, loving, etc. To meet this objection one would have to be able to defend an affirmative answer to the question: can one describe what it would be like to ascertain that some specifically located ("encountered") being is unlimitedly powerful, wise, etc.? Can we, even in principle, envision a test, or a series of tests for deity being performed, either terrestrially or eschatologically? I am inclined to think that we can, at least with respect to some of the traditional divine attributes. An omniscient being would perforce know any and all known facts; an omnipotent being would perforce be capable of doing anything which is not logically contradictory; an omnipresent being, according to one construal of 'omnipresent,' would perforce be able to effect His will at any given place and future time, and so forth. To be sure, we might be unable, in practice, to set up identity-tests for deity in the same way that we can set up chemical or electronic tests for the presence of plutonium in a sample of ore. But it is not absurd to suppose that God might perhaps accede to *showing* us, either at our behest, or unsolicitedly, that He is God, that is, that He has unlimited power, wisdom, etc. Is there not some scriptural warrant for this supposition in Gideon's test of the Lord in Judges 6:33ff. and Elijah's test at Mt. Carmel in I Kings 18:20ff. Still, even if "God" were to demonstrate His power, wisdom, etc., there remains this logical difficulty. There would be no point in time, either terrestrially or eschatologically, at which the question as to whether a specific, "encountered" being is God is *conclusively* settled, since a being who is, or does, certain things for *however* long a period of time might suddenly *cease* being or doing those things. One would never *know* in the sense which is, perhaps, only rarely employed in ordinary language—that of being certain that one is not mistaken—that this specific being is God. But is *that* kind of knowing really required for the type of case in question? Surely we can envision receiving such overwhelming weight of evidence, either terrestrially or eschatologically or at both times, as to settle the question to the extent that this sort of question could be settled at any given point in time at all.

To return now to the main line of argument; while the claim that religious experience would verify the statement that God exists *might* hold where that statement is construed along the lines of Immanence-theory, it does not hold where the theistic assertion is construed along the lines of more traditional Christian orthodoxy. Immanence-theory, perhaps because its theological formulation gravitates toward pantheism or panentheism has generally been overshadowed within Christian orthodoxy by a different theological point of view. For a discussion of this point, particularly the early Church-Fathers' rejection of pantheism, see G. L. Pestige, *God in Patristic Thought.*[43] This more official point of view holds to that sort of distinction between God and the world, as well as everything occurring in the world, such that whatever one might conceivably have direct acquaintance with, one *cannot* have direct acquaintance with God. The phrase "that sort of distinction ..." is intended to ward off the suggestion that pantheism makes no distinction at all between God and the world, a suggestion which would probably be false for most varieties of pantheism. The *sort* of distinction here being attributed to orthodox Christian theology is the thesis that while God may properly be spoken of as having created the world, as having sustained the world, as sustaining the world even now, God may not properly be spoken of as Himself being located in the world, nor as being a part of the world, nor as being an "underlying principle" of the world.

In its sternest form, this theological viewpoint becomes a declaration of God's utter and absolute transcendence. "Never forget," writes St. John of the Cross, "that God is inaccessible, Ask not therefore how far your powers may comprehend Him, your feelings penetrate Him."[44] Dionysius the Areopagite writes, "The highest and most divine things which it is given to us to see and to know are but the symbolic language of things subordinate to Him who Himself transcendeth them all...."[45] John Chrysostom offers a stronger formulation: "... the difference between the being of God and being of man is of such a kind that no word can express it and no thought appraise it."[46] Chrysostom's writings contain stronger formulations still, as, for example: "We call Him the inexpressible, the unthinkable God, the invisible, the inapprehensible; who quells the power of human speech and transcends the grasp of mortal thought; inaccessible to the angels,

[43] G. L. Prestige, *God in Patristic Thought* (London: S.P.C.K. edition, 1952), pp. 28-32.
[44] *Avisos y Sentencias Espirituales*, N. 51. Quoted in Underhill, *Mysticism*, p. 98.
[45] *De Mystica Theologia*, i. 1. Quoted in Underhill, *Ibid.*, p. 79.
[46] Quoted in Otto, *The Idea of the Holy*, p. 181.

unbeheld of the Seraphim, unimagined of the Cherubim, invisible to principalities and authorities and powers, and, in a word, to all creation."[47] Commenting on a passage from Dionysius, St. Thomas Aquinas writes: "We deny firstly anything corporeal about Him and secondly anything intellectual or mental, at least in the respects in which this element is found in living creatures, as for instance, goodness and wisdom. And then there remains in our intellect only that God is and nothing further. Finally we remove even the idea of 'being' itself, insofar as this idea of 'being' is present in creatures, and then God remains in a dark night of ignorance, and it is in this ignorance that we come closest to God in this life, as Dionysius (*De Divinis Nomin.* vii) says. For in such mists, they say, does God dwell."[48] Finally, consider a striking passage from *The Mystical Theology* of Dionysius the Areopagite, Chapter V, concerning the thesis "*That He Who is the Pre-eminent Cause of everything intelligibly perceived is not Himself any one of the things intelligibly perceived*":

> Once more, ascending yet higher we maintain that It is not soul, or mind, or endowed with the faculty of imagination, conjecture, reason, or understanding; nor is It act any of reason or understanding; nor can It be described by the reason or perceived by the understanding, since It is not number, or order, or greatness, or littleness, or equality, or inequality, and since It is not immovable nor in motion, or at rest, and has no power, personal essence, or eternity, or time; nor can It be grasped by the understanding, since It is not knowledge or truth; nor is It kingship or wisdom; nor is It one, nor is It unity, nor is It Godhead or Goodness; nor is It a Spirit, as we understand the term, since It is not Sonship or Fatherhood; nor is It any other such as we or any other being can have knowledge of: nor does It belong to the category of non-existence or to that of existence; nor do existent beings know It as It actually is, nor does It know them as they actually are; nor can the reason attain to It to name It or to know It; nor is it darkness, nor is It light, or error, or truth; nor can any affirmation or negation apply to It; for while applying affirmations or negations to those orders of being that come next to It, we apply not unto It either affirmation or negation, inasmuch as It transcends all affirmation by being the perfect and unique Cause of all things, and transcends all negation by the pre-eminence of Its simple and absolute nature —free from every limitation and beyond them all.[49]

[47] *Ibid.*, p. 180, n. 1.

[48] Quoted in Coburn, "The Hiddenness of God ...," pp. 711-712, from J. Mondin, "Analogy Old and New" (unpublished doctoral dissertation, Harvard University, 1959), pp. 245-246.

[49] *Dionysius the Areopagite on Divine Names and The Mystical Theology*, trans. by C. E. Rolt (New York: The Macmillan Co., 1920), pp. 200-201. I have suppressed several brief unessential footnotes in the translated text. Two cryptic comments, however, might be remembered. Keyed, respectively, to the very beginning and the very last statements, Dionysius comments that "It is not (1) a Thinking Subject; nor (2) an Act or Faculty

Miss Underhill labels the strand of Christian thought illustrated by these passages "emanation-theory,"[50] since the assertion of God's utter and absolute transcendence is historically associated, she reports, with Neo-platonic themes prominent in the development of patristic theology. "The Absolute Godhead," she writes, "is conceived as removed by a vast distance from the material world of sense; the last or lowest of that system of dependent worlds or states which, generated by or emanating from the Unity or Central Sun, become less in spirituality and splendour, greater in multiplicity, the further they recede from their source. That Source—the Great Countenance of the Godhead—can never ... be discerned by man. It is the Absolute of the Neoplatonists, the Unplumbed Abyss of later mysticism; the Cloud of Unknowing wraps it from our sight. Only by its 'emanations' or manifested attributes can we attain knowledge of it. By the outflow of these same manifested attributes and powers the created universe exists, depending in the last resort on the *latens Deitas*: Who is therefore conceived as external to the world which He illuminates and vivifies."[51]

Whatever its historical origins, the asserted distinction between God and all of that which putatively exists or occurs in consequence of God's existence and disposition (His "will," "grace," "providence," etc.) seems to have been very much part of the Christian proclamation from the beginning. From the cryptic announcement of Genesis 1:1—"In the beginning, God created the heavens and the earth"—to the more muted confession of Timothy 6:15-16—"... the blessed and only Potentate, the King of kings, the Lord of lords; who only hath immortality, dwelling in the light which no man can approach unto; whom no man hath seen, nor can see..."[52]—this distinction between God and the entire universe which owes its existence, character, and perdurability to Him found fertile soil in the mind of Chrysostom and the other Greek and Latin Fathers. Sprung from the theological reflexes of the early Fathers, the distinction has surfaced again and again, has grown and spread out into the mainstream of Christian theological, confessional, and devotional writings ever since. The distinction, in short, has gradually become locked into Christian orthodoxy. Otto reports that "The insistence upon the 'inconceivable and incomprehensible' in God did not

---

of Thought; nor (3) an Object of Thought," and "It is (1) *richer* than all concrete forms of positive existence; (2) more *simple* than the barest abstraction."

[50] Underhill, *Mysticism*, p. 96.

[51] *Ibid.*, p. 97.

[52] See also I John 4:12: "No man hath seen God at any time...." See Prestige, *God in Patristic Thought*, Chapter II: "Divine Transcendence," especially pp. 25-32.

cease to be a point of honor in Christian theology with Chrysostom. The forms this protest took did indeed vary : it appears as the assertion at one time that God stands above the reach of all possible predication whatever, and so is Nothingness and the 'Silent Desert'; at another, that He is ἀνώνυμος, πανώνυμος, ὁμώνυμος; at another, that He can indeed be made the subject of predication, but only insofar as all attributes are mere '*nomina ex parte intellectus nostri*; or again, the sternest form of all, it reproduces the line of thought of Job, as can be seen now and then in Luther in his notion of the *deus absconditus*—the thought, namely, that God Himself is not only *above* every human grasp, but in *antagonism* to it."[53] This theme, which is often theologically articulated as a thesis to the effect that God—at least the first Person of the Trinity—is transcendent or hidden, is now an inexpungable part of orthodox Christian faith. *If* one holds to the existence of God, *so construed*, then Wilson's argument fails. For whatever "status" might be claimed for religious experience from this theological point of view, religious experience cannot be said to offer direct acquaintance with God, and hence cannot be said to constitute verification of the statement that God exists.

Because of the importance of "religious experience" in Christian devotion, particularly experiences called omen-ous experiences, most Christians might indeed say—in fact *do* say—that during prayer or Communion, etc., "God Himself is present," or something to that effect. But for those Christians who are in sympathy with the full sweep of themes constituting the classical Christian tradition, such a claim is one which, for assorted reasons, they would normally be disposed eventually to withdraw. Generally speaking, the more theologically sophisticated a Christian is, the more he will tend to substitute for that claim *not* the claim that, say, "The Holy Spirit is present," but some still more guarded claim, something to the effect that "religious experiences" are occasioned by the *activity* or the *workings* of the Holy Spirit.

RETROSPECT. The job set for this chapter has been to examine several different contemporary claims as to how certain crucial theological sentences which make putative statements might be tested. The position shared by Alasdair MacIntyre, I. M. Crombie, and John Hick that "There is a God" or that "God loves us" might conceivably be falsified terrestrially, commends itself to these authors for the reason that the "facts of evil" look, on the surface, as though they count against the truth of the theistic claim. But

[53] Otto, *The Idea of the Holy*, p. 185.

"counting against," it was urged, is not equivalent to *falsifying*, and the surface plausibility of their position stems from a confusion of two quite different notions. When the distinction is drawn, the claim loses force and the appeal of their view dissolves. Indeed, as Crombie himself seems to admit, a dedicated Christian theist could surely not irrationally refuse to allow that *any* terrestrially-experienced extremity of pain or misfortune would constitute the falsification-condition for the sentences in question. The obstacle for the theist is that, given the traditional concept of God, his acceptance of the belief that an infinitely wise, powerful, and benevolent God can turn whatever may befall him to his own well-being makes it logically inappropriate for him to accept calamity of any kind, magnitude, or duration as showing that there is no God or that, say, there is a God but that He is misanthropic. It might be argued that a malelovent God would not, logically could not, really be God, for is it not a part of the traditional concept of God that He is benevolent? This objection may appear trivial, but it is worthy of noting in connection with the main argument under investigation.

The prospect of verifying the statement that there is a God looks more promising were it not for the seemingly insurmountable difficulty posed by one of the most essential, if not *the* most essential, of the attributes traditionally ascribed to God, namely, His transcendence. According to one persistent strain in classical Christian theology, it is of God's very nature to be "wholly other," *different in kind* from anything with which we are familiar or might ever become familiar. But the consequence of that doctrine is this: if we maintain, as many prominent Christian theologians have done, that the being named by "God" is transcendent, and if the argument in chapters three and four is substantially correct, then we lapse into unintelligibility in talking about God *so conceived.* From this it follows that classical Christianity, insofar as it presupposes and is committed to the existence of such a God, presupposes and is committed to something which is supposed to have factual significance and to be true, but which does not have factual significance and is neither true nor false.

The upshot is this: unless some way can be found either to demonstrate how theological sentences might be Verified, or to vitiate the argument upon which this requirement is based, then the statement that there is a God, together with every sentence which logically presupposes the truth of that sentence, is unintelligible, factually speaking. Attempts to reconcile latter-day Positivism and classical Christianity have not, thus far, been successful. The problem posed for Christianity by the Positivists is still unresolved.

CHAPTER V

DILEMMAS

"To what non-trivial objections, sir, do you think that the position you have advanced is open?" Could I fairly reply to this question, as a speaker once replied to me when I posed it after his address, "Sir, it is not my job to criticize my own position where I think it weakest; that's your job!"? Yes and no.

The reply is both evasive and appropriate. For the question generates an uncomfortable dilemma. If one concedes the force of sufficiently fundamental objections to his position, he appears to forfeit it altogether, or make its continued affirmation effete. But if one maintains that the steps of his argument are essentially unexceptionable, particularly when a great many members of the philosophical and theological community are no longer advancing them, then he appears cavalier about those considerations which have in fact prompted equally probing thinkers to dissent from his line of argument. One would like to acquire that reflective generosity of mind and breadth of sympathy which acknowledges suasive force to the arguments of one's critics, even on points which are lethal to one's own reasoned position. At the same time, one would also like to find a way, consistent with one's own deepest analytical intuitions, to be spared the uniquely unwelcome burden of refuting oneself.

Of course, one cannot have it both ways; you cannot both retain your cake and throw it away. Perhaps a compromise would be in order. In the interests of currency, completeness, and fairness to some sides of the issues other than those endorsed here, it would be appropriate to conclude this study with at least a glance at some of the problems and unsettled questions of the central argument. The theological and philosophical issues discussed in advancing the argument of this book are manifestly too complicated to permit a responsible exploration of all the important objections unearthed in fifty years of continuous discussion. But it is fitting that I close with at least a token look at some of the plausible arguments on the other side.

While much of the radically empirical spirit of Positivism has slowly been absorbed into the philosophical reflexes of two generations of thinkers touched by its claims, it is also true that most of the central doctrines of the mainline Positivists have been widely attacked and generally forsworn. As a philosophic movement, Positivism has gone out of style. Accordingly it is easy to overestimate the extent to which its central doctrines have been annulled. My own suspicion is that many of its doctrines have been quietly adopted on a fairly wide scale, "quietly" because something about some of their doctrines continues to ring true even after particular formulations have been discredited. The testability criterion is a case in point. Logical Positivism has been a massively influential force in the development of contemporary theory of knowledge, ethics, philosophy of science, analytic philosophy, and the philosophy of religion. But to concede this is not to deny the unacceptability of the many conceptual crudities in the classical Positivists' program which have been progressively exposed and supplanted by more sophisticated formulations.

Two tasks, then, remain. First, I will provide a summary of the argument both so that it can be seen in its entirety and so that the considerations advanced in the concluding sections will be less likely to be construed as a recanting of the claims I endorsed in chapters two, three, and four. Second, certain objections to crucial steps in the argument will be mentioned. The purpose here is mainly, for reasons of balance and currency, to *note* rather serious objections to the line of argument advanced here. The objections will not be discussed in the detail they merit, and my reply to these objections in each case will neither silence nor disarm them. My intention is to show that we face genuine dilemmas in the resolution of certain issues crucial to the argument. Without withdrawing the resolution of the issues here favored I have tried to show why some have preferred to resolve them differently.

A. SUMMARY OF THE ARGUMENT

I have examined one of the central doctrines of Logical Positivism, together with the implication which the Positivists thought this doctrine carried for religious belief of the sort they took Christianity to involve. The two focal questions are, first, whether the Positivist doctrine under scrutiny is sound and, if so, in what form; second, whether the doctrine, if it be sound, poses any challenge to the intelligibility of that sort of religious belief which Christians hold.

In answering the first question, it was suggested that the form of the

Positivist doctrine advanced by David Rynin—a statement is Meaningful if and only if it is either verifiable or falsifiable or both—is substantially sound, although it is not entirely trouble-free. The second question was prefaced by addressing the prior question as to what sort of religious belief the adjective "Christian" may arguably be held to cover. I concluded that any interpretation of "Christian belief" which would permit a person to entertain belief of that type and, at the same time, not believe in the existence of God, is arguably not-Christian, or at least not traditionally or classically Christian. Christianity which escapes Positivism by clipping its theistic roots forfeits too much. Some have held, however, that Christianity *is* essentially theistic, and by virtue of that fact its fundamental tenets *are* imperiled by Positivistic claims; some of the arguments of these defenders of Christianity were examined. The conclusion was that whether or not Christianity is vulnerable to the attack depends upon what sort of being it is which Christians purport to name by "God." In accord, perhaps, with the immanence-strain prodigally evidenced in traditional Christian thinking about God, Christian theologians have sometimes held that "God" names a being who is accessible, at least in principle, to human experience, partially knowable by direct acquaintance. I suggested that a doctrine of this sort is *not* vulnerable to the Positivist attack. Some Christian theologians hold, however, that God is to be distinguished from the world and from everything that happens in the world in such a way that "God," properly speaking, names a being which is inaccessible, even in principle, to human experience. In its most austere form, this distinction becomes a thesis to the effect that God is utterly, absolutely transcendent. I have not attempted to estimate just how widely this thesis has been maintained by Christian thinkers, although it was suggested that it, or something very much like it, constitutes a prominent part of classical Christian doctrine. This sort of doctrine *is* vulnerable to the Positivist attack. Three *prima-facie* plausible attempts to show that the statement that there is a God is Verifiable were examined and rejected; rejected, that is, for the doctrine of God which was attributed to traditional Christianity.

I have not attempted to explore two other ways in which one might try to show how the statement that there is a God might be Verified. First, one might conceivably construct a case for eschatological *falsification*. The case would require elaboration, however, in such a fashion as to nullify the objection which was brought against the notion of terrestrial falsification. It is doubtful that one could build the sort of case that would silence the demurral of the dedicated Christian believer in the face of even eschatological calamity. Second, one might also try to construct a case for eschatological verification conceived along the lines of a "Beatific Vision of God." Such a case, however, would necessitate abandoning the doctrine of God's transcendence, at least as regards the afterlife. Perhaps examination of the relevant, abundant theological documents on this topic would disclose that an intelligible case might be made, and has perhaps already been made, for a Beatific Vision of God which somehow preserves *some* of those features of the Godhead—majesty, hiddenness, mystery—which cluster under the descriptive banner of "transcendence" and which Christians have most often considered indefeasible. No one, to my knowledge, has replied in this way to Positivism, but it would advance the current stage of the discussion if someone would try to develop the case for verification *via* the Beatific Vision.

B. OBJECTIONS AND DILEMMAS

Consider now some noteworthy objections, and the dilemmas they pose, first to the testability claims advanced in chapters one and three, then to the theological claims advanced in chapters two and four.

1. Conclusive Verifiability

Even if Verifiability were conceded to be a necessary condition of a genuine statement of fact, it is claimed that *conclusive* Verifiability is too strong a requirement for any statement of fact to satisfy. If "Verify" is understood to mean "*show* to be true (or false)" or, more formally, if the Verification of statement *S* requires that there be a logical relation of *entailment* between a finite set of observation-sentences O^1, O^2 ... O_n and the statement *S* which they will be taken to Verify—such that it would be contradictory to assert the truth of the observation-sentences and to deny the truth of *S*—then *that* condition fails because it requires too much. It is too strong a requirement due to three interrelated considerations.

a. *Perceptual misfires.* For conclusive Verifiability to obtain we would have to be sure that our observation-sentences are true. But because of factors such as illusions, hallucinations, hypnotically-induced states, dreams, the possibility of momentary or prolonged private and public systematic delusions and the like, we can never know that some given perceptions are veridical and hence that our observation-statements are true.

b. *Open-texture.* Most of our empirical concepts are vague or suffused with the *possibility* of vagueness.[1] Our empirical concepts are not absolutely precise; we can never be certain that we have included everything in our

[1] Waismann, "Verifiability," pp. 119-121.

definition that should be included to cover all the cases of the application of the term in question. We limit our terms for a certain range of experiential contingencies and leave them undetermined in other directions. Thus we cannot foresee all the possible circumstances in which a statement employing an empirical term would be true or false. "The incompleteness of our verification is rooted in the incompleteness of the definition of the terms involved, and the incompleteness of the definition is rooted in the incompleteness of empirical description; that is one of the grounds why a material object statement *p* can *not* be verified conclusively, nor resolved into statements S^1, S^2, ... S_n which describe evidences for it."[2]

c. *The INEC-factor* (*i*ndefinite *n*umber of *e*xperiential *c*onsequences). Even material-object statements, which are typically taken to be paradigms of Meaningful sentences, include within the scope of their meaning—or, if one is nervous with that formulation, include as part of their Verification-condition—innumerable observational consequences for properly placed observers. To Verify such a statement conclusively, it would seem that we would be required to run check on *all* its relevant observational implications. So if Verification would not be complete with *one* good observation, neither would it be complete with a very large number of them. This is so because material object statements are characteristically *unendingly* subject to the test of further experience, inasmuch as the truth of any such statement has an indefinite number of experiential consequences.[3] Thus we could never finish the job of verifying any material-object statement. There would never be a time at which all the relevant evidence is in, a time at which no further experience could confute the statement's truth.

It is thus claimed that we cannot achieve conclusive verification for even our most paradigmatic empirical statements. If we require verifiability (or falsifiability) for bonafide statements at all, it is urged, let us hold out for weak verifiability (or falsifiability), for *confirmability* (or disconfirmability), according to which the linkage between statement *S* and the observation-sentences which provide evidence for its truth is such that the truth of the latter does not entail the truth of *S* but only provides some reason—a weighty, but not conclusive reason—for thinking that *S* is true.

What prompts us to say that conclusive Verification is impossible to

[2] *Ibid.*, p. 123. Also see W. P. Alston on a similar point in his *Philosophy of Language* (Englewood Cliffs, New Jersey: Prentice-Hall, Inc., 1964), pp. 95-96, and Michael Scriven's discussion in his "Definitions, Explanation, and Theories," *Minnesota Studies in the Philosophy of Science*, ed. by Herbert Feigl, Grover Maxwell, and Michael Scriven (Minneapolis, Minnesota: The University of Minnesota Press, 1958), pp. 99-195.

[3] Alston, *Philosophy of Language*, p. 76.

achieve, then, and hence mistaken to require, is that perceptual misfires, open-texture, and the INEC-factor conspire to render unsatisfiable the supposed entailment-relation between typical statements of fact and the evidence for them.

However, what prompts us to say that conclusive Verification is *not* a mistaken requirement for Meaningfulness is the following: (a) If we could never be sure that our perceptions are veridical, the requirement of conclusive Verification fails, as alleged. But in fact we can be sure that our perceptions are veridical, at least much of the time. Surely we have quite reliable ways to detect the perceptual irregularities that need to be avoided to insure veridical perception. When we do avoid these irregularities, and are sure that we have done so, then our perceptions are veridical, and Verification is not on this account open to question. (b) Open-texture is not a problem for Verification directly; moreover, it is only a problem for Verification indirectly insofar as we have not found it desirable or necessary to precise more fully some of the concepts that figure in the statements we wish to Verify. But if we have not determined all that we could mean or choose to mean when we employ a term, it is hardly surprising that we should sometimes find ourselves having trouble deciding whether a statement employing the term is true or false. The problem with open-texture reminds us only that we are occasionally victims of our own linguistic permissiveness; but we can cease to be victims by elaborating, according to our need, the criteria for the application of terms. Thus, certain kinds of linguistic indeterminacy could be eliminated by linguistic decisions fashioned according to need. Some indeterminacy will normally remain, of course, since we will not normally find it needful to finish the job of defining a term for an indefinite number of conceivable employments. We can decide about the applicability or non-applicability of a term for the test-cases that arise, when they arise, and we can employ any considerations we like and exact any degree of precision which suits our purposes. We cannot specify all our purposes in advance. But why should we be required to do so? (c) The INEC-factor might be indeed lethal to the notion of conclusive Verifiability in practice [4], but it poses no special problems for complete Veri-

[4] However, see John Austin's argument that conclusive verifiability is not impossible, in his *Sense and Sensibilia* (Oxford: Oxford University Press, 1962) Galaxy Book edition, 1964, pp. 117-123. "Does 'This is a telephone' *entail* 'You couldn't eat it?' Must I try to eat it, and fail, in the course of making sure that it's a telephone?" For the same contention see his earlier article, "Other Minds", *Proceedings of the Aristotelian Society Supplementary Volume* XX (1946); reprinted in Flew, ed., *Logic and Language* II [pp. 123-158], pp. 132-142.

fiability *in principle*. Obviously it is impossible in practice to run check on an indefinite number of experiental consequences, but is it also impossible in principle to do so? It is impossible in practice to count all the living gulls; is it impossible in principle to count them? (See below.) Is conclusive Verifiability achievable or not? Some factors prompt us to say yes and others to say no.

2. *Verifiability in principle*

The Verifiability principle, it is urged, appeals to an incoherent, perhaps self-contradictory sense of "possible" in "possible to Verify," to an unprincipled sense of "in principle" in "Verifiable in principle." Extrapolating from the sense of some other dispositional words ending in "...able"[5]—e.g., "dooable," "understandable"—one would think that "Verifiable" must mean "*able* to be Verified," which suggests that someone actually *could* Verify a Verifiable statement. We are reminded that this need not mean Verifiability in practice. What is important, we are told, is that someone might conceivably confront the relevant facts, that we should, accordingly, admit the Meaningfulness of "Brutus killed Caesar," "There are mountains on Mars," and "By 2000 the average age will be 92." But no one could conceivably confront the facts which would constitute the verification-condition of "Dinosaurs existed before men" and "Atomic warfare, if not checked, will exterminate all living things" and the Positivist should quit pretending that anyone could. On any intelligible reading of "Verifiable in principle" these statements should be disallowed because they are not Verifiable *at all.* It is obviously not possible to Verify statements pertaining to states of affairs from which humans are excluded not merely because it is not *physically* possible—to do so would involve violating certain laws of nature—nor because it is not *technologically* possible—in the present state of technology there would be no way of doing it—but because it is not *logically* possible—it involves a contradiction—since if observers (Verifiers) are excluded, so is Verification, and so is Verifi*ability*. "Verifying," John Hospers writes, "is something we do and it would require someone present to do the verifying."[6] Again, but for a quite different reason, "The universe and everything in it doubles in size every twenty-four hours" is not Verifiable either. In this case it is not that no one could conceivably get at the facts but that there is no standard of comparison, which makes it impossible

[5] Some, but not all: compare "edible," "negligible."

[6] John Hospers, *Introduction to Philosophical Analysis*, second ed., 1967, p. 263. See also p. 268.

for anyone to ascertain whether the readily accessible facts are or are not as they are alleged.[7]

What prompts us to say, then, that the Verifiability principle involves some self-contradictory or plainly incoherent thinking about "possibility" is that some quite clearly Meaningful sentences are claimed by neo-Positivists to be Verifiable in principle, whereas they are not in fact Verifiable at all; they are claimed to be such that one might *possibly* Verify them, whereas they are in fact such as to exclude anyone from doing the Verifying, with the consequence that their verification-condition requires the realization of an unattainable possibility, which is to say, the impossible.

However, what prompts us to say that the Verification principle does not involve an incoherent understanding of the possibility of Verification is the following. A *prima-facie* statement may be not-Verifiable in principle—it may not be possible to Verify it—for either of two importantly different reasons: (1) certain observations *would* collectively Verify it *if* they were performable,[8] although they are not performable and never could be, or (2) there are not even *any* imaginable or conceivable or describable empirical conditions which would constitute its Verification. Only cases that fit the second description are disallowed by the Verifiability principle;[9] the counter-examples cited fit only the first description. The puzzle is what we should say about examples where Verification fails for the first reason, whether the Verifiability principle gives, or fails to give, a perspicuous rendering of the conditions of their Meaningfulness. The force of requiring ascertainable truth-conditions for bonafide statements is to require their Meaningfulness to depend on a concatenation of Verificational data of an observational *sort*, not to require that someone ever be in a position to gather this data. The logical possibility of Verification required for Meaningfulness is not the possibility of someone's actually getting at the state of affairs in question, but merely the possibility of knowing what it would be like to get at it. That is to say, when a Verification fails for the first reason the statement may yet be Verifiable, though when it fails for the second reason, the statement may be presumed to be un-Verifiable, and hence Meaningless.

[7] However, see Hempel's interesting discussion of the hypothesis of an expanding universe in his *Philosophy of Natural Science* (Englewood Cliffs, New Jersey: Prentice-Hall, Inc., 1966), p. 97. For a classical positivist treatment of this case see F. Waismann, *Principles of Linguistic Philosophy*, ed. by R. Harré (New York: St. Martin's Press [first published, 1935], 1965), pp. 326-327.

[8] That is, they have imaginable, conceivable, or describable empirical truth-conditions.

[9] Some of the early Positivists would also have disallowed the first. That view, happily, did not prevail.

Yet there still seems to be a difference, it might be claimed, between the possibility that a particular state of affairs obtains and the possibility that someone might find it out. What does this difference suggest for the issue at hand? Consider the questions, (i) Does some statement *S* describe a logically possible situation? and (ii) Is it logically possible to test statement *S*? Are these sufficiently different questions that one might answer the former in the affirmative and the latter in the negative? This is not easy to decide; for the latter question, if the former be answered affirmatively, sometimes seems to merit both a "yes" and a "no." Does "There were dinosaurs before there were men" describe a logically possible situation? Yes.[10] Does it describe a logically possible situation which it is also logically possible to test? When we realize that we know perfectly well what it would be like to observe dinosaurs and fail to observe men, we think that "yes" is the correct reply. To our objectors we seem to have slipped in an observer. When reminded that to give an affirmative answer we have had to imagine the emplacement of an observer in a situation where none is permitted, we are inclined to reply that any imagined observer's emplacement is not seriously meant, that it does not violate the sense of the example, and that this is one of a whole set of caviling objections which miss the nerve and spirit of the Positivist enterprise. But there are times when, feeling analytically parsimonious, we conscientiously resist envisioning any phantom observer, when we stick literally to the terms which the example specifies; then we think that "no" is the better reply, we maintain that we understand the statement without making the slightest tacit reference to the conditions of its verification, and we attack those who project a phantom observer as having violated the conditions of the case.[11] Is an imagined observer there or not? Does it matter? That is, if the Verificationist has to project a ghost-Verifier to cover cases inaccessible to real Verifiers, is this a trivial projection or is it really quite damaging to the Verificationist's case? Does the Verifiability principle utilize some illicit notion of possibility in "possible to Verify"? Some considerations prompt us to say yes and others to say no.

3. Ad hoc exceptions

A principle which allows an exception, it will be argued, is not a principle which commands respect. A testability criterion which cannot be formulated in such a way as to include even all those cases which common sense insists must be included is obviously bankrupt. The Verifiability prin-

[10] Contrast "There are married bachelors."

[11] See Ayer and Copleston, "Logical Positivism—A Debate," pp. 746-747.

ciple, supplemented by the argument provided, may fairly be said to meet some of the traditional objections to earlier formulations, but it meets its Waterloo with unrestricted universals containing mixed quantification—"For every substance there exists some solvent"—since there could never be a time at which the finite number of observations made thus far on the finite number of samples considered thus far would have either established or excluded their truth. They patently *could* be true, or perhaps false, yet they violate the criterion. Two counter-claims might arise: (1) if the Verifiability principle makes an exception for mixed-quantificationals, why not make exceptions as well for theological statements? One good *ad hoc* exception deserves another. (2) The Verifiability principle is flatly faulty and is no more entitled to be the moving power behind an argument allegedly discrediting the Meaningfulness of theological sentences than it is entitled to discredit the Meaningfulness of mixed quantificational statements.

What urges the conclusion, then, that the Verifiability principle is unacceptable is that its canons torpedo a certain class of obviously Meaningful sentences which then have to be rescued by an *ad hoc* exception.[12]

Two replies, however, may soften this objection: (1) If exceptions are made for mixed quantificationals, exceptions must be similarly made *for cause* across the board. Yet not just *any* cause will suffice to countenance an exception. Mixed quantificationals are simply another member of the class of statements which fit description-(1) in the section above; that is to say, they are such that certain observations would collectively Verify them *if* they were performable, although the relevant observations are not performable and could never in fact be performed. Exemptions would have to be made indifferently for any other special case of this type, for theological statements too, if they fall under description-(1). The argument would have to be heard. (2) The problem with Verifying mixed quantificationals emerges from their unrestricted *scope*, from their covering an indefinite number of cases, not from any inherent obscurity in their meaning which impedes our knowing what to look for on the supposition that they are true. Mixed

[12] Apparently Mr. Rynin is no longer disposed to exempt mixed quantificationals from the Verifiability requirement; perhaps he never really was. In "Cognitive Meaning and Cognitive Use" (1966) he appears to withdraw quite fully what looked like an earlier, guarded inclination to "include them [mixed quantificationals] in the class of cognitively meaningful statements in terms of the criterion of possessing truth-conditions" even though they do not fully qualify. He currently urges what he calls their "cognitive *use*" in that they provide heuristic guides for scientific discovery. His earlier intuitions, if indeed he ever held those credited to him in chapter four, seem to me to have been much better. Mixed quantificationals may indeed have heuristic use too, but surely they may also intelligibly be claimed not merely to appear to be, but to be, true or false.

quantificationals were exempted not because a denial of their Meaningfulness is counter-intuitive, but because their unrestricted scope obviously does not impair their Meaningfulness, even though it does prohibit their Verification-in-practice. We could have equally well argued—although Rynin does not—that mixed quantificationals are Verifiable *in principle* since we know what it would be like to Verify a sentence like "For every substance there exists some solvent": To have Verified this statement would be to have found a substance which *forever* yields to no solvent, or to have never found a substance for which we could not also find its solvent. Admittedly, there would be no point in time when all the data are in, no time after which future data could no longer overturn our present verdict. Yet, are not these features already quite solidly and unexceptionably locked into the notion of "Verifiable *in principle*"? What are we to say? Does "For every substance there exists some solvent" have truth-conditions of an ascertainable sort which are, accordingly, acceptably viewed as ascertainable in principle though not in fact? Is "For every substance there exists some solvent" an exception to the Verifiability principle or not? Some considerations prompt us to say yes and others to say no.

4. The translatability criterion

Philosophers have by and large abandoned hope of producing an acceptable formulation of a general criterion of factual significance. Those who still pursue the program nowadays at all have tried to formulate the criterion, following Carnap,[13] so as to apply not to *whole* declarative sentences, but to the *terms* which appear in them. The program has had its difficulties and, as we shall see, has been chastened into making one significant major concession, but it is too influential in contemporary philosophy of science to be passed over entirely. What is required for Meaningfulness, it is said, is that the terms comprising a sentence be meaningful and that they be combined in syntactically acceptable ways. The syntax is specified as the standard notational devices of modern symbolic logic, stemming from the *Principia Mathematica* of Whitehead and Russell. How does one ascertain whether the non-logical terms are meaningful? The guideline, very loosely stated, is that the terms must be themselves observational terms or else *translatable* into observational terms.[14] Sentences are Meaningless only if they contain

[13] Carnap, "Testability and Meaning."

[14] For a critique of the notion of translatability, see I. Scheffler, *The Anatomy of Inquiry* (New York: Alfred A. Knopf, 1967), pp. 152-162.

meaningless—that is, empirically untranslatable—component-terms, or if the terms are unacceptably combined.

The motivation for this "ideal language" program, as it is sometimes called, comes principally from an attempt to vindicate the procedures and posits of the natural and social scientist. It is not simply that whatever the man in the white laboratory coat says is acceptable. It is rather that the string of the scientist's successes in explaining and predicting events in the organic and inorganic world is sufficiently arresting and appreciated, largely for the sake of the technology which it feeds, that we want to grant to the scientist as much conceptual freedom as his work requires. From some quarters, moreover, there has also arisen a fairly strong inclination to understand the scientist's discursive apparatus as not merely pragmatically, instrumentally effective—which it is—but as cognitively significant. The plain fact is, however, that much of the scientist's work will not pass muster on the older formulations of the testability principle. The reason for this is that the theories advanced to help explain and predict events at the observational level contain terms which do not themselves refer exclusively to observables. Nevertheless, it is thought that the scientist is neither charlatan nor magicmaker, that his explanatory apparatus is importantly different from that of the "metaphysician," and it is also thought that there should be a way of showing that this is so. The translatability criterion is an attempt, accordingly, not to make the theoretical work of the scientist *look* Meaningful, but to show that it *is*. That is to say, it is an attempt to formalize the intuition that although most of the scientist's theoretical work floats further above the observational plane than the classical Positivists appear to have noticed, or would have liked, the scientist does in fact subject his theoretical apparatus—though not in the simple way sometimes thought—to those selfsame empirical controls which the Positivists attempted to canonize in the testability-criterion. The difference between the earlier and the later program is that the translatability-criterion, at least in its chastened, liberalized form, explicitly tries to make accommodation for unobservables.

The translatability criterion merits closer examination. Its thesis is that a sentence is Meaningful only if it is translatable into the formulations of some specified language whose legitimate sentences are priorly assumed to be Meaningful. Informally, this amounts to the claim that a Meaningful sentence must either be, or else be translatable into, a sentence or set of sentences which are already known to be Meaningful. More formally, sentence *S* is Meaningful if and only if *S* is translatable into language-*L*—an empiricist's language—such that the components of *S* are specifiable, directly or indirectly, in the sense-vocabulary of *L* and are syntactically well-formed. L is defined, as is any language, by reference to vocabulary and syntax. The former is usually subdivided into a set of primitive and a set of non-primitive elements (I and II below). The unchastened version of L, then, might typically be characterized as follows:

I. *Lexicon*: A primitive descriptive vocabulary consisting of a stock of first-level observation-terms designating primitive observation-predicates, plus names for observed particulars (individual constants).

II. *Direct Definitions*: A stock of higher-level defined terms. Definitions give the permissible modes of introducing new descriptive terms into L by specifying the formal relations which must hold between any descriptive term which is neither an observation-term nor an individual constant and the primitive observation-terms of L:

a. Second-level terms: "Explicitly defined terms" are of the logical form $A =_{df} f$ and g and h. Explicit definitions are formulated in the base observational vocabulary and provide individually necessary and jointly sufficient conditions for the application of the terms so defined.

b. Third-level terms: "Operationally defined terms" ("Contextually defined terms," "Definitions-in-use"). Dispositional terms, such as "hard," "brittle," "soluble," etc., are operationally defined. (Carnap's celebrated notion of "partial reduction sentences").

III. *Syntax*: A set of sentential connectives and operators, plus a set of rules permitting (1) sentence-formation out of I and II, and (2) the formulation of inferences between the sentences of L. The syntax provides the structure of L by specifying which combinations of words yield sentences and which modes of deduction between the sentences of L are acceptable.

If language-L, as specified above, had proved acceptable for the purpose for which it was fashioned, the translatability-criterion would have had two advantages: (1) It would rule out, from the beginning, sentences which contain empirically vacuous terms—e.g., "Gremlins cause airplane accidents"—and would rule in, from the beginning, sentences which were troublesome for other versions of the testability criterion—e.g., "All crows are black," "For every substance there exists some solvent," "There were dinosaurs before there were men," etc. (2) It would also rule out, on syntactical grounds, sentences whose non-logical terms satisfy the translatability condition but which are combined in unaccredited ways, e.g., "The multitude greens Harry because nine when doors" and even, allegedly, "Quadruplicity drinks procrastination."[15] As Scheffler notes, "Control over the vocabulary of ... a particular base language would eliminate nonsensical terms ... while control over its syntax would eliminate nonsensical combinations of remaining signs."[16]

To achieve adequacy as a characterization of modern science, however, it is now generally conceded that the vocabulary of *L* will have to be expanded to include those notions which occur within advanced theorizing known as "theoretical constructs."[17] As defined exclusively by I, II, and III, *L* is not yet rich enough to accommodate the posits and procedures of science as we know it today. Scientific theories are more and more likened unto interpreted hypothetical-deductive *systems*. An uninterpreted axiomatized system is adopted, given an empirical interpretation, and deductive relationships are drawn. Theoretical constructs are introduced into the vocabulary of *L* as *postulates*. Their purpose is to help explain the lower-level laws which, in turn, are themselves used to explain and predict what we can observe. Theoretical terms may be *indirectly* defined, of course, by reference to other theoretical terms. But they are not themselves subject to observational check and are not introducible by any kind of direct definition (explicit or operational). Higher level theoretical constructs permit the deduction, through lower level laws, of observational consequences and thus function integrally in the explanation and prediction of events on the observational plane. But it must be kept in mind that theoretical terms are not observational terms and are not reducible to or definable in terms of them; they are introduced *by postulation*, are capable of partial interpretation, and are "testable" only indirectly, by checking deducible consequences. To understand some theoretical component *C* one has to understand the entire theory of which *C* is a part. If *C* is embedded in a statement which, though it is untestable, yields testable consequences when the statement is taken together with other statements, then *C* is an acceptable component of the system. Scientific postulates are not themselves testable, then, but the *system* of which they are a part is. The upshot is that one can attribute truth or falsity to a theory, on this chastened criterion, even though it contains components which are not empirically cashable and statements which are not themselves ascertainably true or false.

The implication of this chastened form of the criterion for the claims of the theologian are very interesting indeed. The distinctive feature of the

[15] *Ibid.*, p. 158.

[16] *Ibid.*, p. 155.

[17] See *supra*, Chapter 3, C, 2, pp. 104-111.

translatability criterion has been lost, of course. For the *unit* of cognitive significance has become neither a set of primitive empirical terms into which all the other non-logical terms are translatable, nor a set of sentences formulable by them, but the entire interpreted system. As Hempel points out, the expanded translatability criterion is also extremely permissive: "It is satisfied by the system of contemporary physical theory combined with some set of principles of speculative metaphysics, even if the latter have no empirical interpretation at all."[18] On this criterion, then, that part of the theologian's apologetic enterprise which has been under scrutiny in this study looks more capable of success than it looked on older formulations. For while it might have been thought that the unobservables essential to theology would have been ruled out of court from the beginning by the translatability criterion, it turns out that they might be acceptably introduced by postulation. *Provided* that certain other connections can be made—connections with the plane of observation—Christian theological "theory" will have been shown to have the same methodological credentials as the theory of the scientist. To demonstrate this would require showing that a theological system is *relevantly* like a scientific system. The challenge, in particular, would be to show that (1) the unobservables within theology function within that system, as they do in scientific theory, in such a way as to generate "testable consequences"—testable lower-order theological statements which would provide the confirmation-disconfirmation conditions for the theory; (2) a theological system responds, in the hands of its custodians and renovators, to situations of conflict between the anticipated and the observed in the same fashion that a scientific theory responds, in the hands of its custodians and renovators, to observational anomalies. Thomas Kuhn, among others, has shown that a good scientific theory is not simply *abandoned* when some anomaly shows that some particular conjunction of premises cannot be true; theories are adjusted internally, then readjusted again, to accommodate anomalies at the observational plane.[19] Because of their internal plasticity, theories are rarely abandoned when one of their testable consequences is falsified; they are abandoned only when they become too ponderous and cumbersome internally, and when a *better* theory has been formulated.[20] The relevant theological task would be to

[18] Carl Hempel, *Aspects of Scientific Explanation* (New York: The Free Press, 1965), pp. 113-114.

[19] Thomas Kuhn, *The Structure of Scientific Revolutions* (Chicago: The University of Chicago Press, 1962 [second edition, 1971]), Chapters VI-VIII.

[20] Standards of excellence for scientific theories are much in the forefront of current discussion in the philosophy of science.

show (a) what sorts of internal adjustments are occasioned within theological theory and by what sorts of anomalies, (b) what kind of theory, if any, might be likely to qualify as a "better" theological theory, and on what grounds, than the one to which the theologian is committed, and (c) what sorts of anomaly might compel sufficiently cumbersome internal adjustments to effect the defeat of a theological theory and the shift of allegiance from one theological theory to another.

What is the implication of the translatability criterion for the argument advanced in chapter four? (1) If we hesitate to admit unobservables into theories, or if, unable to resist so strong a tide, we submit to their admission but are nevertheless unable conscientiously to countenance the Meaningfulness of theories containing theoretical constructs, then one alternative still open is to adopt an instrumentalist view of such theories. Some have found this attractive, though it has not been endorsed here. (2) If we concede that theories which contain theoretical constructs can somehow, even on our deepest intuitions, intelligibly be called Meaningful, we can assuage the remnants of our nervousness about this concession by remembering that such theories have testable consequences which, if they obtain, confirm the theory—though they do not verify it—but, more importantly, if they do not obtain, *falsify* the theory in the sense that it compels either its withdrawal completely or the renovation of some part of it. This view has been endorsed in chapter three. (3) If we prefer (2) to (1), then on the principle that what's sauce for the goose is sauce for the gander, we should welcome the claim that a theological theory might conceivably be shown to be structurally and methodologically like the scientist's theory and Meaningful for the same reasons. However, if one has reasons to think that theological theory is immune from falsification, then the program of providing supportive argumentation for the claim of (3) will appear, however welcome, doomed to eventual failure. But is it the case that theological theory, as claimed in chapter four, is unfalsifiable? Perhaps that claim should be re-examined.

5. Falsifiability and theological statements

Some will insist that at least some of the theological statements of Christianity—notably the statement that God exists or that a cluster of core-statements expressive of the fundamental claim or claims of Christianity—are Meaningful on the Verifiability criterion since they are falsifiable. To be sure, it will be conceded, a Christian is ordinarily committed to his religious beliefs with a degree of tenacity which could scarcely be called meagre. Admittedly, too, his conviction about the truth of his religious beliefs, or some subset of them, is typically so *non-tentative*, so *unprovisionally* geared to the sorts of events and experiences which can plausibly be understood to be evidence-for or evidence-against those beliefs, that it sometimes *looks* as if *nothing* could nullify it. A Christian's faith, in short, is one of total, unreserved commitment. Nevertheless, it will be urged, faith is not inexhaustible; it is theologically naive to claim that it is, theologically monstrous to claim that it should be. Committed though he be, a Christian holds his faith because he has reasons for doing so; among his reasons some are perhaps more central than others in the sense that if *those* reasons should collapse it would also tumble his faith. It is difficult to espy just what these reasons are, to say nothing of assembling a complete list of them, but whatever they are, a Christian will rest his faith on them distributively. Among them, however, the following would surely be included: (1) that the Biblical teachings are historically correct, at least in the gospel narrative, or perhaps, in certain central parts of it (notably, the resurrection); (2) that in general wickedness is punished and virtue rewarded, and (3) that adversity can be turned into occasions for growth and joy. It is flatly contrary to fact to maintain that Christians continue to have faith in the absence of weight-bearing, quasi-evidential factors such as these. When such elements give way, if they do, faith typically does also. Howard Root writes:

> More than once men have said that if they were obliged, through historical enquiry, to disbelieve the main events of the Gospel narrative, their faith would go. Whether this is a theologically sound view does not matter. It is a part of ordinary religious usage. We can say that in some sense belief is tentative. Nor have we adequate reason for saying that this sort of tentativeness is incompatible with honest and sincere worship. There would be something odd about saying that people do not and cannot ever allow anything to count against their belief. This is the remark which the verificationists wished to elicit.... It is the plain fact that believers sometimes cease to believe; or equally to the point, they sometimes change their beliefs quite radically. It is also the fact that they are often ready, even eager, to offer explicit reasons for these changes and are not content simply to point to some authority. Are we then to say that because their belief was not permanent they were never really believers at all? How then should we know that we are believers in this absolute sense? Is the future so open to us that we can never discover that our belief (or some part of it) was in some sense tentative? [21]

While it may be true, then, for some theologically misshapen variety of Christianity that a "Christian" could go on holding his beliefs no matter what happens, it is not true of authentic Christianity, which enjoins no such thing. A Christian is simply not obliged to hold his beliefs *come what may*. That kind of commitment is not faith, but madness.

[21] Howard Root, "Metaphysics and Religious Belief," *Prospect for Metaphysics*, p. 75.

What prompts us to say, then, that the statement that God exists is falsifiable is that Christians do characteristically abandon that belief when they abandon certain of their crucial historical beliefs or fail to see any rough congruence between moral-spiritual worth and manifest destiny or fail to find natural and moral evil to be the occasion for improving and enriching the human condition.

However, what prompts us to say that the statement that God exists is not falsifiable are the following considerations. There may be some issues on which it is important to take our clues for what Christians ought to do from what Christians do—being a pacifist, perhaps. But the issue at hand does not appear to be one of these. *Of course* Lord Jim abandoned ship, as did the other officers on the bridge; the question is, was he justified in doing so? It is understandable—even forgiveable, perhaps—that he jumped, but in the jumping he renounced his responsibilities as executive officer. The issues are similar in the theological case. Christians give up their faith for cause, yes. Certain contingencies prompt them to abandon ship. But what contingencies *justify* their doing so? This matter should be subject to theological, not psychological, adjudication. The relevant theological doctrines are the doctrine of God's love and forgiveness on the one side, and the doctrine of God's judgment, his punishment for sin, on the other. While it is certainly true that a manifest destiny drenched with suffering and pain would typically provide a believer with cause for jumping ship—it might even look to him like a falsification of the claim that God loves us, or even that God exists—it is also true that it would *not* provide *justification* for his jumping ship, since terrestrial infelicity, perhaps even eschatological infelicity, when coupled with the doctrine of the ubiquity and gravity of sin, may always faithfully be interpreted as a corollary of God's justice, hence not as a falsification of the statement that God exists. "Hell" and "Purgatory," after all, are very ancient, revered theological doctrines. Now ordinarily the demands of justice are eventually met; further suffering, after *some* point, could fairly be interpreted not as God's punishment for sin but as "God's" malice, hence falsification after all. Yet this is not an ordinary case of punishment since (a) sin is taken to be an infinite, or at least incalculable, offense against God's holiness; hence (b) there would be no point in time at which the Christian could be assured that he does not merit further punishment, and this is so because (c) while it is said that God loves us, it is also said that God chastens those He loves, and that God's ways are not our ways, nor are our ways His. What prompts us to say that the statement that God exists is not falsifiable is that the doctrines of the sinfulness of man, the justice of God, and the "otherness" of God appear to make it logically inappropriate for a Christian to interpret any contingency at all as incompatible with God's moral governance over the world, hence not as a disproof of it, hence not as a falsification of the theistic claim. If things got bad enough, would Christians give up the ship? Yes. Would they be justified in giving it up? Psychologically, yes; theologically, no, because the condition which would justify it cannot be known to have been satisfied. Three factors combine to guarantee its unsatisfiability : (i) the possibility of eventual deliverance, (ii) the appropriateness of perhaps unlimited punishment for sin, and (iii) the unfathomable otherness of God. To remain constant when the evidence screams "Jump!" may not be madness, but faith. Then we are reminded, "But our sins have been washed away," and we are inclined to think that constancy in the face of heinously adverse evidence *is* madness, not faith. Yet we recall, "His ways are not our ways." What are we to say? Is commitment in spite of ruinous evidence faith or is it madness? It becomes a matter of balancing theological doctrines one against another. Is the doctrine that God exists—God as understood in Christianity—falsifiable? Some considerations prompt us to say yes and others to say no.

6. The transcendence of God

The fundamental theological error of my over-all argument, it will be said, is that of attributing *radical* transcendence to God as God is understood in Christianity. Among the many themes running through the fabric of Christian doctrine there is indeed the theme of God's transcendence. Now and then theologians from all periods in the history of Christian thought will assert a radical contrast between God and utterly anything else whatsoever. "God," it would be thought, names a being which is "totally other," ineffable. But these are not, it may be said, the representative voices of the tradition. Clearly, the Bible does not teach God's ineffability; one could glean perhaps a score or more of passages to support this theme, but many hundreds to deny it. The whole soteriological thrust of Christianity requires that God be *not* wholly other, that he be characterized rather by certain humanly intelligible attributes—power, wisdom, justice, love—which are evidenced particularly in God's plan for the redemption and salvation of man, attributes which, were they to be stripped of meanings continuous with their ordinary usage, would lose their soteriological power. Besides, worship demands an accessible deity, not a remote one. The entire devotional life of the Christian would make not the least sense if we supposed that God is different in kind from anything we have experienced or now know or could ever experience or know. One can maintain the vital distinction between Creator and creature which has always been important to Christian theologians without denying a qualitative resemblance between man and God. A proper accent on the transcendence of God requires only accenting the relative distance between God and the creature, not the asserting of an absolute difference of *quale* or kind between them. To hold that God is transcendent is merely to hold such theses as that (1) God is immaterial, very much like minds are immaterial, although He might reveal himself through material forms; that (2) God is Creator and Sustainer of the world (hence "beyond," "outside" the world) only in the sense that His mode of existence is self-sufficient, rather than dependent; that (3) God has various attributes—eternity, immutability, omnipotence, omniscience, and the moral attributes—which contrast with their finite human counterparts not in kind but in degree; etc. If God were wholly other, God would be utterly unknowable, indescribable, incapable of acting in or on the world. "A completely transcendent God, a God who is really *wholly* other would be out of all relation to us, and therefore quite unknowable and quite irrelevant to us."[22] The theme of radical transcendence is utterly inconsistent with the fundamental themes of Christianity. The God of Christianity is not a metaphysical something-I-know-not-what, a spooky, impersonal superbeing hovering spacelessly, timelessly outside the universe. God is a "Thou" differing in number and *quantus* from the universe and its contents which are existence-dependent upon Him. The doctrine of the *imago-dei* proclaims that although God created the world itself out of nothing, He created *man* in God's own image and likeness. Accordingly, a corollary of the doctrine that "in a special way man imitates the nature of God" is that one might fairly extrapolate from the nature of man to understand the nature of God, or at least begin to understand God's nature. The God of Christianity is neither unknowable, inaccessible, nor ineffable. "I and the Father are one." "God is the father of our Lord Jesus Christ, judge, comforter, savior, forgiver, provider, redeemer, and faithful friend."

What prompts us to say that God is not ineffable, then, is that God's ineffability is not taught by the scriptures, that Biblical, credal, and devotional documents have always ascribed to God quite determinate characteristics, and that a denial of these characteristics would evacuate the gospel of its soteriological significance.

However, as needful as the determinate characteristics of God admittedly

[22] Langdon Gilkey, *Maker of Heaven and Earth* (Garden City, New York: Doubleday & Company, Inc., 1959; Anchor books ed., 1965), p. 96.

are for facilitating the church's typical evangelical and devotional employment of the doctrine of God, that doctrine also contains other elements whose prominence and recurrence within the history of Christian thought seems to warrant an equal claim to indefeasibility. The Christian doctrine of God is a vector of many forces. As prominent as the theme of God's determinateness, though not evangelically as "marketable," so to speak, is the theme of God's indeterminateness. This is not to say, of course, that God's qualitative "otherness" from everything finite is the cheeriest or the most often emphasized of the doctrines definitive of the kerygma. It is only to say that in every period of the evolution of Christian thinking, from the muted voices of the New Testament to the thundering enigmas of Karl Barth, Christian theologians have found reason to maintain the essential otherness of God, His indissoluble incomprehensibility. They have maintained this theme right alongside of, and in the face of, the quite antipodal theme of God's possession of determinate, intelligible characteristics. Whether both themes can be enfolded into a coherent doctrine of God is of course the basic theological problem one small aspect of which I have tried to address in this book. It is the fundamental point at issue not only between Christians and their critics, but also, and increasingly, within the ranks of the custodians of Christian thought themselves. And it should not be thought that this is a new problem for Christian dogmatics; it was one of the fundamental generative enigmas for the evolution of Christian doctrine during the Patristic period. For the purposes of the present book I hope it has been sufficient, in the context of recent apologetic efforts influential enough to have changed the very content of Christian doctrine, to have *remembered* the historical fundamentality of the strain within Christian thought which asserts God's ineffability and to have assessed its relevance for the specific issues probed here.

However, since the concept of God's transcendence is so widely under attack nowadays,[23] most splashily by the "Death of God" theologians, perhaps I should at least broach the normative question as to whether the Christian theist's problems with Positivism could viably be dispatched, as some would suggest, by an explicit repudiation of the doctrine of God's transcendence. Christian doctrine is no more slave to the past than are the sartorial habits of the Vatican-guard or the choice of the language of the liturgy. If evolution can change the outer face of Christianity, then why not the inner face as well: why not also the innermost spine of Christianity—the

[23] See Alasdair Kee's interesting discussion in his *The Way of Transcendence* (Baltimore: Penguin Books, Inc., 1971).

doctrine of God? Might the Christian systematician subtract from the doctrine of God the theme of divine ineffability—and discard that theme—while at the same time remaining faithful to the deepest *theo*logical intuitions of his doctrinal progenitors? The line between acceptable doctrinal evolution and apostasy is admittedly difficult to draw, but might it be drawn this side of God's ineffability?

Given the problems shouldered by not doing so, it is a tempting option to take. The question to be considered carefully before doing so, however, is what sort of linkage obtains between the feature of God's transcendence and certain other features of the concept of God which assuredly could not be forfeited without apostasy. In particular, could one continue to hold all that is implied by the doctrines of God as *Creator* and God as *Holy* without maintaining God's transcendence? The interrelation of doctrines within Christianity is an extremely complex matter; nothing said here is meant to minimize that complexity or to suggest that any particular connection is either obvious or invariably fixed. It seems evident to me, however, when I ponder the interrelation of classical Christian doctrines, that whatever else God is within Christianity, God is a metaphysical and moral absolute and that, accordingly, God's transcendence is a natural corollary of God's creatorhood and his Holiness. Admittedly, these two latter doctrines perform a diversity of jobs within the doctrinal corpus, but one of the jobs they seem quite fundamentally to do, stated very roughly, is this: God's createrhood guarantees God's otherness *in kind*, while His holiness guarantees God's otherness *in degree*; together they insure God's essential ineffability. As creator of heaven and earth, God can scarcely be anything less than trans-categorial, beyond the forms of thought and the categories which we employ to characterize the natural order—time, space, causality, substance, individual, person, etc. God is "outside" that order and all its contents, "different from" every determinate object, person, event, characteristic, or phenomenon, since God functions as creator and/or "ground" of everything that is. "God ... transcends all essential marks of creaturely status."[24] Hence, God is different *in kind* from anything one might describe, confront, imagine, conceive of, etc. But God is also different *in degree*; his

[24] Gilkey, *Maker of Heaven and Earth*, p. 89. See also p. 94 and n. 11 on p. 75: "This assumption that there is a fundamental distinction of nature or substance between God and His creatures, so that no creature can be said to be "made out of God", had been long implicit in Christian thought and life. It reached its clearest explicit form, however, in the argument with the Arians. Although the Arian controversy is not about this issue, what is significant is that the argument between the two sides assumes the absolute distinction of substance between God and creatures."

"holiness" is that characteristic or set of characteristics by virtue of which God is supremely exalted and praiseworthy by contrast to all other things.[25] The supreme exaltation of God would appear to require nothing short of such contentions as that (1) God's being infinitely exceeds the being of His creatures and that by virtue of its exemption from all *finite* limitation, the divine being is discontinuous with finite beings and any and all properties which characterize them; that (2) God's mode of existence is so eminent that mere sentient creatures, whose *intellect* as well as whose *will* is "fallen" (sinful), are restricted in their capacity to apprehend and comprehend Him with their impaired conceptual apparatus; that (3) God's moral and dispositional attributes are so different in kind, in amount, and in manner of operation from those we attribute to finite beings when we apply the same descriptive adjectives to them that we cannot seriously hope to understand attributes in the former domain by reference to, or extrapolation from, attributes understood in the latter domain;[26] etc. The holiness of God, Langdon Gilkey claims, is not a property of God among other properties; it is a kind of intensifying factor for all His properties, an intensifier which raises each property to such a degree of eminence as to insure its opacity to human understanding and insures its essential difference as applied to God from what it would mean were it to be applied to something less exalted than God:

Holiness is not primarily a moral attribute, as if it meant merely the perfect goodness of some superbeing with a white beard. Rather it refers to that absolute "otherness" which distinguishes the divine from all that is creature, and so characterizes every aspect of God. Holiness is the word that refers to the *divine* aspect of any attribute asserted of deity, *the quality which makes any attribute essentially different in God than in other things*, the quality that raises anything, be it power or love or anger, to the *nth* degree when it is applied to God. Thus God's goodness is "holy," His being is "holy," His anger is "holy," His love is "holy." *Holiness, therefore, points to the unconditioned, the transcendent element of deity which absolutely distinguishes God from all creatures*; holiness is the "Godness" of God.

[25] In this connection I should again like to commend Ninian Smart, *Reasons and Faiths*, Chapter 1; R. C. Coburn, "The Hiddenness of God ..." and "The Concept of God," p. 73.

[26] This generates one line of reply to the problem of theodicy. To the extent that one construes God's moral and dispositional predicates as different in kind from those predicated of men, to that extent it seems tempting to think that *the mere underscoring of those differences* is sufficient to defuse the traditional problem of trying to reconcile God's omnipotence, omnibenevolence, and omniscience with what appear to be massive doses of evil and suffering in the world.

Thus holiness and the divine transcendence are ideas very closely associated in theology; *so far as God transcends His creation, so far is He holy.*[27]

What prompts us to say, then, that God is ineffable is that certain other very fundamental Christian doctrines seem to require it; if God is a metaphysical and moral absolute, then God is ineffable. But then we shake ourselves and remember other themes equally fundamental to Christianity; we realize that if God is really ineffable, assuredly He is not the God of Christianity. If God is transcendent, then God is not God; but unless God is transcendent, God cannot be God. What are we to say?

It is to dilemmas such as these that the issues of the argument lead us.

[27] Gilkey, *Maker of Heaven and Earth*, p. 89 (Italics mine). Professor Gilkey's recent book—*Naming the Whirlwind: The Renewal of God-Language* (Bobbs-Merill, 1969)—forwards a different kind of theological analysis. What is said about God is now governed by certain methodological controls which he adopts—phenomenological and linguistic controls: "Ours", he says, "has been ... a phenomenological analysis of the *experience of* the unconditioned ...; In another sense, it has been an analysis of the *language about* the unconditioned ..." (p. 415. Italics mine). Given these controls it is natural that the analysis comes out more this-worldly. If I understand his approach and the claims it generates I find nothing here which amounts to a withdrawing of the theologically spartan view enunciated *about God* in the striking passage cited above.

SELECTED BIBLIOGRAPHY

A. BOOKS

Alston, W. P. *Philosophy of Language*. Englewood Cliffs, New Jersey: Prentice-Hall, Inc., 1964.

Austin, John. *Sense and Sensibilia*. Oxford: Oxford University Press, 1962.

Ayer, A. J. *The Problem of Knowledge*. Baltimore, Maryland: Penguin Books Inc., 1956.

— *Language, Truth, and Logic*. New York: Dover Publications, n.d. (first published, 1936; second ed., 1946).

— ed. *Logical Positivism*. Glencoe, Illinois: The Free Press, 1959.

— *et al.*, eds. *The Revolution in Philosophy*. London: Macmillan & Co., Ltd., 1957.

Aulén, Gustav. *The Faith of the Christian Church*. Philadelphia: The Muhlenberg Press, 1948.

Barker, S. F. *Induction and Hypothesis*. Ithaca, New York: Cornell University Press, 1957.

Braithwaite, R. B. *An Empiricist's View of the Nature of Religious Belief*. Cambridge: Cambridge University Press, 1955. The Ninth Arthur Stanley Eddington Memorial Lecture.

Bridgman, P. W. *The Logic of Modern Physics*. London: Macmillan & Co., Ltd., 1928.

Brunner, Emil. *The Christian Doctrine of God. Dogmatics*, Vol. I. Trans. by Olive Wyan. London: The Lutterworth Press, 1949.

Cohen, Morris R. and Nagel, Ernest. *An Introduction to Logic and Scientific Method*. New York: Harcourt, Brace and Co., 1934.

Danto, Arthur and Morgenbesser, Sidney, eds. *Philosophy of Science*. Cleveland, Ohio: The World Publishing Co., 1960.

Edwards, Rem B. *Reason and Religion*. New York: Harcourt, Brace, and Jovanovich, 1972.

Edwards, Paul and Pap, Arthur, eds. *A Modern Introduction to Philosophy*. Glencoe, Illinois: The Free Press, 1957 (rev. ed., 1965; third ed., 1973).

Feigl, Herbert and Sellars, Wilfrid, eds. *Readings in Philosophical Analysis*. New York: Appleton-Century-Crofts., Inc., 1949.

Ferre, Frederick. *Language, Logic, and God*. New York: Harper and Row, Publishers, Inc., 1961.

Flew, Antony, ed. *Essays in Conceptual Analysis*. London: Macmillan & Co., 1956.

— ed. *Logic and Language*, two volumes (first series, 1951; second series, 1953). Oxford: Basil Blackwell.

— and MacIntyre, Alasdair, eds. *New Essays in Philosophical Theology*. London: SCM Press, Ltd., 1955.

— *God and Philosophy*. New York: Dell Publishing Co., 1966.

Gilkey, Langdon. *Maker of Heaven and Earth*. Garden City, New York: Doubleday & Co., Inc., 1959.

— *Naming the Whirlwind: The Renewal of God-Language*. New York: The Bobbs-Merrill Co., 1969.

Hempel, Carl G. *Aspects of Scientific Explanation*. New York: The Free Press, 1965.

— *Philosophy of Natural Science*. Englewood Cliffs, New Jersey: Prentice-Hall, Inc., 1966.

Hepburn, Ronald. *Christianity and Paradox*. London: Watts, 1958.

Hick, John. *Faith and Knowledge*. New York: Cornell University Press, 1957 (second ed., 1966).

— *The Existence of God*. New York: The Macmillan Co., 1964.

— *Philosophy of Religion*. Englewood Cliffs, New Jersey: Prentice-Hall, Inc., 1966 (second ed., 1973).

Hospers, John. *An Introduction to Philosophical Analysis*. Englewood Cliffs, New Jersey: Prentice-Hall, Inc., 1953 (second ed., 1967).

James, William. *The Varieties of Religious Experience*. New York: Random House, n.d. (first published, 1902).

Kee, Alasdair. *The Way of Transcendence*. Penguin Books, Inc., 1971.

Kraft, Victor. *The Vienna Circle*. Trans. by Arthur Pap from *Der Wiener Kreis*. New York: The Philosophical Library, 1953.

Kuhn, Thomas. *The Structure of Scientific Revolutions*. Chicago: The University of Chicago Press, 1962 (revised ed., 1970).

Lazerowitz, Morris. *The Structure of Metaphysics*. London: Routledge & Kegan Paul, 1955.

Lewis, H. D. *Our Experience of God*. London : George Allen & Unwin, Ltd., 1959.

Linsky, Leonard ed. *Semantics and the Philosophy of Language*. Urbana, Illinois: The University of Illinois Press, 1952.

MacIntyre, Alasdair. *Difficulties in Christian Belief*. London: SCM Press, Ltd., 1959.

— *The Unconscious*. London: Routledge & Kegan Paul, 1959.

Martin, C. B. *Religious Belief*. Ithaca, New York: Cornell University Press, 1959.

Mascall, E. L. *Words and Images*. London: Longmans, Green & Co., 1957.

Miles, T. R. *Religion and the Scientific Outlook*. London: George Allen & Unwin, Ltd., 1959.

von Mises, Richard. *Positivism. A Study in Human Understanding*. Trans. by the author from his *Kleines Lehrbuch des Positivismus*. New York: George Braziller, Inc., 1939.

Mitchell, Basil, ed. *Faith and Logic*. Boston: The Beacon Press, 1957.

Munz, Peter. *Problems of Religious Knowledge*. London: SCM Press, Ltd., 1959.

Nagel, Ernest. *The Structure of Science*. New York: Harcourt, Brace and World, Inc., 1961.

Otto, Rudolf. *The Idea of the Holy*. Trans. by John W. Harvey from *Das Heilige* (first published, 1923). New York: Oxford University Press, 1958.

Pap, Arthur. *An Introduction to the Philosophy of Science*. Glencoe, Illinois: The Free Press, 1962.

Passmore, John. *Philosophical Reasoning*. London: Gerald Duckworth & Co., Ltd., 1961.

Pears, D. F., ed. *The Nature of Metaphysics*. London: Macmillan & Co., Ltd., 1957.

Popper, Karl R. *The Logic of Scientific Discovery*. Trans. by the author from his *Logik der Forschung*, 1934. London: Hutchinson & Co., Ltd., 1958.

Prestige, G. L. *God in Patristic Thought*. London: William Heinemann Ltd., 1936; S. P. C. K. edition, 1952.

Quine, W. V. O. *From a Logical Point of View*. Cambridge, Massachusetts: Harvard University Press, 1953.

Ramsey, I. T., ed. *Prospect for Metaphysics*. London: George Allen & Unwin, Ltd., 1961.

Scheffler, Israel. *The Anatomy of Inquiry*. New York: Alfred A. Knopf, 1967.

Smart, Ninian. *Reasons and Faiths*. London: Routledge & Kegan Paul, 1958.

Underhill, Evelyn. *Mysticism*. New York: Harcourt, Brace & World, Inc., 1955. First published, 1912.

Waismann, F. *Principles of Linguistic Philosophy*. Ed. by R. Harré (first published, 1936). New York: St. Martin's Press, 1965.

Wieman, H. N. *The Source of Human Good*. Chicago: The University of Chicago Press, 1946.

Wilson, John. *Language and Christian Belief*. London: Macmillan & Co., 1958.

Wittgenstein, Ludwig. *Tractatus Logico-Philosophicus*. London: Routledge & Kegan Paul. Ltd., 1922.

— *Philosophical Investigations*. Trans. and ed. by G. E. M. Anscombe from *Philosophische Untersuchungen*. New York: The Macmillan Co., 1953.

B. ARTICLES

Austin, John. "Other Minds." *Proceedings of the Aristotelian Society Supplementary Volume*, Vol. XX (1946).

Ayer, A. J. "Demonstration of the Impossibility of Metaphysics." *Mind* (1934).

— "Verification and Experience." *Proceedings of the Aristotelian Society*, Vol. XXXVII (1936-1937).

— and F. C. Copleston. "Logical Positivism—A Debate." A radio debate on the Third Programme of the British Broadcasting Corporation, June 13, 1949.

Buchdahl, Gerd. "Science and Metaphysics." *The Nature of Metaphysics*. Edited by D. F. Pears. London: Macmillan & Co., Ltd., 1957.

Carnap, Rudolf. "Ueberwindung der Metaphysik durch Logische Analyse der Sprache." *Erkenntnis*, Vol. II (1932).

— "Die Physikalische Sprache als Universalsprache der Wissenschaft." *Erkenntnis*, Vol. II (1931).

— "Testability and Meaning." *Philosophy of Science*, Vols. III (1936) and IV (1937).

— "Truth and Confirmation." *Readings in Philosophical Analysis*. Edited by Herbert Feigl and Wilfrid Sellars.

Coburn, Robert C. "The Concept of God." *Religious Studies*, Vol. II (1967).

— "The Hiddenness of God and Some Barmecidal God Surrogates." *The Journal of Philosophy*, Vol. LVII (1960).

Crombie, I. M. "The Possibility of Theological Statements." *Faith and Logic*. Edited by Basil Mitchell.

— "Theology and Falsifications." *Socratic Digest*, Vol. V (n.d.).

Feigl, Herbert. "Empiricism versus Theology." *A Modern Introduction to Philosophy* (1957). Edited by Paul Edwards and Arthur Pap.

— "Logical Empiricism." *Twentieth Century Philosophy*. Edited by D. D. Runes. New York : Philosophical Library, 1943.

— "The Mind-Body Problem in the Development of Logical Empiricism." *Revue Internationale de Philosophy*, Vol. IV (1950).

Flew, Antony; Hare, R. M.; and Mitchell, Basil. "Theology and Falsification." A symposium published in *University* (1950-1951).

Hempel, Carl. "The Logical Analysis of Psychology." *Revue de Synthèse*, 1935.

— "Problems and Changes in the Empiricist Criterion of Meaning." *Revue Internationale de Philosophie*, Vol. IV (1950).

Hepburn, Ronald. "Demythologizing and the Problem of Validity." *New Essays in Philosophical Theology*. Edited by Antony Flew and Alasdair MacIntyre.

Herbst, Peter. "The Nature of Facts." *Australasian Journal of Philosophy* (1952).

Hick, John. "Theology and Verification." *Theology Today*, Vol. XVII, No. 1 (1960).

Lewis, C. I. "Experience and Meaning." *The Philosophical Review*, Vol. XLIII (1934).

— "Some Logical Considerations Concerning the Mental." *The Journal of Philosophy*, Vol. XXXVIII (1941).

MacCorquodale, Kenneth and Meehl, Paul E. "Hypothetical Constructs and Intervening Variables." *The Psychological Review*, Vol. LV (1948).

MacIntyre, Alasdair. "Visions." *New Essays in Philosophical Theology*. Edited by Antony Flew and Alasdair MacIntyre.

Marhenke, Paul. "The Criterion of Significance." *The Proceedings and Addresses of the American Philosophical Association*, Vol. XXIII (1950).

Mitchell, Basil. "Modern Philosophy and Theology." *The Socratic*, Vol. V (1952).

Nagel, Ernest. "Principles of the Theory of Probability." *The International Encyclopedia of Unified Science*, Vol. I, No. 6 (Chicago: University of Chicago Press, 1939).

Quine, W. V. O. "Two Dogmas of Empiricism." *Philosophical Review* (January, 1951).

Root, Howard. "Metaphysics and Religious Belief." *Prospect for Metaphysics*. Edited by I. T. Ramsey.

Rynin, David. "Cognitive Meaning and Cognitive Use." *Inquiry*, Vol. IX (1966).

— "The Dogma of Logical Pragmatism." *Mind* (July, 1956).

— "Vindication of L*G*C*L*P*S*T*V*SM." *Proceedings and Addresses of the American Philosophical Association*, Vol. XXX (1957).

Scheffler, Israel, "Prospects of a Modest Empiricism." *The Review of Metaphysics*, Vol. X, Nos. 3-4 (1957).

Schlick, Moritz. "Meaning and Verification." *Philosophical Review*, Vol. XLV (1936).
— "Positivismus und Realismus." *Erkenntnis*, Vol. III (1932-1933).
Stace, W. T. "Metaphysics and Meaning." *Mind* (1935).
Waismann, F. "Verifiability." *Aristotelian Society Supplementary Volume*, Vol. XIX (1945).
Wisdom, John. "Gods." *Proceedings of the Aristotelian Society*, (1944-1945).

INDEX